GENERALS in the CABINET ROOM

GENERALS in the CABINET ROOM

How the Military Shapes Israeli Policy

Yoram Peri

UNITED STATES INSTITUTE OF PEACE PRESS

Washington, D.C.

The views expressed in this book are those of the author alone. They do not nec-essarily reflect views of the United States Institute of Peace.

UNITED STATES INSTITUTE OF PEACE
1200 17th Street NW, Suite 200
Washington, DC 20036-3011

First published 2006

Printed in the United States of America

The paper used in this publication meets the minimum requirements of American National Standards for Information Science—Permanence of Paper for Printed Library Materials, ANSI Z39.48-1984.

Library of Congress Cataloging-in-Publication Data
Peri, Yoram.
    Generals in the cabinet room : how the military shapes Israeli policy / Yoram Peri.
      p. cm.
    Includes bibliographical references and index.
    ISBN-13: 978-1-929223-81-7 (softcover : alk. paper)
    ISBN-10: 1-929223-81-1 (softcover : alk. paper)
    ISBN-13: 978-1-929223-82-4 (hardcover : alk. paper)
    ISBN-10: 1-929223-82-X (hardcover : alk. paper)
    1. Civil-military relations—Israel. 2. Israel—Politics and government—1993- 3. Israel. Tseva haganah le-Yisra'el—Political activity. I. Title.
    JQ1830.A38.C5855 2006
    322'.5095694--dc22
                                  2005035175

To my beloved wife and closest friend, Pnina

Contents

Foreword

Israel's political system frequently baffles foreigners and sometimes Israelis as well. A raucous, multiparty parliamentary democracy operates without a written constitution but under partial constraint from several individual "Basic Laws" and a respected Supreme Court, which, speaking as the High Court of Justice, has often intervened in recent years to block or modify actions by either the Knesset or the Israel Defense Forces (IDF).

A small, besieged nation, Israel is surrounded by hostile and often aggressive neighbors and has fought eight wars in its fifty-eight years—and yet it has managed to maintain its democratic system. Dogged with security threats, it has not fallen victim, as have so many other new states, to military coups or authoritarian regimes. Indeed, the powerful IDF remains subject to civilian control by the prime minister, the cabinet, and the Knesset (and increasingly, since 1996, the Supreme Court). But how has the military's power been kept in check? This is but one of the important questions addressed by Yoram Peri in *Generals in the Cabinet Room*. Building on and carrying forward his 1983 seminal work, *Between Battles and Ballots: Israeli Military in Politics*, Peri draws on extensive firsthand research to lay bare the labyrinthine relationships that have evolved between Israel's military professionals and civilian political leaders and institutions. While he focuses mainly on events from the early 1990s to the present, he includes some fascinating examples of the military-civilian relationship that are drawn from earlier eras to illustrate that conflicts between Israel's military and political leaders have been part of the country's political history since its earliest days.

As Peri aptly demonstrates, Israel's history is suffused with the overriding theme of national security, which has always given the IDF's chief of general staff (CGS) a strong voice in the nation's political councils and a permanent public stage. It is no accident, of course, that only three of the sixteen men who have served as CGS have *not* later entered politics after retirement and that of the last four prime ministers elected, three have been former senior generals. To underscore the nature of this interplay between Israel's military and political elites, Peri describes some fascinating encounters between IDF leaders and their civilian "superiors" that not only reflect large egos but also fundamental political and strategic disagreements. But he stresses that in those moments when the military voice overwhelmed the civilian, determined military leaders were only filling a vacuum of indecisiveness created by divided, weak political leadership. One poignant example of this casts a long shadow over the present-day dilemma of Israeli settlement in the West Bank. It took place during Yitzhak Rabin's first stint as prime minister, when an essential member of his fragile coalition government was the National Religious Party, which advocated Jewish settlement in the West Bank. As Peri states,

> In the "Sebastia Affair" of 1975 . . . members of the Gush Emunim settlers group founded—for the first time and in an illegal manner—a settlement in Samaria. . . . Rabin, who saw this as a challenge to his government, demanded that CGS Gur disperse the settlers. But Gur objected on the grounds that doing so either would require the use of force and likely lead to bloodshed, or would result in soldiers refusing to follow their orders. Rabin yielded, the settlers won, and the incident is now considered a watershed moment, establishing an important precedent for future Jewish settlements in the occupied territories. It exposed the government's weakness and made clear to the settlers that through the use of force they would be able to impose their own will on the government. This is, in fact, what they have done ever since. . . . Rabin candidly admitted to me that he never forgave himself for having yielded to Gur on that day.

This passage is not only indicative of the type of information and insight Peri offers in this work, but it is also indicative of why Peri has long been regarded as the foremost scholar on the evolving role of the military in Israeli society. As the passage demonstrates, his close association with key players within Israel's military establishment and political elite has enabled him to draw extensively on their private views in analyzing the history and issues that lie behind the headlines. Elsewhere, for example, through his interviews and conversations with decision makers, he is able to provide unique insight into the role played by military intelligence assessments and senior military officers in setting Israel's foreign and defense policy, tracing the military's shift from being a proponent of the peace process to being an advocate of the hard line. In particular, Peri details how the military's changing view of Yasser Arafat and his true intentions affected the decisions of Israel's political leaders, helping push Israel away from negotiations after the failure of the Camp David Summit in 2000 and the outbreak of Israel's "eighth war," the al-Aqsa intifada.

Just as the IDF's policy preferences have changed with Israel's internal and external environment, so too have many of its revered strategic doctrines that were long held unassailable. Faced with a conflict that is not amenable to purely military solutions, the IDF—as Peri explains—has been forced to revise how it relates to the enemy. Throughout the book, he touches on the impact that Israel's struggle—or low-intensity conflict (LIC)—with the Palestinians has had on the IDF and Israel's political system. While the country's old military doctrines had been designed to cope with threats from regular armies from surrounding states and to avoid wars of attrition by ensuring quick, overwhelming victories, LICs by definition last a long time, which means that political, economic, and social factors are as important as military ones in determining the outcome of such a conflict. This reality of Israel's ongoing conflict with the Palestinians, in Peri's analysis, has served only to draw the IDF leaders more and more into the domestic political arena. Without "a clear strategic directive," he states, "the military is sometimes forced to determine its own . . . and the policy it adopts does not always correspond to the wishes of the elected government." Indeed, Peri is convinced that "the ongoing occupation and counterinsurgency warfare will increase friction between the military and civilian society, and the IDF will sink deeper into the political mire." He concludes that as long as "a democratic Israel rules over the Palestinian people, Israeli civilian society will remain split over the future of the territories."

Peri's analysis of how this "military-political partnership"—or "symbiotic pattern of joint responsibility"—has evolved in a democratic state offers a fascinating piece of history, as well as a real contribution to a better understanding of how Israeli policymaking actually occurs. His final chapter offers recommendations for reforms in the Israeli system that might help stem the flow of influence from politicians to officers and that merit close attention by Israeli policymakers, although he himself admits he is pessimistic that they will be adopted while Israel remains in a permanent state of war. He also states that many of his conclusions have relevance beyond Israel, which is a view I share. After all, we are currently in a new era in which LICs are being fought around the world. One way or another, the United States is and will be involved in many of them. Although the American and Israeli political systems are light years apart and our military establishments are vastly different, some of Peri's observations about this new era shed light on trends in our own society. While his thoughts about certain parallels between what is happening in Israel and what is happening in the United States are only delicately implied, we should read some things between the lines. As long as we are engaged in an endless, worldwide war against terror, Peri's account of the way endless warfare has affected Israel's democracy provides a cautionary tale for us as well.

Ambassador Samuel W. Lewis

Acknowledgments

I AM DEEPLY GRATEFUL to many people who helped me in this research. First I would like to thank the fine people at the United States Institute of Peace, in particular Joseph Klaits and John Crist of the Jennings Randolph Program for International Peace, where I was a fellow researcher in 2001. I would also like to thank other members of the Institute with whom I shared ideas and examined facts, especially the Institute's experts on Middle East affairs, Judy Barsalou and Steven Riskin, as well as my editor, Nigel Quinney, my translator, Hazel Arieli, and my research assistant, Gur Hirshberg. I owe a debt to my colleagues, who share with me long years of research on civil-military relations: Charles C. Moskos, Eliot A. Cohen, Louis Goodman, and others in the United States; and a group of Israeli researchers, led by the father of military sociology in Israel, Moshe Lissak, and two bright scholars of civil-military relations, Kobi Michael and Yagil Levy. My gratitude also extends to the Fulbright Fund, of which I was a senior member in 2000, and to my colleagues at the Chaim Herzog Institute for Media, Politics and Society at Tel Aviv University.

GENERALS in the CABINET ROOM

Introduction

WHEN THE BERLIN WALL CRUMBLED in 1989 and the Iron Curtain collapsed, optimism spread throughout the world. Politicians and intellectuals saw these events not only as the "end of history"—the end of the Cold War and a great victory for liberal democratic values—but also as an opportunity for establishing a new world order, a future devoid of war. After all, since the end of World War II in 1945, more than 160 wars had been fought worldwide, in which 28 million people had been killed. Did humanity not deserve to begin a new "postwar" era and to build a "postwar" society? Soon, however, those envisioning such possibilities came to realize that their optimism was no more than wishful thinking. The drive to war, so deeply engrained in mankind's genetic code, is not easily purged.

During the 1990s alone, there were fifty-seven major armed conflicts in forty-five locations.[1] Today, at the beginning of the twenty-first century, one out of every fifteen countries—with a combined population of one billion, or one-sixth of humanity—is involved in one kind of war or another: guerilla war, insurrection, civil war, revolutionary war, secessionist war, or international terror war. In Congo alone, the death toll since that country's civil war began in 1998 has been estimated to be as high as 4.7 million. Though its death toll has been greater than that of any other ongoing war in the same period, the conflict in Congo is otherwise typical of today's wars. The combatants are mostly irregular militias, their victims are mostly unarmed, and the fighting is lengthy: it has gone on for more than five years. Whereas a century ago most conflicts occurred between nations, and 90 percent of casualties were soldiers, today almost all wars are civil wars, and 90 percent of the victims are civilians. The aspiration for peace has not yet overcome the primal drive to war.

The optimistic wave that spread around the world at the end of the twentieth century—the supposed end of the war age—was amazingly

3

similar to the wave that swept over intellectuals in Europe at the end of the eighteenth century, when liberals and evolutionists, as well as Socialists and Communists, believed that the historic function of wars had been exhausted. However, the optimists of the 1990s, like those of two hundred years earlier, made a grave error in judgment. Wars have not disappeared; they have just changed in nature. Today, terms such as "fourth-generation warfare," "low-intensity conflict," "subconventional war," and "perceptual warfare" are commonly used. These new conflicts demand a shake-up of the analytic approach as well, since these conflicts are so different from the old wars. They are not being conducted between regular armies but, rather, between civilian societies. Soldiers have been replaced by irregular fighters, many of whom do not wear uniforms. The purpose of these wars is not, as it was in the past, to conquer territories or to wipe out military formations. Rather, they are fought in front of the cameras, to gain the sympathy of the international community and to shape civilian consciousness. Under such circumstances, the distinctions between war and peace fade; war is conducted at the rear, and even the relationship between strength and weakness has changed. Subconventional warfare, for example, can diminish the strength of a conflict's dominant party and actually empower an otherwise weaker side.

New Boundaries between the Military and Society

The common denominator in all these changes is the social context of war: the connection between the military and civilian society—that is, the association between war and society, and the tension between military strategy and politics—and hence the relationship between generals and politicians. For the new wars, like peacekeeping and peace building, are conducted under politically saturated circumstances, in which the military and civilian spheres now interact. This situation requires renewed discussion about a topic that has been marginalized too long—the civil-military relationship.

The tension between political thought and action, which are entrusted to civilian leaders, and the art of war, which is entrusted to military experts, has occupied social thinkers since the beginning of modern democracy. How can the elected, the people's representatives, control those who wield the weapons? Can civilian leaders curb the desire for war in those who choose the military as a lifelong career? And, most important, can civilian leaders limit the political power of military leaders, preventing them from dictating policy and keeping them under the authority of the state?

A concise and generally popular answer to such questions was provided 170 years ago by the military theorist Karl von Clausewitz, who famously wrote in his book *On War* that "war is the continuation of politics by other means." Therefore, war has to be subordinate to statesmanship, and warriors must always be subordinate to politicians. Or, to quote Maj. Gen. (res.) Israel Tal, a military theorist and developer of Israel's Merkava tank, the military component is forever just one part of the whole of national might: "The military leadership represents the part, while the national political leadership represents the whole, the inclusive vision of the nation's resources in its striving for survival."[2]

In the second half of the twentieth century, political scientists, political philosophers, and military sociologists all searched for rules and principles for determining a normative system to govern relations between democratic armies and their civilian superiors. The term that they adopted as a regulative principle was *professionalism*. The professional soldier—a description that also became the title of a book by Morris Janowitz, a pioneer of military sociology—is a military officer who specializes in preparing for and conducting war. He has a great responsibility toward society, and, being professional, he receives operational autonomy and a freedom to act according to his professional principles. In return, however, he must understand that politics is beyond the scope of his authority. He must remain neutral in a political sense and accept absolutely civilian authority.

The concept of professionalism, which has been used to marry the arts of war and statesmanship and to ensure the subordination of the military echelon to the political echelon, was developed by the founding fathers of the discipline of civil-military relations. But, even among them, approaches varied. Samuel Huntington distinguished between two types of civilian control over the military: subjective control achieved through rules and principles that ensure the maximization of civilian power, and objective control achieved through professional officers' internalizing that they must operate exclusively in the military domain and that they must be politically neutral.[3] A rather different take was presented by Samuel Finer, another founding father, at All Souls College, Oxford University.

He wrote of mature democracies in which military men ride on horse-back and are permitted to be involved in, but not to interfere in, politics. They are permitted to exert influence to a certain extent and even to pressure the civilian government. But they are barred from blackmailing the government, from getting involved in determining who will be in power, and, above all, from seizing power themselves.[4]

While such theories of civil-military relations held during the Cold War years, they were forgotten with that war's end. It became increasingly clear that such ideas did not suit the new era, an era in which military units are sent on peace missions and nonuniformed fighters conduct subconventional, low-intensity warfare. When a photograph of one helicopter strike in the heart of a refugee camp, or even the conduct of a single infantry soldier at a checkpoint on the way to Baghdad or Bethlehem, can be transmitted by satellites, in real time, to millions of homes around the world, it becomes difficult to distinguish between strategic political decisions and military operative action. Such conventional distinctions become much less relevant, as do the mechanisms that previously defined the division between civilian leaders' responsibilities and generals' responsibilities. Politics and military action become much more integrated, and therefore both the military's desire for an autonomous status and the presumption that professionals in khaki will abstain from involvement in politics are no longer realistic.

The new situation has alarmed those who worry about the future of democracy. Even a decade ago, explicit warnings were made and concern was warranted. "Beware!" proclaimed those who observed the U.S. armed forces at the time. "The U.S. military is now more alienated from its civilian leadership than at any time in American history, and more vocal about it," wrote one observer.[5] "It seems clear that the United States is now experiencing a weakening in civilian control of the military," another remarked.[6] The same critic went even further and speculated whether continuing in such a manner might end in a military putsch.[7]

Similar voices were heard in Israel during the late 1980s and 1990s. "Tactics have taken over strategy" (that is, the operational perception of the military imposed itself on, and dictated the overall political thinking of, politicians), wrote a critical sharp-eyed observer of the Israeli defense establishment.[8] Using more subtle language, but with equally profound implications, Major General Tal described the weakening of the government's status vis-à-vis the military: "When the government wants to assess situations or, alternatively, to set policy, it relies on the same source—the IDF [Israel Defense Forces] General Staff—which it is itself supposed to oversee, whose recommendations it is supposed to critically analyze, and which it is supposed to guide."[9] However, very soon such observers realized that a normative collapse had not taken place but, actually, that a new relational system had been created.

Such developments brought on by the new era require new theoretical reflection, in Israel and around the globe. Discussion must ensue, and care must be taken in doing so, especially given the sensitivity of such subjects in democracies. Indeed, rather than discussing who decides and who executes policies, or how best to ensure the subordination of officers to politicians or the civilian control of the military, scholars already have begun using terms such as "shared responsibility," "concordance," and "an unequal dialogue."[10]

To sum up, at the beginning of the twenty-first century, observers have increasingly recognized that boundaries separating politics and politicians from fighters in democracies have become blurred and that the influence of politicians on military decisions has been much greater than previously believed. At the same time, however, the influence of military officers over the design of national policy has been more intrusive than previously believed, and the potential for military influence on foreign policy and international relations has been greater than had been thought. Contemporary democratic theory must account for the fact that military organizations have become heavyweight players in the running of state affairs and exert vast influence in the international system.

At the beginning of the current decade, the *Washington Post*'s military correspondent, Dana Priest, set out on a journey to report on the activity of the commanders of the U.S. military's global command posts. Offering eyebrow-raising conclusions in her book, *The Mission,* she revealed that U.S. policies in various regions of the world are determined more by the generals who command U.S. operations there than by the State Department via its ambassadors. The generals have human and economic resources at their disposal, she reported, that are two or three times the resources available to diplomats, and they have contacts not only with foreign militaries but also with heads of state. They are concerned with matters extending far beyond narrowly conceived security issues, Priest disclosed.

It is thus no wonder that she referred to the generals with a term from the Roman Empire: "proconsuls."[11]

While Priest was examining the military's political status in the American empire, an insurgency took place in the territories Israel has occupied since 1967. The collapse of the peace talks between the Palestinian Authority and the Israeli government in the summer of 2000 led to the outbreak of the second uprising, called the "Al-Aqsa intifada." This latest chapter in an almost hundred-year conflict between Jews and Arabs was the catalyst for this volume's research. Over the proceeding chapters, I examine how the professional Israeli military has coped with the difficulties of this new war. In particular, I address the following questions: What relationships have existed between the military and the government in Israel? What has been the division of labor between politicians and generals? To what extent has the IDF influenced the setting of Israeli foreign and defense policies? And how has the IDF's altered role affected its relations with civilian society?

The conclusions of this research have relevance beyond Israel. Israel, as I see it, is a notable case study, as it can cast light on the general worldwide pattern mentioned above. Those who wish to understand the new relationship between war and statesmanship, and between generals and politicians, and those who want to examine in-depth the political influence armed forces have in the current era, should turn to the Holy Land. While the principles of parliamentary democracy have not been undermined and while democratic procedures continue to be practiced in Israel, a situation in which there is a symbiotic pattern of joint responsibility has emerged, an unequal dialogue, or, as I prefer to call it, a pattern of political-military partnership.

From the beginning of the intifada in September 2000, the IDF was not just the operational arm that conducted the war against the Palestinian Authority and Palestinian organizations. It also had a central role in setting Israeli foreign and defense policy, wielding influence at the suprapolitical level, the strategic level, and the operational level, no less than at the tactical military level. It acted as a central political player and was a partner in policymaking. It did not get involved in politics as an organization outside of politics might do; in fact, it has been involved in politics as an inside partner, a stakeholder, as it were. On several occasions during the course of the war, for example, Israelis reading their morning papers learned about deep disagreements between the defense minister and the chief of general staff (CGS), as though the CGS was not a public servant subordinate to the country's elected representatives but rather a political player equal to them in weight and status. Frequently, the IDF's position was accepted at the end of the day, even though the CGS had not forced politicians to act against their wills and had reiterated democratic norms, affirming that in a functioning democracy, it is, of course, the political echelon that determines policy.

As my research expanded, I discovered that this state of affairs did not begin with the Al-Aqsa intifada but had already existed in the beginning of the 1990s. It became clear to me that the military was a principal decision maker determining both Israel's conduct during its eighth war and its conduct in the peace process ten years earlier. As I read more documents and interviewed more central players from the peace process of the 1990s, a picture emerged of an IDF with its own clear vision for the Middle East, a view that the IDF encouraged successive Israeli governments to adopt. To conclude, the Israeli case is instructive about the true nature of today's new relationship between the military and the state, between generals and politicians, and between politics and the art of war. The model of political-military partnership that developed in Israel at the end of the twentieth century might well anticipate similar civil-military relations in democracies throughout the twenty-first century.

The Book's Structure

This book was written with the general public in mind, not just specialists in civil-military relations. Therefore, while it is not altogether devoid of theory, it uses little theoretical terminology. Thus, the first chapter presents key questions on civil-military relations in Israel. It describes research conducted in this area and discusses one of the most frequently asked questions on this subject in the past decade: is Israeli society militaristic? With great detail, I disprove in this chapter the thesis that the IDF's position in politics is compatible with the instrumental model, demonstrating that the military is not simply the instrument of political authorities. I argue that another model exists in Israel, one based on a political-military partnership.

Chapter 2 describes the geostrategic changes that occurred in the Middle East in the late 1980s, prompting the IDF to recommend a revolutionary transformation in Israel's policies toward her Arab neighbors. I argue that the military was an important catalyst for reversing the government's policy; because of its influence, the government decided to open negotiations toward a peace settlement, even at the cost of giving up territories captured in the Six Day War in 1967.

Chapters 3 and 4 cover an issue that has seldom been raised in studies of the IDF: its political dimension. Chapter 3 analyzes the IDF structure and clarifies how the IDF gained its vast political prowess. In addition to exploring the importance of the Planning and Policy Directorate, I also examine the unique role of the Military Intelligence Directorate (MID), which is responsible for gathering intelligence on Israel's adversaries, ultimately determining the way Israel's entire political class perceives the world. In the period under study—the 1990s until summer 2005—two factors led the MID to become an especially powerful influence on the design of Israel's foreign policy: the malfunction of the political leadership, which faced a protracted political crisis and lacked a clear vision for a political solution, or the courage to actualize such a vision, if one existed; and the MID's dominance within the intelligence community at large. Chapter 4 describes how the IDF acted as a political machine during this period.

The IDF decided in the late 1980s that it would be to Israel's advantage to engage in a peace process, and Prime Minister Yitzhak Rabin included the IDF as a major policymaking and negotiating partner. In 1996, however, the picture changed. Chapter 5 examines how Rabin's assassination and the rise to power of the Likud Party, headed by Benjamin Netanyahu, led to a halt in the peace process and to a rupture in the relationship between the military and its political captain. The disagreement between the military and political echelons regarding issues of national security brought an unprecedented reaction from Israel's military elite, which actively—though democratically—participated in routing Netanyahu from power in 1996. The return to power of a left-of-center government, headed by former IDF chief of staff Ehud Barak, sparked the resumption of the peace process. However, as described in chapter 6, it was eventually curtailed because of the failure of the Camp David summit in July 2000 and because of the outbreak of the intifada in September of that year. In response to these events, the IDF formulated a new, tough, and unyielding policy toward the Palestinian uprising. Just as the IDF had earlier been an initiator and an active partner—not only an implementer—in advancing the peace process, it now became an influential and outspoken advocate of the new hard line. It promoted this view to such an extent that, by the end of Barak's term in office, some, including cabinet ministers, saw the IDF as the tail that wagged the dog.

Chapter 7 describes the tensions between the government and the military that continued during Ariel Sharon's first government, from 1999 to 2002. When this national-unity government was confronted with international constraints, its schizophrenic makeup and "dual policy" led to inconsistent positions. This created tension between CGS Shaul Mofaz and the prime ministers he served under—first Barak, then Sharon. The tension and resulting conflicts that are described in chapters 6 and 7 were caused not just by personal friction but also stemmed, to a large degree, from the new type of warfare Israel faced: low-intensity conflict.[12] Chapter 8 analyzes the IDF's counterinsurgency warfare as a manifestation of this type of conflict, as a war that is characteristic of our present era.

Chapter 9 further describes Israel's policy toward the intifada, in its various stages, both before and after Operation Defensive Shield in March 2002 and from the appointment of Moshe "Boogy" Ya'alon as CGS in 2003 to the summer of 2004. During Ya'alon's tenure, the friction between the military and the political echelons continued and became more overt. Although the IDF carried out Sharon's policies, at times the military and political echelons disagreed about what Israel's policy should be regarding the Palestinian Authority and its prime minister Mahmud Abbas (Abu Mazen), the security fence, and disengagement from the Gaza Strip. In the end, this tension led Sharon and Mofaz to essentially fire Ya'alon by not extending his term in office for another year, as is common practice.

Chapter 10 examines Mofaz's and Ya'alon's conduct as CGS from a historical perspective. Here the description of the intifada's chronological development pauses, and we move to an analysis of the CGS's special status as a major political player in Israel. The historical events analyzed in this chapter illustrate the role played by previous chiefs of staff, especially in the political decision making required for moving from war to a peace involving the ceding of territory. Moshe Dayan's position in the 1950s and Mordechai Gur's position in the 1970s are explored; though they are not unique, they are especially interesting.

While chapters 1 through 10 focus on the political arena, with the government on one side and the military on the other, the broader civilian sphere is examined in chapters 11 and 12. A low-intensity warfare, such as the intifada, is conducted not just against the hard core of the resistance but also against the civilians in whose midst the insurgents operate. Therefore, this raises questions concerning the justification of the war *(jus ad bellum)* and of the means used and measures taken *(jus in bello)*. The issues of "purity of arms," a moral obligation not to hurt innocent civilians during military operations, and conscientious objection, and the criticism of and protest against the burden of reserve duty, all raised questions regarding the IDF's identity and the legitimacy of its operations. This caused a change in its perception of how to end the war. Toward the end of 2003, these issues brought about another shift in IDF policy: the IDF recognized that its iron-fist policy against the insurgents might reduce the level of Palestinian violence but would not end the conflict and that "a political horizon" was also needed.

Sharon also realized that the status quo would not bring an end to hostilities and recognized the heavy toll of the continuous occupation and the growing impact of conscientious objection on Israeli society. This led Israel in the summer of 2005 to unilaterally withdraw from the Gaza Strip and dismantle Jewish settlements there, bringing a symbolic end to yet another stage of the conflict.

Chapter 13 provides a postmortem of the intifada and analyzes Palestinian and Israeli claims of victory. While Israel succeeded in preventing the Palestinians from attaining most of their major strategic goals, it was not able to achieve its own strategic objectives. It brought neither a Palestinian surrender nor a change in the Palestinians' goals, which is the main objective of counterinsurgency warfare. This chapter also further describes the tension in political-military relations created by the intifada.

The last three chapters resume the theoretical analysis of the model of the political-military partnership. Chapter 14 presents reasons for the strain between the two cultures that exist in Israel—the security culture and the diplomatic culture. The practical distinction is not between generals in khaki and civilians in pinstriped suits but between these two cultural coalitions, each of which includes representatives from both the military and political sectors. While the dominance of the security culture has distinguished the Israeli case since the state's founding, chapter 15 illustrates the negative impact of this culture, both on the Camp David summit in 2000 and on the course of the al-Aqsa intifada, from its beginning until the summer of 2005. Although the Palestinians' share of the blame for the failure of Camp David and the unfolding of the second intifada is greater by far, Israel's security culture made Israel a partner to the failure and continued violence. However, one should bear in mind that this book does not attempt to judge Palestinian policy or to compare it with Israeli policy, as my intent here is not to analyze Palestinian society or political culture. Rather, my focus is on Israel's military and polity. The book's final chapter summarizes this research and presents some recommendations for improving the relationship between the generals and their political bosses.

The democratic view is that generals should assist decision makers in the halls of government but that they should not sit as equals around cabinet tables. The military's substantial influence on Israel's policymaking and the friction between its generals and its government stems not from any intention on the IDF's part to grab the reins of power from the politicians, but from the weakness of the political echelon caused by the intractable conflict with the Palestinians.

As the government had no blueprint for a political solution to the problem created by the Palestinian uprising, it expected the IDF to provide a military answer, even though, according to IDF thinkers, "the correlation that existed in conventional warfare between military gains and political achievements" does not apply to low-intensity conflicts, and even though the Israeli-Palestinian conflict was not amenable to a pure military solution.[13] Indeed, after four years of fighting, the IDF succeeded in preventing the Palestinians from realizing the intifada's original goals, but it could not quell the fighting altogether and is still compelled to fight a war of attrition that is contrary to the fundamental tenets of its national-security doctrine.

The nature of *la guerre révolutionnaire* is such that military considerations have a secondary importance. But in the absence of a clear strategic directive from the government, the military is sometimes forced to determine its own, thereby fulfilling a function that, according to democratic theory, is supposed to be provided by the political echelon. The IDF is forced to act on a political plane, and the policy it adopts does not always correspond to the wishes of the elected government.

Therefore, as long as a democratic Israel rules over the Palestinian people, Israeli civilian society will remain split about the future of the territories, and the IDF will continue to pay the price for the protracted conflict and the politicians' lack of courage to make historic decisions. Israelis view the IDF as their shield, and thus it enjoys their broad support. But the ongoing occupation and counterinsurgency warfare will increase friction between the military and civilian society, and the IDF will sink deeper into the political mire.

Background and Methodology

The research leading to this book was conducted during a three-year period. Partial findings were first presented in a report titled *The Israeli Military and Israel's Palestinian Policy*, which was published in 2002 by the United States Institute of Peace.[14] As a result of the large response I received to that article's publication, I extended and updated the research through the summer of 2005.

The study is based on many primary sources and documents collected from the IDF and other Israeli security agencies and governing institutions, as well as on a long series of in-depth interviews with senior figures from the Israeli military-political elite. The list of interviewees presented in the appendix does not include a very large number of senior officers who are still serving and therefore asked to remain anonymous. This situation often accompanies research on current security matters. Similarly, I am not able to quote certain documents I received from sources in the security system, documents underlying various assertions appearing in this work.

One of the ways to overcome this methodological difficulty is to refer to other publications, particularly newspapers that covered the subject. Generally speaking, I refer to newspaper articles only when they cite specific information I also possess from internal sources that cannot be quoted. I have used this method in the past, although I should note that in recent years the defense establishment has shown a greater willingness to be scrutinized and criticized by external academics, and so I have been able to cite more primary sources than previously. For example, in the past year, several research studies on the intifada have appeared in Hebrew that cite materials that had been classified when I commenced this study. The publication of these books now allows me to reveal some of the material I had at my disposal during the early stages of my research.[15]

A Final Note

When my first book on the IDF, *Between Battles and Ballots: Israeli Military in Politics*,[16] was published in 1983, readers were surprised by some of my claims. However, the warning I raised in that book, that the continuation of the occupation would deepen political involvement of the IDF and create a more problematic relationship between the military and society in Israel, has proved to be accurate.

Israeli society has managed, despite its current situation, to preserve a democratic institutional structure. Even so, the occupation and especially the nature of the ongoing war with the Palestinians are threatening Israel's democratic soul and its moral fabric. It may well be that, in comparison to the way other democracies act or are currently acting in similar situations, Israel should be praised for its conduct. But, when aspiring to follow superior values, the comparison to others should not suffice—values should not be relative but absolute. This is undoubtedly the case for a nation that brought the Bible to mankind and that aims to raise its own children based on the ancient morals of the prophets.

This book focuses on events since the early 1990s, a time when many hoped that a hundred years of conflict between Israel and its surrounding neighbors was soon to end. Unfortunately, that decade ended with a cursed war in which Israelis and Palestinians continued, driven amok, to shed each other's blood. But the state of affairs on the day of this book's publication should not extinguish hope. In the words of the late Yitzhak Rabin, winner of the Nobel Prize for Peace and a statesman and friend with whom I was fortunate to share many hours of conversations over these matters, "For us, the acceptance of the existing state of affairs should not even be considered an option. It must be out-and-out rejected."

1

Civil-Military Relations in Israel

Is Israeli Society Militaristic?

For the first twenty years after the establishment of the state of Israel, there was no Israeli institution, apart from the kibbutz, that was as esteemed as the IDF. The IDF was not only precious to Israelis, it was also highly esteemed by foreign observers, since it was a citizens' army that drafted almost nine out of ten Israelis, including women, and was involved in civilian activities, such as education, immigrant absorption, and nurturing popular culture. Essentially, the IDF was a reserve military with a civilian ethos, wherein civilians donned uniforms one month per year. Each officer began his career as a regular soldier, and an informal—and to a certain extent evenly balanced—relationship existed between officers and soldiers. Adding to its popularity was the fact that it had won seven wars over the course of fifty-five years and had remained strong through endless violent attacks on soldiers and civilians.

Social and political researchers, familiar with theoretical and comparative literature on war and the military, were impressed even more by another IDF phenomenon: notwithstanding its own might, the IDF accepted the authority of the political echelon and was not involved in politics. According to the researchers' analysis, the Israeli case disproved the Cold War garrison-state hypothesis, which had been developed by Harold Lasswell in the 1950s. Lasswell asserted that conditions of prolonged war in a country would make the military so strong a social organization that its political power would be aggrandized, civilian authority would be weakened, and the democratic character of the warring society would be endangered. Such a society—even if it was not actually engaged in war but only preparing for it—would, according to Lasswell, turn into a closed society ruled by military elites.[1]

The Israeli case, these researchers claimed, disproved Lasswell's thesis on a number of counts. They pointed out that, despite the fact that Israel's national-security requirements imposed restrictions on human rights, civil liberties, and democratic practices, and despite the fact that Israel's military was its largest organization and the wealthiest and most powerful body in the state, Israel continued to maintain democratic procedures and had kept its civilian spirit. It did not become a praetorian state ruled by a political military but remained a nation in arms, in which military service was seen not just as a duty but also as a civic virtue. In the researchers' view, Israel did not transform into a warmongering nation like Sparta but pursued peace, like ancient Athens.[2]

While the IDF had such a positive image, Israelis considered it taboo to use the term "militaristic" when describing their nation. Whoever dared to use it was suspected of harboring ideological, anti-Israeli biases, and of generally being a hostile political adversary, having in all likelihood Communist, pro-Soviet sympathies. That, for example, was the attitude toward an article written by Shulamit Carmi and Henri Rosenfeld in 1989. In it they wrote that since Israel's War of Independence in 1948, Israeli leaders had abandoned the road to peace and instead had preferred the occupation of Palestinian lands, the expulsion of their inhabitants, and the use of force in international relations. The authors maintained that Israel had a militaristic policy because it had decided to integrate with the Western camp. If, however, Israel's leaders had aligned with the Soviet camp and had chosen to pursue Israeli-Arab cooperation, Carmi and Rosenfeld argued, Israel would have stayed clean and pure.[3] This analysis was spectacularly naive, pitting the "forces of light," those advocating a Jewish-Arab partnership in support of the Soviet Union and thus comprising a part of the "progressive" camp, against the "forces of darkness," those who viewed Israel as a Jewish national state, with a capitalist economy, that inevitably would join the West's militaristic and imperialistic camp. It is no wonder that the article was tossed onto the academic rubbish heap and years would pass before it was rediscovered.

Until the 1980s, virtually all researchers of Israeli society belonged to a school of thought that praised Israel as a model—worthy of imitation—of a nation in arms.[4] This little nation was thought of as a democracy that was able to both defend itself and successfully preserve its soul. War was considered an external factor, imposed on the Israelis by their Arab neighbors, who objected to the very existence of a Jewish state on holy Muslim land. Israeli foreign policy, despite its great reliance on military force, was considered justifiable because hostile neighbors wished to "throw the Jews into the sea," as Radio Cairo's propaganda explicitly declared on the eve of the Six Day War in the summer of 1967. The Israeli security doctrine was seen as one in which force was a last resort, thus justifying only wars of "no choice." The doctrine was defined as defensive, and offensive tactics were understood as a necessary response to Israel's lacking strategic depth. Further, the officers' corps was considered heterogeneous and was thought to lack a "military mind."

However, in the 1980s there was a paradigm shift in the study of Israeli society. For the first time, a young generation of "new historians," critical sociologists, and radical political scientists presented a new approach that depicted Israeli society in a very critical way. The historians overturned the concept that the Palestinians and Arab states were the cause of wars. Instead, these historians blamed Israel for creating the Palestinian refugee problem through the expulsions of 1948 and 1967. They blamed Israeli leaders for having a stake in continuing the conflict, for rejecting peace initiatives, and for preferring the use of force rather than a political settlement that would require compromise. The radical sociologists did not directly address Israeli foreign policy, but they did cast doubt on the assertion that Israel is an enlightened, liberal, peace-seeking society. They claimed that Israel was not a liberal democracy but an ethnocracy, that is, an ethnic democracy that was violating the rights of the Palestinian minority.

This criticism did not only address Jewish-Arab relations. The radical school often used the notion of "war and state-building," emphasizing the role of the military and wars as constitutive factors of Israel's society and state, both institutionally and culturally.[5] These critics did not view the military as the major melting pot of Israeli society, as members of the previous school had viewed it: "The functionalist theory, which regards the military as an important factor in the modernization and construction of the state and integration of different classes and ethnicities, has been shattered. . . . The military itself creates different hierarchies, not only between men and women, but also among men from different nationalities, ethnicities, and classes. The state uses a human resource policy based on ethnic considerations in order to preserve its authority and the existing political order."[6]

Critics have also used theories of internal colonialism and postcolonialism to describe what they saw as the exploitative methods used by the Ashkenazi political elites, who, in order to remain hegemonic, excluded the "other," the Mizrahi Jews, immigrants of Middle Eastern origin. According to this analysis, "security-ism," a softening of the idea of militarism, is a necessary facet of the white-Ashkenazi-male-colonialist-Zionist project. Israel was no longer seen as a modern Athens but was compared to Sparta. The Israeli-Arab conflict itself was explained not as one that was imposed on Israel from the outside by an external enemy but as a built-in reality nurtured from the inside, a survival mechanism for the military and state elite.

The researcher who has done the most to advance this particular school of thought is Yagil Levy. His book published in 2003, *The Other Army of Israel: Materialist Militarism in Israel*, explains the basis for his paradigm. According to Levy, Israeli militarism is not an exceptional, pathological phenomenon of Israeli society but rather an organic part of it, a means of constructing its unequal social and political power relations. "Materialistic militarism is a tool in the hands of dominant social groups. It is used in order to justify their position within the political arena and to validate the social status, identity, and privileges granted to them by this position."[7] According to Levy, the fostering of the IDF, glorifying of war, and nurturing of the violent conflict between Israel and the Arab states and Palestinians are all techniques used by Ashkenazi-white-Zionist men to maintain their high social status and to protect the existing social order.

Some scholars have specifically argued that the source of Israeli militarism is the civilian sector, not the military. Baruch Kimmerling, for example, explained the macho nature of Israeli society as a result of "cognitive militarism":

> Professional-militarism should contract the role of the military to its most restricted instrumental tasks, while civilian militarism will expand the boundaries and the roles of the military far beyond the notion of the

"preparation of the armed forces for future war with the best available material and human resources." The main bearers of civilian-militarism are the civilian government, civilian elites, and all or most of the members of the collectivity.

With respect to this type of militarism, it is not necessary that the military, as an institutional structure, governs the political sphere; nor is the military necessarily stationed at the center of a statist cult. In contrast, civilian militarism is systematically internalized by most statesmen, politicians, and the general public as a self-evident reality whose imperatives transcend partisan or social allegiances.

The gist of civilian militarism is that military considerations, as well as matters that are defined as "national-security" issues, almost always receive higher priority than political, economic, and ideological problems. Thus, dialectically, making peace is also a military matter. Moreover, while professional-militarists perceive war as an end in itself, civilian militarized politicians perceive war as a Machiavellian "continuation" of diplomacy and domestic policy.[8]

But others attributed Israel's militarism to the role that the military plays in Israeli society. Thus, Uri Ben-Eliezer, another scholar of this critical school, has turned the term "nation in arms" on its head. This term, which for the first generation of researchers implied a "beautiful Israel," was used in his work to characterize Israel's militaristic aspects. When Israel is called a "nation in arms" in Ben-Eliezer's work,

> it is said to be an organization of military, society, and politics according to the model developed in Europe in the nineteenth century as a result of the close proximity that existed then between the state and war on one hand, and nationalism and militarism on the other. The model was used as a means to draft the widest range of enthusiastic people for war. . . . In a nation in arms, military, war, occupation, and control are expropriated from the narrow professional domain that is separate from society and become part of a project that all of society is involved in.[9]

One prominent characteristic of a nation in arms, according to Ben-Eliezer, is

> cooperation between the military and political echelons. This is based on a common view that political problems have to be solved by force and on a tendency to see the military route as the preferred and most efficient way to solve conflicts and disputes among nations. . . . The military, in a nation in arms, is nonpolitical in a partisan or factional sense, but it is diligent in realizing ethnonational politics. It is indeed its expropriation from sectarian politics that gives it a seal of approval for the

great political influence it wields, influence which it usually achieves without having to resort to drastic means like a military putsch or the establishment of a military regime.[10]

Finally, Ben-Eliezer concludes by stating that a nation in arms has

> a large compulsory draft, a large reserve military with great involvement in wars and the preparation for them, a war industry and a war economy, and a national culture that sanctifies the military solution to political problems and that places the military and the soldiers at society's center.[11]

Levy followed this line of thought and noted a seemingly paradoxical issue within Israel: how does the military remain bounded by civilian control when militarism exists within Israeli society itself? In explaining this phenomenon, he states:

> Contrary to what has been surmised by most students of military-civilian relations in Israel, state agencies molded arrangements of control over the IDF not **despite** but **due** to the militarization of society and politics. At the broader theoretical level, contrary to the existing scholarship on militarization, it can be argued that if militarization can simultaneously increase the state's capacity to extract internal resources and the military's own gains, militarization can **restrain** rather than **enhance** the autonomous power held by the military.[12]

Since the beginning of the 1990s, this radical vision of Israeli militarism has extended beyond the walls of academia, due to the publication of books in Hebrew by Motti Golani, Ofer Shelah, Yagil Levy, and Majed al-Haj and Uri Ben-Eliezer.[13] The taboo of mentioning the concept of "militarism" disappeared, and the subject is now routinely discussed within the country. For example, nowadays an article about "Israeli militarism" can appear in a respectable newspaper such as *Ha'aretz* without the sky falling. While more continues to be written about this subject, *Generals in the Cabinet Room* examines a fundamental issue regarding militarism, focusing on one element only—how the military shapes policy. It questions whether the military is under effective civilian control or whether the military is involved in politics beyond the legitimate degree accepted by democratic theory. It also asks to what extent the military transmits militaristic values into the civilian value system. To better understand these issues, we need to familiarize ourselves first with the instrumental model of political-military relations.

The Instrumental Model of Political-Military Relations

Conservative scholars that dominated the research of civil-military relations in Israel until the 1990s did not doubt that political control over the IDF was effective, that officers submitted to the authority of the political echelon, and that they did not even entertain the possibility of taking control of the centers of national decision making. To explain the Israeli case, they used concepts borrowed from the founding fathers of the civil-military relations field: U.S. sociologist Morris Janowitz and political scientist Samuel Huntington, their British colleague Samuel Finer, and a small group of experts from the 1960s and 1970s who did comparative research on the military.

Following Janowitz's theories, Israeli military sociologists emphasized the institutional characteristics of the Israeli officer corps: it is highly professional and, following the basic principles of military professionalism, accepts civil supremacy and authority. The IDF officer class, these sociologists explained, is not recruited from a separate social group but rather reflects society as a whole; it is neither corporatist nor alienated from civil society, which are two necessary conditions for intervention in politics.[14] Other explanations of the Israeli case were based on Huntington's theories and emphasized the institutionalization of politics in Israel. Israel was classified as having a "developed political culture," to use Finer's words, wherein both "objective" and "subjective" civil control of the military exist.[15] In other words, there are mechanisms of civil control that act on the military from the outside and mechanisms that operate within the military itself, such as the internalization of obedience to political leadership.

What explains the Israeli phenomenon, according to all of these scholars, is that Israel is a nation in arms and the IDF is a citizens' army: the armed forces reflect the entire mosaic of Israeli civil society; the early retirement of officers (in their mid-forties) prevents the formation of a closed military caste; the reserve service prevents alienation and isolation of the military from civilian society; and the integration of the military in the civil system prevents the growth of corporatism. In fact, the military lifestyle in Israel hardly differs from the civilian lifestyle, as reflected in the casual dress of reserve soldiers who fill city streets. This existence of permeable boundaries between the civil and military spheres creates harmony in civil-military relations. According to this line of thought, such permeability exists not just between the military and the various social spheres but also between the military and the political sphere. Therefore, despite what the garrison-state thesis might predict, Israeli society is not militarized. To the contrary, Israel's military has become civilianized.

It was this harmony in civil-military relations, the IDF's characterization as a citizens' army, and the existence of permeable boundaries between the civil and the military spheres that led researchers to argue that a clear hierarchy exists in Israel between the civilian echelon and the military echelon subordinate to it. These researchers maintained that "the opening of channels of communication between the two elites ensures the continued civil control of the military elite and serves as a functional defense against the danger of injury to the democratic character of Israeli society."[16] Therefore, those who view civil-military relations as harmonious assert that the relationship between civilian officials and military officers follows the instrumental model, whereby

- the military is an executive tool for implementing policies determined by the government;
- the military is disconnected from the political system and particularly from its parties;
- the military is subject to an efficient national oversight structure.

But to what extent did scholars who argued that this pattern exists in Israel indeed describe reality and not just their own wishes, hopes, and aspirations? Since the establishment of the IDF, the founding fathers of Israeli politics made an explicit effort to fortify the instrumental model. This is why David Ben-Gurion, the first prime minister and defense minister of the young state, did not hesitate, even at the price of civil war, to dismantle the military organizations of several parties, including his own, and to establish a unified military responsible to the government in the midst of the War of Independence in 1949. Fortunately for him, civil war was avoided when Menachem Begin, the leader of the underground Irgun, decided not to return fire on the IDF soldiers who sank the *Altelena*, the ship on which he was trying to import arms for his fighters.

After the establishment of the Israeli state, Ben-Gurion continually repeated his perspective on the military's position in the state:

It is not up to the military to decide on the state's policy, regime, laws and governmental arrangements. Moreover, it is not up to the military to decide on its own rules, structure and courses of action, and it certainly should not decide whether there will be peace or war. The military is not more than an executive branch, the Defense and Security branch of Israel's government. . . . Organizing the military and designing its nature, these are all under the sole control of the civil authorities: the government, the Knesset and the voters. . . . The military is entirely subjugated to the government.[17]

This concept was also reiterated in the pronouncements and writings of the shapers of Israel's security system, from Ben-Gurion to Yitzhak Rabin and later Ariel Sharon. Today this lesson is impressed upon young military cadets, who also hear it repeatedly when they later serve as generals and as members of the General Staff. At the meeting of the General Staff on January 3, 1994, for example, CGS Ehud Barak specifically pointed to this ideal after the government decided to open negotiations with the Palestine Liberation Organization (PLO):

The IDF does not determine policies. It does not have a policy on the questions: Is this process good or bad? Is this the process that should exist? The duty and responsibility of the IDF vis-à-vis the political echelon is to make clear, in advance, loudly and clearly, what is the security reality that is going to emerge as the result of the agreement. . . . On the other hand, we should be careful to avoid taking positions, and we should not make manipulative use of the sensitive and central security issue in Israeli existence. We have to be very cautious not to steer the government or to put pressure on an elected government toward policies that are different from its own.

Under consideration today are momentous decisions. The elected government has the authority to take these decisions. The government is empowered to do things which some of us, as individuals, may view as bad. Our responsibility is to carry out the government's instructions in the best possible way, to execute what has been agreed upon, and not to reach a situation whereby we try—knowingly or otherwise—to dictate to the government the nature of the political arrangement.

Barak also made this argument almost a decade later, when he retrospectively analyzed his own term as prime minister. From his perspective, "The relations between the military and the political echelons in Israel are basically healthy, even if they are not perfect." But when he made a similar comment in the spring of 2003, some were surprised. Among them was one of Barak's close friends, former deputy CGS and head of the National Security Council, Maj. Gen. Uzi Dayan.[18] Using somewhat soft language, Dayan advocated that "In order to protect its democracy, Israel needs a sharp and definitive line drawn between the military and the political echelons."[19] He detailed many cases in which weakness at the political level brought about "unwanted behavior" from the military, such as spending more than the budget granted by the Knesset, enabling the construction of illegal settlements in the territories, and not carrying out a strict policy aimed at preventing maltreatment of Palestinians in the territories.

Moreover, Dayan argued, the military is also the leading force in cabinet deliberations over nonmilitary strategy issues and has great influence over the decisions at such meetings. Why, he asked, was it necessary to have the military examine U.S. president George W. Bush's political plan widely known as the "road map"? And why was the opinion of military personnel more important than that of civilians when the policy concerning Arafat's future was discussed? In the end, Dayan did not hesitate to address concepts once considered taboo, concluding that there is a politicization of the military and a militarization of politics.

So who was right in this debate, Barak or Dayan? Does the instrumental model really exist, or is it more an ideal than an actual pattern of behavior? And even if the military has no intentions of dictating policies to the elected government, can it adhere to this under conditions of prolonged war? Indeed, in the past few years, those who question to what extent the instrumental model fully and accurately describes the reality in Israel have increased in number. They include not only scholars from the radical school but also present and past pillars of the Israeli security establishment, such as Ephraim Halevy, former head of the National Security Council and Mossad, former deputy chiefs of staff Tal and Dayan, and other scholars and researchers, such as Yehuda Ben-Meir, a fellow at the Jaffee Center for Strategic Studies at Tel Aviv University.

In his 1995 book *Civil-Military Relations in Israel,* Ben-Meir took issue with some of the arguments I raised in my 1983 book, *Between Battles and Ballots,* but he basically endorsed my central assertion that civil control of the military is not free of flaws. He even developed and extended that assertion:

> In certain areas civilian involvement is maximized beyond what is
> accepted and common in Western countries. This is especially so with

regards to the actual conduct of military operations. At the same time, civilian involvement is barely present in other areas. In particular, strategic planning and, to a lesser degree, force development suffer from military over-involvement and domination, at both the decision-making and organizational levels.[20]

Ben-Meir also pointed out the three main trouble spots in Israeli civil-military relations: the lack of constitutional and legal clarity as to formal aspects of the system; the lack of civilian input into strategic planning; and the lack of a proper balance between the military and civilian echelons of the defense organization.[21] Support for this position can also be found in *Civil Control of the IDF*, a recent study by Maj. Gen. (res.) Aviezer Yaari, who for many years was responsible for the defense system in the Office of the State Comptroller.[22]

The observation that the Israeli scenario is a partnership and does not follow an instrumental model reflects a general trend in today's research on civil-military relations. Scholars who subscribe to this latest school criticize the traditional theorists for having almost deterministic assumptions about society, while social reality is in fact fluid and dynamic. Every society is in a constant process of change, they point out, which also blurs the boundaries between the civil sphere and the military. These scholars submit that theories in the past saw a clear separation between the military and politics as a key to successful civil control. The new theories, however, assert that in present times the military and the civilian sectors are intertwined more than at any other time in the past, that the operations of civil-military coalitions and associations are based on common values, and that as a result varied scenarios are possible. Some will lead to separation between the military and civilian echelons; others might lead to shared responsibility or even partnership between the two.

What also draws criticism from scholars of current civil-military relations is the term "professionalism" and the Huntingtonian and Janowitzian assertion that a professional military is distant from the political arena. At the turn of this century, scholars cited the weakness of this term and called for its reexamination. Some have argued that, although professional officers are a product of the military culture, any attempt to apply a unified professional pattern to all officers is stereotyping. Officers do not constitute a homogeneous group any more than members of any civilian group. They are divided into military subprofessions, in which each officer has his or her own identity.[23] Further, the noncombat activities of post-modern militaries, such as peace building and peacekeeping, and the new wars, counterinsurgencies, and wars of the fourth generation, render problematic the word "professionalism." This is due to the blurred boundaries between the political and military fields of action and between the political and military professions. No wonder some scholars have even proposed changing the training of officers to expose them to the art of politics and its principles and to give them the skills that will equip them for "diplomacy in uniform."[24]

Military historian Eliot A. Cohen also holds that the distinction Huntington drew between military professionalism and statesmanship is dubious. Cohen argues against using the generalized term "professionalism," citing examples that demonstrate the wide variation among different officer groups and different militaries. But the focus of his criticism has been aimed at the tight and inseparable connection between military thought and strategy, and statesmanship and politics. He points to the 1991 Gulf War as an example, maintaining that the political echelon could not escape the necessity of active involvement in the conduct of the war and directly conducted military operations; for, just as Winston Churchill said fifty years earlier, at the end of the day real statesmanship and military strategy are but one.[25]

The Impact of the Prolonged Occupation

A political-military partnership existed in Israel during the prestate period, when the Israeli armed forces were born. From its inception in the 1920s and 1930s, the Haganah—the predecessor of the IDF—was a revolutionary army, particularly the Haganah's elite force, the Palmach. In such an organization, as with the Chinese Red Army, the Cuban Army, and Marshall Tito's partisans in Yugoslavia, there is from the outset a blurring between the political and military dimensions.[26] Although Ben-Gurion, as the first prime minister and defense minister, abolished the partisan military organizations and established a unified force under the authority of the government and the Knesset, the political-military partnership continued to exist after 1948. Later, this partnership would evolve in response to three factors: the protracted war, the occupation of the territories and the political crisis that resulted, and the ensuing two rounds of low-intensity warfare, namely, the first intifada, which lasted from 1987 to 1992, and the second intifada, which began in September 2000.

As I already have shown in *Between Battles and Ballots,* the protracted war did not turn Israel into a garrison state but certainly impacted the quality of its social and political arrangements. The centrality of security, the extensive human capital and social capital invested in the military, and the country's institutional interests created in Israel a social structure different from that of democracies living in peace. Though the democratic nature of Israeli society has been preserved and the military continues to subscribe to democratic values, Israel exists as a nation in arms and, therefore, lacks integral boundaries between its military and society. This has inevitably led to the militarization of certain societal spheres and the politicization of the military in other spheres.

Although the IDF's initial de-politicization process had continued into the 1960s, the Six Day War and the occupation that followed brought the IDF back into the depths of the political quagmire. First and foremost, the IDF became an occupying military in charge of the administration of daily life in the occupied territories. Beyond having strict security roles and responsibilities for maintaining public order, IDF officers also became military governors, responsible for the welfare of the Palestinian population, which numbered more than 3.5 million by the beginning of the twenty-first century. Directly following the occupation of the territories in 1967, though, the IDF's commanders assessed that they would not stay in the territories for much longer, and therefore the CGS did not initially get involved in modeling policy there.[27] This assessment changed drastically in 1980, when then prime minister Menachem Begin replaced the resigning minister of defense, Ezer Weizman. Without the strong presence of Weizman, then-CGS Rafael Eitan's influence over policy became that much greater and the IDF became a leading decision maker.

According to Maj. Gen. (ret.) Shlomo Gazit, who after serving as director of Military Intelligence (DMI) became the coordinator of activities in the territories, the first intifada completed this process of turning the CGS into a dominant factor in the territories. From this point on, the head of the Central Command—a position always occupied by a major general—has been actively in charge of the settlements in the territories, with his decision making and behavior being directly influenced by his relationships with the settlers. This is also the reason why the commander of the army's division in Judea and Samaria—a position always occupied by a brigadier general—and his subordinated commanders ultimately became the ones who would decide the conditions under which the Palestinians, as well as the Jewish settlers, would live. [28]

What intensified the IDF's political involvement was the highly controversial nature of Israel's position in the territories. A heated national debate raged over such issues as relations with the Arab states and the Palestinians, Israel's permanent boundaries, the future of the territories, and the character of Israeli society, its political regime, and collective identity. All of these questions have stood at the center of Israeli politics since 1967, and the military, whether by choice or not, has been involved in all of them. The various security and civil problems that the occupation created, which Israeli society could neither resolve nor escape, in turn created a protracted political crisis. Israeli society was divided between Left and Right, the peace camp and the nationalist camp. The fragmented party system could generate neither a stable coalition government nor powerful leaders with the will and ability to make difficult decisions. Taking active initiative entailed such a heavy political price that few leaders were prepared to risk it, and then only rarely. For example, when one of them, Yitzhak Rabin, finally had the courage and displayed the will and ability needed to cut the Gordian knot, his peace policy was approved in the Knesset by only the smallest of margins, 61 to 59; he was then delegitimized and eventually assassinated on November 4, 1995.

The Israeli leadership's inability to solve the territorial problem—and in many cases the belief that under the guise of indecision Israel could establish facts on the ground and strengthen the Jewish presence in the territories—has also created political flaws within the country. In the territories, this is noticeable in the nonimplementation of the rule of law and in the power a small group of settlers have in dictating policy. In the Israeli party system, this is seen in the weakening of the parties as the locus of national decisions and in the strengthening of extraparliamentary groups. In the governing system, this is apparent in frequent changes of government: since the onset of the peace process with the Madrid conference in October 1991, Israel has had no fewer than six prime ministers. In the security sphere, this has been expressed in the weakening of the mechanisms of civilian control. As a result, the military was sucked into filling the political leadership vacuum; its political power grew, and its involvement in national policymaking expanded. Therefore, it was not the military's political ambitions but civilian politicians' weakness that brought it there.

The most recent step in the intensification of the political-military partnership came about when the occupied Palestinian population ceased being passive and began a struggle for national liberation. In the first intifada, the military found itself conducting counterinsurgency warfare against a civilian population engaged in a revolutionary war. In other words, the military was engaged in political warfare. Such a reality would create serious problems for any professional military. In this case, the military had responsibilities of a civilian nature in the occupied territories, including policing and pacification activities, actions for which it was not built or trained. Thus a crisis of self-identity and self-image developed. Furthermore, the involvement of the military in counterrevolutionary warfare, which is by definition political warfare, forced it to develop a military doctrine that includes political elements. In such a situation, the military inevitably loses its neutral, all-national apolitical stance. The split in Israeli opinion about the occupation brought about circumstances in which any position the military took would pit it against one segment of the population. When the military has had to reach conclusions due to political leaders dodging responsibility, it finds itself so pitted.

Finally, as I will demonstrate, the modus operandi of the military in a low-intensity conflict inevitably damages its relations with the political echelon above it. This crisis intensifies whenever there is disagreement between the political and military echelons about the means and nature of actions for quelling the insurgency and about finding a solution to the political problem that created it. This was the situation from which the military was trying to disentangle itself when the first intifada erupted at the end of the 1980s. The fact that the early negotiations, which resulted in the Oslo Accords and brought about the mutual recognition of Israel and the Palestinian national movement, were carried out without the knowledge of the IDF brought about the impression that the IDF was not interested in the peace process. The truth was quite different. The IDF was the main factor pushing the Israeli government into this process. But why?

The sociologists of the radical school have an explanation, expressed in the sharpest manner by Levy. According to him, Israel's Ashkenazi-bourgeois elite reached the conclusion that its social interests were no longer benefiting from, but rather were being damaged by, the continuous war. The Israeli economy, then entering the globalization era, was creating opportunities for the Western-secular elites to produce better material resources, helping them to establish their stratificational position and to preserve society's hierarchical inequality. In this state of affairs, the war and militarism were becoming an obstruction. For this reason, the IDF elite also adopted the process of demilitarization of Israeli society, which was reflected in the diminution of the IDF through the reduction of defense budgets and mainly through the efforts to reach a peace accord.[29]

The IDF officers reject this explanation and claim that the change in their attitude toward war was a consequence of an "objective" change in the external environment. They argue that these changes in Israel's circumstances opened the window of opportunity for a diplomatic accord. The two explanations do not invalidate each other; many social phenomena have been explicated in one way by the anthropologists observing society from the outside and in a different way by those being observed themselves. As for me, I tend to regard Levy's explanation as describing the consequence of changes rather than their cause. I believe that the IDF's decision to push for a peace process derived more from the dead end it found itself in as a result of the continuous "colonial situation" and from its desire to step out of this state of affairs. The term "colonial situation," as coined by historian Emanuel Sivan, does not imply that Israel deliberately set out on a campaign to conquer the territories. Unlike wars conducted by colonial powers in past centuries, the Six Day War was a just war that was forced on Israel. Yet the continued Israeli occupation of the territories, the establishment of Jewish settlements there, and the resistance of the indigenous population have compelled the Israeli government to rely on the sword.[30]

However, this situation quickly became a burden for the military. Instead of devoting efforts and resources to preparing for future war, it had to invest its energies in keeping the territories. The officers well knew that power alone would not be able to quell insurgency and achieve tranquility. They also knew that being an occupation army put it at the center of a national dispute, something the officers had always wanted to avoid. The only solution, therefore, was to end the occupation. Indeed, toward the end of the 1980s, the IDF believed that a situation had developed that made this option possible.

2

The Geostrategic Transformation of the 1990s

The Impact of the First Intifada

The IDF saw a radical shift in Israel's geostrategic position following a series of international events at the end of the 1980s and early 1990s,[1] leading it to argue for a peace initiative. This began with the collapse of the twenty-year-long status quo in the occupied territories with the outbreak of the first intifada in September 1987 and the PLO's public declaration a year later that it renounced its opposition to the existence of the Jewish state. The PLO indicated it would adopt a new approach that envisioned two independent states living side by side with a Palestine composed of the territories occupied by Israel in 1967. Additionally, the fall of communism had a great impact on Israel's geostrategic situation: Syria lost its support from the Soviet Union, without which it could not go to war against Israel. As a result, Syria began to change its international orientation, making overtures toward the United States and, in 1991, actually joining the U.S.-led coalition against Iraq. Equally important, this war, which brought about an Iraqi missile attack on Israel, ended any possibility of Iraq establishing a strong northern front against Israel.

However, Israel's political leadership remained fixed in its old, rigid ideology and was incapable of seeing the cumulative effect of these dramatic changes. At the time, U.S. secretary of state James Baker described his impressions to Zalman Shoval, Israel's ambassador to the United States, upon returning from the region: "A number of Arab countries demonstrate a certain degree of flexibility and are beginning to think in terms of promoting the political process."[2] But Israel's prime minister, Yitzhak Shamir, rejected this interpretation. Pressured by the United States, Shamir ultimately agreed to Israel's participation in the 1991 Madrid Peace Conference, but made clear his country's negotiating principles had not changed: the PLO would not be allowed to participate in the conference either directly or indirectly; the formula of "land for peace" would not be a precondition for the negotiations; and there would be no agreement to a Palestinian state.[3] A few years later Deputy Defense Minister Ephraim Sneh, a member of the Labor Party, rightly characterized Shamir's understanding of the Madrid Peace Conference as a photo opportunity designed to serve him and U.S. president George H. W. Bush, each of whom had an eye on upcoming elections.[4]

In contrast to the political leadership, the IDF reacted quite differently to this series of events and was among the first to interpret the effect of the emerging reality on Israel's geostrategic situation. The IDF concluded that the first intifada engendered a radical change in the Israeli-Arab conflict, leading the IDF to finally adopt the "war between nations" school of thought. Even before the establishment of the state of Israel in 1948, there had been an ongoing dispute between two schools of thought in the policy sphere. The first, the "war between states" school, argued that the source of the Israeli-Arab dispute was the refusal of the Arab states to recognize Israel's existence and that peace would come only if this policy changed. According to this school, the Palestinian problem needed to be solved in the framework of a peace treaty with Jordan. The second school, seeing a "war between nations," argued that the Israeli-Palestinian dispute was at the heart of the broader Israeli-Arab dispute and that Israel could achieve normalized relations with the Arab states only if the Palestinian problem were resolved.

When Rabin first became prime minister, he, as a disciple of Ben-Gurion and Golda Meir, was an ardent supporter of the "war between states" school, which was dominant in Israel before the first intifada. However, the intifada led him to recognize that the Palestinians were a nation fighting independently to shape their fate, and he eventually concluded that Israel should relate to the Palestinians as an independent actor, a partner.[5] Although the Israeli public popularly perceived Rabin as transforming from a hawk into a dove in the 1990s, this perception was mistaken. As early as 1967, Rabin understood the constraints on Israel's ability to impose an end to the conflict and had been ready for a territorial compromise in exchange for a peace agreement.[6] His major transformation in the 1990s involved his joining the "war between nations" school of thought.

Rabin's prominence during the 1990s, which only increased after he became a "martyr of peace" with his assassination in November 1995, led to his being seen as the one person primarily responsible for initiating the peace process. While it is true that without his backing Israel would not have embarked on a new path in its relations with the Palestinians or begun the Oslo process, the change in Israel's geopolitical and geostrategic thinking was also brought about by another party—the Israeli military. This has not received due attention from scholars of Israeli society or the Arab-Israeli conflict. While the political leaders of the Likud Party continued to oppose the "war between nations" concept, or what they called the "Palestinist view," even after the outbreak of the intifada a change was taking place in the geopolitical and geostrategic outlook of the military. In March 1989 DMI Amnon Shahak submitted to the cabinet his National Intelligence Estimate (NIE, also known as the "Annual Review of the [Security] Situation"), in which he stated explicitly that the intifada was directed and led by the PLO. This conclusion angered the Likud ministers and Knesset members, who were not prepared on any account to grant legitimacy to the PLO—a group they viewed as a solely terrorist organization. Shahak was accused of interfering in politics and of being influenced by dangerous leftist attitudes. Some Knesset members even demanded his dismissal.

As a result of the intifada, the IDF reached another conclusion that was no less radical. While the political Right demanded that the IDF put an end to the Palestinian uprising, the IDF itself realized that it could not do so without using methods far beyond those acceptable in Western democracies and in the value system of Israeli society. CGS Dan Shomron drew heavy flack from the nationalists when he stated this explicitly; it was a public acknowledgment of the limits of the IDF's power to solve the Palestinian problem. The IDF could use force to prevent the Palestinians from compelling Israel to withdraw from the territories, could lower the level of Palestinian violence, and could contain it to buy the political echelon time to reach a peace agreement. But, in the final analysis, the IDF concluded that only a political solution could bring an end to the intifada.[7]

The intifada thus redefined the framework of political discourse on two of the major subjects that divided Israeli society between Left and Right, Labor and Likud, and the peace camp and the nationalist camp: the PLO and the occupied territories. The issue was not only whether to cede the territories but also whether to recognize the PLO and eventually agree to the establishment of a Palestinian state. In this new discourse, the military stood firmly in the pro-recognition, pro-peace camp.

The New Threat: The Outer Circle

Another significant change occurred in the IDF's view of Israel's foremost security threats. The main threats to Israel's existence as a state (its "fundamental security," in Israeli terminology) had previously come from the Arab countries of the "first circle," primarily Egypt, Jordan, and Syria. Yet the 1979 peace treaty with Egypt, the covert collaboration on security with King Hussein of Jordan, and the weakening of Syria following the collapse of the Soviet Union reduced these threats significantly and led to a change in a central component of Israel's defense doctrine. Traditionally,

> Israel aimed to achieve its principal goal—acceptance by its Arab neighbors—through the cumulative effect of limited but clear-cut battlefield victories, that might eventually convince its adversaries of the futility of efforts to eliminate it. During wartime, Israel sought to destroy enemy forces and seize territories for use as a bargaining chip in postwar negotiations, and as a means of achieving more secure borders that would enable it to absorb an enemy surprise attack without risking its survival. This would also, Israeli planners hoped, enable it to create a more stable postwar status quo.[8]

By the beginning of the 1990s, however, a new security situation had developed. The failure of the war in Lebanon and the lesson of the intifada —that there was a high price for holding the occupied territories—showed, in Rabin's words, that Israel could no longer set for itself a defense policy that included imposing a peace settlement of its choosing on a routed or defeated Arab country. At the same time, the changes that took place regarding Jordan and Syria, as well as the Palestinian willingness to recognize

Israel's existence, strengthened the possibility that the countries of the first circle would accept a peace agreement with Israel. Such an agreement was then even more imperative, in view of the new threats posed by the states of the "second" circle. These states—Iran, Iraq, and Libya—threatened Israel with Scud missiles, as well as with weapons of mass destruction.

IDF planners reached an unequivocal conclusion: it was necessary to make an agreement with the states of the first circle, even at the cost of territorial assets, so Israel could focus on improving its preparedness for a possible war with the countries of the outer circle. This was vital, not only to avoid a situation in which the first-circle countries would ally themselves with those of the second circle, but also to gain strategic advantage. Specifically, such an agreement might allow the Israeli military to fly over Jordan or Syria and might even permit the IDF to station land forces on Jordan's eastern border in the event Iraqi forces advanced toward Israel.

Changes in the Defense Doctrine

The IDF viewed an agreement with the Palestinians and the states of the first circle as not only a means of giving Israel an advantage in a possible attack from second-circle countries but also as a way of eradicating the desire of these bordering countries to act against Israel in the first place. The more Israel reduced Palestinian terror without hurting its vital interests, the harder it would be to arouse hostile action against Israel. A new strategic situation would be created and hostility toward Israel from Benghazi to Tehran would probably decrease, asserted IDF strategic planners.

This outlook was reinforced in the IDF's review at the end of the 1980s, by which time the IDF had gained an adequate perspective for evaluating the benefits derived from peace with Egypt. This evaluation reinforced the view that peace—no less than the occupied territories—could provide security. In the words of Maj. Gen. Doron Almog, former head of the Southern Command, "Peace was perceived as a strategic asset."[9] In fact, the treaty with Egypt gave Israel many strategic benefits. It removed Israel's most significant military opponent and weakened the Arab coalition, which thereafter became quite divided, and made it possible for Israel to cut its defense budget, disband military units, and reduce the overall size of its forces. Moreover, Israel received increased defense assistance from the United States, leading to an upgrade in military equipment, three new airfields, and a strengthening of U.S. defense guarantees. But perhaps the primary outcome was a revolutionary change in the IDF's perception of war.

Following the Yom Kippur War in 1973, when three thousand Israelis were killed and more than twice that number wounded, Israel's defense policy planners realized that a saturated battlefield and use of a mass army in future wars of assault and friction would create unbearable attrition. The solution, enhancing the IDF's ability to hit enemy targets without direct human contact on the battlefield, was a radical change in Israeli military doctrine. As a result, Israel took steps to provide the IDF land force with technological superiority over the armies of the Arab states, an advantage it had not previously possessed. Peace with Egypt made it possible to divert huge resources to embark on a project to develop what was described as a "small smart army"; the project brought about many innovations and a revolution in military affairs. Today, in the early years of the twenty-first century, no military in the world is more highly developed than Israel's. Following the example of the United States, the state had reached an advanced stage of Revolution in Military Affairs (RMA).[10] Israeli military capabilities and equipment now include precise, guided ordnance; vertical envelopment; long-distance missiles; special forces that can hit numerous targets simultaneously; and many other novelties and innovations in command control and communications, such as those used by the United States in the war in Iraq in 2003.

The change in defense doctrine also included another element related to the definition of war goals. Whereas in the past the two primary goals of Israeli commanders were the destruction of rival military powers and the taking of territories, with the end of the Cold War, the first goal became more important than the second. For example, the loss of Soviet support in Egypt and Syria made the destruction of these two countries' military equipment more important from a strategic standpoint because the hardware could no longer be quickly or easily replaced. This, in turn, made the goal of conquering and occupying territory less attractive.

Further, the Six Day War and the Lebanon War showed not only that it was difficult to relinquish conquered territory but that it was also no less difficult to rule it, especially in light of civilian resistance. The IDF also understood that Israel's territorial holdings only increased its neighbors' suspicion that the Jewish state had expansionist intentions, thus intensifying enmity toward it. This provided another reason for the territorial dimension's decline in strategic significance. Such enmity was exemplified in the Iraqi missile attack on Israel's home front during the Gulf War, which pushed Israel beyond its "strategic depth." Shimon Peres summed up the situation in Israel frankly: "The traditional doctrine, based on territory, is proven inefficient when it is facing the knife and the missile."[11]

However, the new military doctrine also had to take into account other factors, some of them paradoxical. For example, just when the military balance between Israel and its neighbors had tilted immeasurably in Israel's favor, it became increasingly clear that there were limits to Israel's power. In particular, the U.S. refusal to let Israel join the coalition against Iraq, Israel's inability to react to the Iraqi missile attack (contrary to its long tradition of retaliation), and the weakness displayed by the Israeli home front in the face of the attacks revealed chinks in the armor of Israel's power. The decline in Israeli society's traditional readiness to tolerate a long-term war as a mobilized society added to these difficulties.

Shifts in the Value System

A security doctrine is not simply a military matter. It must take into account the civilian environment in which the military operates. This is particularly true of a citizens' army based on reserve duty. At the end of the 1980s, the IDF had to consider the changes that had occurred in Israeli society. First, the societal rift with respect to the future of the territories had widened: an increasing number of groups expressed a diminished willingness to risk their lives to maintain the occupation. The military's preoccupation with retaining the territories and governing their populations placed it in the center of a public debate in which it drew criticism from the Right and the Left—and sometimes from both sides at once.

Other factors also contributed to the erosion of the military's status. Since the Yom Kippur War, in which the term the "mishap"—the failure of intelligence to see that Egypt and Syria were about to launch a surprise attack—came into currency, some Israelis began to charge that the military was not fulfilling its responsibilities. The failure of the Lebanon War, Hizbullah's success in southern Lebanon, and a long string of operational failures, including ones by elite IDF units, diminished the high regard in which the military had been held for so long. A change occurred in the culture of the Israeli media as well: both print and broadcast journalists increasingly subjected the military to intense scrutiny, no longer spoiling it with the "soft" coverage it had been accustomed to.[12] This change in attitude toward the military was part of a greater transformation in values that Israeli society was undergoing. Those opposed to the transformation argued that it was due to fatigue, self-indulgence, and the desire for an easy life. Others viewed the change as a healthy expression of normalization and of Israel's shift from a mobilized society—or a fighting society—to a society more sensitive to quality-of-life concerns, where postmaterialist values and an individualist orientation were replacing the collectivist orientation of the past.[13]

However the value shift was assessed, there was no mistaking its having taken place. Enthusiasm and motivation for military service diminished, especially within the reserve ranks. The percentage of those serving in the military decreased, which led to increased complaints from those who were serving that they were bearing an unfair share of the burden. Since the beginning of the present decade, for example, no more than 50 percent of recruits have finished their entire period of military service. The rest either were not mobilized at all or were discharged before their terms ended. The military increasingly became perceived, therefore, as a source of negative values and of societal problems, and it lost its status as an autonomous, exalted institution above civilian criticism. The harmony that had existed in civil-military relations had weakened.

Despite this trend, Israelis continued to maintain a high level of confidence in the military relative to other national institutions. Roughly 80 percent of the Israeli public had "confidence" in the military, while only 30 percent professed confidence in the political parties, the media, and the Knesset.[14] However, this confidence could not offset the change that had taken place in civil-military relations: parents of soldiers became increasingly involved with what was taking place in the military; outside institutions and officials such as the Supreme Court and state comptroller weighed in on military affairs in general, whereas the military had previously been autonomous; and the public demanded that investigations of military mishaps and failures be removed from the military's jurisdiction and be undertaken by external bodies. Civilian sensitivity to casualties became so great that the IDF was forced to change its operational patterns, so that the risk to soldiers' lives would be lowered as much as possible.

At a ceremony marking the first anniversary of Yitzhak Rabin's assassination, Shahak remarked on the new social ecology in which the IDF operated, and he lamented that the military and society were alienated from each other. In this dramatic speech that made headlines throughout the country, not least because of the occasion on which it took place, Shahak said,

> In the whirlwind of emotions into which our society has been cast, in the vast confusion that reigns, the Israel Defense Forces—with which you [Rabin] were victorious, and which you so loved, esteemed and believed in—is losing its status. . . . Sharp criticism, emanating from a desire to repair what is wrong, out of love, has given way to alienation. The direct connection between the IDF and the civilian society, a connection which has always distinguished the IDF and has contributed to its strength, has become unfocused and has bred melancholy. Polarization, hedonism, apathy, opportunism and manipulation have infected the national consensus, where they have found, in the military, a punching bag. How far we are from the days when the IDF was a source of pride, a source of respect. . . . We are perceived either as suckers or as millionaires, not to mention the political labels that are ascribed to us. . . . Today, a "successful Israeli" is perceived by many as one who has succeeded in the stock market, invested in real estate, and has stamps on his passport marking ski trips and shopping trips or vacations abroad. The [values of Israeli society] are changing. Dodging IDF service is no longer a mark of shame on draft dodgers' lives, and giving of oneself voluntarily, consciously, out of a desire to contribute, is insufficiently valued. . . . Yes, there is also some good, but the signs of a chipping away at the IDF's status, at the society's fiber, and at its capacity to emotionally withstand crises are worrisome phenomena, and it is imperative that we address them, rather than rest on our laurels.
>
> I therefore call upon all of us, military and civilian alike, to wake up, to be alert and to find in our hearts more mutual respect and appreciation, so that our society will take the military back into its heart. If our society understands that we have no other options and that we only have one IDF, the bridge will be rebuilt.[15]

Indeed, this change in Israeli society's value system was one of the factors that led Rabin to decide to try to reach a political agreement with Israel's enemies, even at a high cost, "so that if, in the future, we will have to go to war again, the public will know that all other options had been exhausted."[16]

Thus, a broad range of factors led the IDF to review its defense policy at the end of the 1980s. The review concluded that changes in the surrounding countries had made peace more achievable and that the strategic value of the occupied territories had diminished. Therefore, ceding these territories would be a fair price to pay for achieving a peaceful accommodation with Syria, Jordan, and the Palestinians.

Major General Sagi's About-Face

The story of Maj. Gen. Uri Sagi, who served as DMI in the early 1990s, is particularly important for understanding the IDF's change in strategy, since he was the first officer who dared to present the new IDF security framework to Prime Minister Shamir. In his diary, Sagi recounts a family experience from just after the outbreak of the first intifada in 1987:

> After a few weeks of frustration, a tri-generational encounter took place at my house, in front of the TV set, between my father, myself, and my son Gal. The picture on the screen at that moment, in which soldiers were confronting violent, hate-filled demonstrations, indiscriminately beating anybody they came across, did not change my father's belief that the Arab disturbances of the 1920s, the massacre of the Jews in 1929, and the bloody Arab revolt of 1936 [against the Brithish authorities], left us with no option but to use force in dealing with our adversaries.
>
> He even mocked: "You in the army don't understand anything. You'll lose everything, and we'll lose the country." I did not react. My son, then thirteen, asked: "Why are soldiers beating and abusing women, children and the elderly? Is there no other way?" I tried to murmur that life is not just black and white, while at the same time I came to see the inadequacy of force as a solution to these problems, if we want to live here with our children, with norms that we can, in good conscience, adopt.[17]

Later, during the Gulf War, Sagi heard similarly conflicting views at the top of the defense establishment on the question of whether Israel should react to the Iraqi Scud missile attacks. After the Scud strike, the air force and special IDF units began exercises in preparation for attacking the missile launchers in western Iraq, but the United States, which feared that Israeli action would endanger its Gulf War coalition, demanded that Israel forgo retaliation. Israeli generals and civilians fell on both sides of the debate. Air Force commander-in-chief Avihu Ben-Nun and then deputy CGS Ehud Barak were in favor of action and received the support of Defense Minister Moshe Arens. Yet CGS Shomron fiercely opposed retaliation and won the support of Shamir, who decided, in the end, not to act.

Sagi analyzed the significance of military intervention, weighed the various factors from an overall strategic and political perspective, and was convinced that Shomron was right. He was worried that Ben-Nun and Barak were urging military action "despite their understanding that that alone would make it harder to reach an overall solution to the firing of Scud missiles. . . . Here we see again a phenomenon that we saw in the war in Lebanon—failure to understand the meaning of military action that cannot achieve its stated objective."[18]

Sagi formally presented this emerging perception to the government in his first National Intelligence Estimate. Among other things, he wrote,

> 1991 was an exceptional year in terms of the changes that took place in the world in general and the Middle East in particular. . . . There were far-reaching changes and profoundly significant processes, whose strategic importance for Israel is equal to that of the wars that we have known hitherto. . . . Following the Gulf War, the short-term Arab military threat to Israel has declined because of Iraq's defeat and the reduced military potential.
>
> The war engendered radical changes in the power relations among the Arab countries. . . . Egypt regained its leading status. . . . Altogether, relations among the Arab states were marked by deep division. . . . The USSR and the Communist bloc underwent a change and ceased to be a political and military support for the radical elements in the Arab world . . . while the United States after the Gulf War remained as the only Great Power, with everyone waiting at its door, and as the one trying to shape a new world order, of which one of the components is peaceful solution of conflicts. . . .
>
> As a result of Iraq's defeat, the awareness that Egypt had previously reached now spread among broad circles, also in Syria, that there is now no practical alternative to political action in solving disputes with Israel.

Indeed, perhaps the most significant ovservation in Sagi's 1991 intelligence assessment related to Syria:

> The changes in the international arena and in the region have ripened into awareness on the part of Assad that there is a need for changes in his policies. In a prolonged stocktaking process, the Syrian leader came to understand that the way he had gone so far would not help him to achieve his aims (return of the Golan Heights, enhancement of Syria's

international and regional status, and promotion of its welfare). . . . Assad recognized that he must replace the concept "strategic balance," which had become an empty slogan with less and less chance of being realized, with a new approach focusing on an attempt to achieve the same goals through a political process led by the United States.

Assad actually referred to peace with Israel as a goal, even if in practice it is a means of advancing toward his goals. . . . It seems that the change also occurred because in Assad's view the timing seems to be an opportunity—perhaps never to be repeated—to take advantage of the potential for improving relations with the West and above all the United States.

Sagi identified what he called a process of increasing openness in Assad's policies, "revealed in increased tactical flexibility: more openness toward the West, a series of changes in Syria's conception of the characteristics of peace talks, resumption of diplomatic relations with Egypt . . . [and] omission of the term 'strategic balance' from his public statements. All these prepared the ground for the last significant change, whose crux was willingness to negotiate directly with Israel in the framework of a peace conference." His report also assessed the situation in the Arab world and provided a fairly clear description of what Israel's policy should be, warning, "In 1991 the danger of overall confrontation initiated by the Arabs is low. . . . [However,] stagnation in the political process is liable to sow the seeds of the next military confrontation, even if this does not happen in the near future."

This was a very brave act on the part of the new DMI. He well understood that Arens and Shamir were the leaders of the hard, uncompromising ideological faction in the Likud. Shamir summarized his attitude to changes in the Arab world in one sentence, which quickly found a place in the pantheon of classic statements by Israeli prime ministers (such as Meir's "There is no Palestinian nation"): "The sea is the same sea, the Arabs are the same Arabs." Even after being compelled by the United States to participate in the Madrid conference, Shamir neither expected nor intended the conference to lead to any kind of agreement, as he later admitted openly.

In a retrospective analysis in 1998, Sagi wrote with restrained criticism:

Perhaps the seven years that have passed [since the Madrid conference] may give us the sense that the time factor is not indifferent and creates circumstances that stem not only from decisions to employ a certain strategy, but also from the inability to decide. Saying "no" to everything and not taking initiative to continue the dynamics of the process creates stagnation, which gives rise to a different, basically negative dynamic, even if the decision makers did not want this to happen.[19]

3

The Political Arm of the Military

The Power of the Intelligence Directorate

In Israel there is no separation between foreign and defense policy. One parliamentary committee, the Foreign Affairs and Defense Committee, oversees both areas, and prime ministers regularly serve simultaneously as defense minister. The prime minister generally relinquishes the defense role only if he lacks the political capital to keep it for himself. In some instances, the prime minister has been forced to give up the defense portfolio to the head of a rival group within his own party, as happened in the 1960s with Labor Party leaders Levi Eshkol and Moshe Dayan, and in the 1970s with Rabin and Peres. In other instances, the prime minister has been forced to surrender the defense role to the leader of the second-largest party in the governing coalition, as occurred with Shamir and Rabin in the 1980s, and Sharon and Ben-Eliezer in 2002. This ascendancy of security over diplomacy was determined by Ben-Gurion at the beginning of the 1950s, when he explicitly stated that "foreign policy has to serve defense policy."[1]

The centrality of security in Israeli society subsumes not only foreign policy but many other domestic and civilian spheres as well. Therefore, the defense establishment has always been a major factor in determining Israel's national policy. Since within this system the military has the upper hand over the civilians in the Ministry of Defense, those wearing uniforms end up being the ones who set the agenda. This is manifest first and foremost in the CGS's position, a situation that I will elaborate upon later. In this chapter, I will describe the major political tools that the CGS has at his disposal—the Military Intelligence Directorate (MID) and the Planning and Policy Directorate.[2] But, for a better understanding of the developments in the 1990s, I will begin with a short historical introduction of these two institutions.

One of the MID's primary tasks is to warn the government about the imminent threat of war, so that the IDF can adequately prepare for any aggressive enemy action. According to Israeli defense doctrine, the reserve army no longer needs up to forty-eight hours to fully mobilize. A misreading of enemy plans—as happened on the eve of the Yom Kippur War in October 1973—could have catastrophic repercussions for the whole state. Therefore, the intelligence corps is a standing corps (like the air force, whose task is to react to an attack until reserve units are mobilized), and it has high priority in budget allocations. This is also why the MID has such high prestige, both inside and outside the military. Because of its significant responsibility, the MID enjoys a substantial political role within Israel and has become both the country's main military intelligence-collecting agency and main analyst of strategic developments in the Middle East and elsewhere. This expanded role was formally expressed in the IDF Supreme Command Orders of 1991, which stated, "The Intelligence Directorate bears a responsibility to the IDF, the Defense Ministry, and the Cabinet, for warning of peace and war, for gathering, researching, and crystallizing the national intelligence assessment of military, terrorism, political, strategic, technological, and economic matters, and for the production and dissemination of data on those matters." Similarly, Maj. Gen. Aviezer Yaari, who headed the MID's research division and later became comptroller of the defense system at the State Comptroller's Office, explained, "The global threats hovering over Israel force the Military Intelligence Directorate to deal with political and ideological issues as well."[3]

The defense establishment, particularly the military, gained prominence in light of the structural political crisis that has existed in Israel since 1967. As the divide between the political Left and Right has made it extremely difficult to achieve a majority vote for any one policy, no government has had the power, the ability, or the desire to set and carry out a comprehensive, long-term strategy. Thus, the most convenient action for governments—from both political camps—has been to remain passive, to hold on to the status quo, and to respond to external initiatives only when there has been no other choice.[4]

This attitude nurtured and strengthened the concept that was becoming accepted by the vast majority in Israel, that the source of the conflict was external and that the conflict was a reality that would change only if a transformation occurred in the policies of the Arab world. This perception lent legitimacy to the absence of political initiative on the part of Israeli governments. What remained was to follow events in the Arab world, to guard against Arab belligerence, and to hope for the day when an Arab desire for reconciliation would appear. And, many asked, what could better observe and analyze what was going on in the Arab world than the MID?

The absence of a civilian intelligence service that paralleled the MID further strengthened the directorate's position. The Agranat Commission, a national commission of inquiry established by the government following the 1973 Yom Kippur War to examine the "mishap," sought to break this military monopoly. But its recommendations to establish a parallel civilian intelligence system in the Foreign Ministry, to upgrade the assessment section of the Mossad, and to appoint a special adviser on intelligence to the prime minister were not implemented. Israel's institutional structure and its political culture continued to rely mainly on those in uniform: the DMI, the MID's research division, and the CGS. Indeed, intelligence reforms have been proposed a number of times during Israel's history—particularly after big military failures—but inevitably such proposals always collapsed, primarily because of the IDF's power and its interest in maintaining that power. The IDF argued that, at the end of the day, it had to be the sole body responsible for presenting the government with the answer to the question of most concern: is war on the horizon? After all, it would have to pay the price if it provided the wrong answer.[5]

The officer who heads the MID, the DMI, has substantial political clout. He is not only responsible for intelligence within the military and, as such, is subordinate to the CGS, but he is also an adviser on intelligence matters to the defense minister, the prime minister, and the cabinet as a whole. While the DMI enjoys a privileged position, the position's dual responsibility has led to several cases of intelligence failure over the decades, raising a number of important questions: Can the DMI meet with the defense minister without the CGS's knowledge? Can the DMI present the prime minister with his opinion if it contradicts that of the CGS? What position should the DMI present to the cabinet if there are disagreements between the CGS and the defense minister?[6]

According to Israeli intelligence doctrine, the MID's work is based entirely on the Marking of Vital Information (MVI), meaning proper intelligence information must be provided to decision makers, particularly on issues they should be informed about. Further, these decision makers, whether senior military officers or senior government officials, have the right and responsibility of determining the types of intelligence information they will receive. Despite this doctrine, however, the DMI and other leaders of the MID were the ones who, over the years, dictated what intelligence decision makers would see or not see; these leaders decided what should be considered vital information, and how it should be classified, and outlined data-collecting plans accordingly. The DMI's formal responsibility over the NIE granted him this high status within the intelligence community and was the cause of recurring frictions with other institution leaders, such as with the heads of the Mossad, the Israel Security Agency (ISA),[7] and the Foreign Affairs' research division. This formal responsibility also awarded the DMI senior status in the political sphere.

For example, the DMI and the head of the MID's research division present the latest intelligence during their weekly meetings with the prime minister, the defense minister, and other policymakers. The research division issues a compilation of reports and daily assessments, a weekly summary, and white papers; however, the most important document the division releases is the NIE. Once a year, this paper is presented to the cabinet and to the Knesset's Foreign Affairs and Defense Committee. Though its primary purpose is to answer the question of whether war is anticipated in the coming year, this document is broad in scope; it is essentially a political document that reviews at length regional and global political processes, as shown in the paper that Sagi presented to Shamir in 1991, which I described in chapter 2.

One of this document's biggest problems, as is the case with all MID estimates, is that the directorate, whose main task is to warn against surprise attacks and to identify threats and other hostile actions against the state and its inhabitants, is habituated to think in terms of worst-case scenarios. The MID tends to overestimate the military aspects and underestimate the social and economic ingredients of the given situation. It also

tends to exaggerate dangers, without identifying opportunities for cooperation, conciliation, or peace. As a result of its overestimation of the enemy's
negative intentions and military abilities, it is inclined to distribute alarm-
ing warnings. According to one observer, "The Intelligence failure to foresee the war in October 1973 resulted in a total and unexamined acceptance
of worst case scenarios."[8] These assessments had been formulated not only
by civilians but also by officers who had advanced through the ranks of
the intelligence community. Maj. Gen. (ret.) Aviezer Yaari articulated this
criticism in a restrained manner: "The situation in which the intelligence
system is constantly warning against dangers should be avoided. . . . It is
difficult but necessary to present both risks and positive developments.
Such an intelligence assessment would be more balanced, better founded,
and its moral and practical implications more meaningful."[9]

The extent to which intelligence assessments determine the government's course of action is an important question. Ostensibly, intelligence
should describe the state of affairs on the other side of Israel's border and
analyze developments there. At best, it is supposed to enable leaders to
determine what is likely to happen if Israel takes one step or another. In
effect, the information presented to the government should lead it to make
certain decisions. However, in most cases the military does not simply
provide estimates; it also provides recommendations regarding courses of
action, giving the military critical influence over policymaking. Shlomo
Gazit, ranked among the most professional leaders to have served in the
MID, described this state of affairs:

> In Israel there is a kind of "monopoly" over security. This is created by a
> combination of the Intelligence estimates and the recommendations sub-
> mitted to the government for a certain policy or course of action. Nowa-
> days, the assessment and analysis of the state of affairs are carried out by
> a military or security intelligence body, and the recommendations of the
> defense system are based on and derive from this estimate.
>
> In such monopoly conditions there is almost no chance for other play-
> ers in the government to present an alternative plan, because no other
> player has the necessary infrastructure for intelligence gathering and
> assessment making. . . . This explains the heavy influence the defense
> system has in designing Israel's policy, and in preventing any attempt
> to suggest and adopt a different policy.[10]

Such a situation might be avoided were there both an NIE from the
MID and a "net assessment" given by an integrative institution that

receives its input from both the military and civil institutions, such as the Ministry of Foreign Affairs and the Mossad. But, as a result of the military's opposition, net assessments were never introduced in Israel; for the same reason, the state has failed to establish a strong National Security Council and to appoint an intelligence adviser for the prime minister.

Dan Meridor, who has handled matters of intelligence and national security and watched these issues closely as a cabinet secretary, a Knesset member, and a minister, candidly described how the military influences the government: "Meetings with military personnel have a fixed scenario. The military representatives present three options: the first could be very effective, but bears many risks and has a low chance to succeed; the second might succeed and bears no danger, but is of marginal effectiveness; and the third, which was the one they preferred from the start. It got to the point where I would just say to them—'start from the third option.'"[11] Lately, a number of other Israeli statesmen have expressed this kind of criticism, whereas in the past only a few dared to do so. Such opinions have become more accepted as more officers have retired from the military and moved into the public arena. For example, Barak has spoken about the direct and monopolistic hold the military has on providing intelligence assessments and recommendations to the government: "There is a danger that the direct connection to the military system might result in a tendency, even an unconscious one, to see the military-technical aspect of reality as having a greater significance within the state of affairs than other components."[12]

Additionally, the DMI's heavy influence on the military is clearly expressed by the fact that three of the last four DMIs—Barak, Shahak, and Ya'alon—became chiefs of general staff. Officers in this position, who are responsible for dealing with threats from the Arab world, tend to see the Arabs as the principal shapers of Arab-Israeli relations, as if Israel's actions had only a marginal impact on the relationship. They also regard the Arabs as forever having ill intentions: "A CGS coming from such a background will assess, judge, and, in fact, offer policies according to these parameters, expanding significantly the power of the DMI as the creator of the national consciousness and policy."[13] Indeed, following the Yom Kippur War, intelligence heads and military leaders in general tended to become more assertive in giving their estimates and more proactive in making policy recommendations.

Military Intelligence: Successes and Massive Failures

For their part, IDF officers, including heads of intelligence services, tend to underestimate their influence: "We only describe and analyze facts. It is not our role to tell politicians what to do. At most, we present them with analyses of what effect their actions might have on the other side's behavior."[14] However, certain senior IDF officers and MID heads think differently. Major General Sagi expressed this contrary viewpoint in his memoirs: "In my opinion, the chiefs of staff, no less than the heads of intelligence, are not only entitled to express their opinions on the significance of strategic, military and political action, it is their *duty* to do so. . . . It is the duty of the professional level to analyze the meaning of [political leaders'] decisions and their outcomes."[15]

Sagi had specific reasons for writing so explicitly. He, like Shahak and Barak, who preceded him as directors of military intelligence, belonged to the generation of officers whose formative military experience had been the surprise attack that started the Yom Kippur War. This event severely shocked Israelis and added to their feelings of vulnerability, so much so that people feared for Israel's existence. The Agranat Commission placed the blame for this tragedy squarely on Israel's intelligence chief, Maj. Gen. Eli Ze'ira, and CGS David Elazar. Even though the MID had monitored the deployment and activities of the Egyptian military for several weeks, it had failed to understand the picture that had been evolving: Israel received warning of the attack from a Mossad agent in Cairo less than twelve hours before the first Egyptian soldiers began crossing the Suez Canal.

However, the commission's findings angered the public, because they did not also hold the country's political leadership accountable for the "mishap." The resulting controversy brought about the resignation of Prime Minister Meir. But the conclusions of the commission had even more serious implications for the IDF. Military officers viewed them as a tough-learned lesson: politicians will disclaim responsibility for any failings in national security and lay blame on the generals. This led to a profound change in the military's attitude toward politicians. Military leaders developed a lack of respect and deep suspicion of politicians, and officers wanted to be more equal partners in making decisions, so they would not fall victim to a failed policy they had no role in formulating.

The impact of this lesson was even stronger than that of the one drawn by the U.S. officer class following the war in Vietnam,[16] since in the Israeli case the Yom Kippur War intelligence failures had threatened the very existence of the state of Israel.

However, over the years, the high status of the DMI has not changed, despite mistakes by many who have filled the role. Although the most dramatic was the "mishap" in 1973, there were many other blunders as well. For instance, the MID did not foresee the Iran-Iraq War that began in 1980. And then, when the ceasefire between these two states was reached in 1988, the DMI estimated that Iraq was in need of a long recovery period, thus failing to predict the Iraqi invasion of Kuwait in 1990. Similarly, the DMI did not foresee the outbreak of the intifada in December 1987 and made yet another error that year when the MID concluded that the movement of Syrian forces in the Golan Heights indicated Syria's intention to attack Israel. The MID did not anticipate developments that were positive for Israel either, such as the PLO's call that began in 1998 tinian conflict. The DMI also miscalculated in 2000, when he concluded that the IDF's one-sided retreat from southern Lebanon would not reduce Hizbullah attacks on Israel.[17] Additionally, erroneous assessments by the MID almost prevented the signing of the peace treaty between Israel and Jordan, claims Ephraim Halevy. He revealed that after the signing of the Oslo Accords, the MID estimated that Jordan could not reach a peace treaty with Israel before Syria did so. Fortunately, Rabin authorized Mossad personnel, Halevy in particular, to continue talks with King Hussein—talks that culminated in a peace treaty between the two countries.[18]

Many of these problems arose because MID officers tended to see risks rather than opportunities and because these officers had undue influence over politicians. These problems intensified even more in the early 1990s—at the dawn of negotiations—when the directorate's ingrained institutional mindset negatively affected diplomatic efforts. Those in favor of reaching a settlement with the Palestinians expressed their concern about this. Deputy Foreign Minister Yossi Beilin, the architect of the Oslo Accords, was particularly blunt:

> The intelligence assessments reach the media immediately, and are perceived as unalloyed truth, in spite of the abundance of refuted assessments concerning the Palestinians, their intentions, the probability of

outbreaks of violence, etc. All of these became conventional wisdom, whether or not they were presented to the Cabinet. They play a negative role in Israeli-Palestinian relations, because they were perceived as though Israel—not necessarily the Intelligence Directorate—was ascribing negative motivations to the Palestinians.

It is unacceptable that Cabinet Ministers should have to apologize to the media when they vote against a military operation, or that they should fear that if they suggest postponing a military operation, it could cost them politically . . . I have no doubt that relations between the military and the Cabinet, and the independence of the military during that period, had a negative impact on our ability to reach an agreement.[19]

Knesset member Yossi Sarid has further contended that "those involved in strategic evaluations strengthen former foreign minister Abba Eban's remark that intelligence communities are inevitably fated to err. And they really have erred very often, apart from exceptional cases."[20] Critics of Israeli intelligence cite its many mistakes as evidence that the assessments of its research division should not be taken as revealed truth. But they also cite other reasons for questioning its assessments. For example, there are often differences of opinion within the intelligence community itself.

The reason for these differences of opinion is that in the end such assessments are a matter of political evaluation and not of scientific truth, particularly when intentions and not capabilities are analyzed. Both Peres and Rabin warned that assessing intentions and situations is more than merely collecting data—it requires political insight. And, in most cases, experienced statespersons possess more such insight than young intelligence officers.[21] Regardless of one's perspective about the individuals in these two groups, one cannot ignore the elusive nature of intelligence information; evaluations are largely influenced by one's worldview, mental makeup, judgment, and political outlook. This, among other things, led Rabin, as prime minister, to request the raw material from which the MID experts drew their conclusions.

As noted, proposals for improving military intelligence have been made from time to time, such as encouraging pluralism in the intelligence community and establishing an integrative body that would take into account both military and civilian perspectives. The most recent intelligence-reform proposal was made by the Investigating Team of the Knesset's Foreign Affairs and Defense Committee, which examined intelligence lapses following the 2003 war in Iraq. As in the United States and

Britain, the intelligence community in Israel determined prior to the war that Iraq had weapons of mass destruction and that Saddam Hussein was planning to attack Israel before or during the war. The committee, which gave its recommendations in March 2004, determined that intelligence findings were not based on reliable information but rather on assessments, assumptions, and speculations. The committee did find that the intelligence work was done in good faith, but it criticized the gap between the self-confident proclamations of the heads of the IDF before the war and their posterior declarations. It also harshly criticized intelligence for not having any information regarding Libya's efforts to develop nuclear weapons, a fact that was exposed only after Libya announced an end to its program.

Throughout the eighty-one pages of its report, the committee criticized the structure and working patterns of intelligence and recommended reforms. Some of the recommendations put forth in the report, such as the appointment of an intelligence adviser for the prime minister, had been made in the past and gone unimplemented, but the report also suggested new, more encompassing, recommendations. For example, one suggestion was to "civilianize" the IDF's 8200 Listening Unit, a military intelligence division that monitors all Arab electronic transmissions, and another was to pass legislation to evaluate and determine the structure of the intelligence community and to redefine the different tasks within it. As expected, both the CGS and the DMI publicly criticized the committee's work methods and the content of its report, and they rejected most of its recommendations.[22]

As the military will continue to have the power to prevent any change in the status quo for the foreseeable future, only some of the committee's proposals will likely be implemented: the military's role as the major player in the formulation of security policy will not change. Before I show how the MID influenced the Israeli government's policy toward the Palestinians in the 1990s, let us turn our attention to the second political machine of the IDF, the Planning and Policy Directorate.

The Role of the Planning and Policy Directorate

Even conservative scholars of civil-military relations in Israel concede that among the different spheres of contact between the political and military echelons, strategic planning is the one least supervised by the government. This arena is characterized by heavy military involvement and a dearth of civilian involvement—indeed, it has been described as a "total monopoly" of the IDF. Such a monopoly is a "most conspicuous weakness in the Israeli governmental system," writes one former director of the MID, Maj. Gen. Aharon Yariv. "The minister of defense is completely dependent on the military," remarks Maj. Gen. David Ivri, a former commander of the air force and longtime director general of the Ministry of Defense. What happens in this sphere is no less than an abdication of civilian authority. "The fact that the military presents civilians with only one option is unbearable," states public-policy expert Yechezkel Dror.[23]

As with the field of intelligence, it is important when considering the field of strategic planning to keep in mind how very broadly Israelis interpret the term "defense"; the IDF deeply penetrates civilian society on economic, cultural, and political levels, affecting significantly but by no means exclusively the country's foreign policy and international relations. Two examples illustrate this well. First, in 1966, the IDF prepared a long-term plan for developing its order of battle. Among the assumptions that formed the basis for its five-year plan were common military principles, such as "the battle must be transferred to the enemy's territory," but also some purely political—if not ideological—ones, such as "Israel will retain all captured territories until full peace is achieved" and "in the peace negotiations, Israel will demand changes in the cease-fire lines of 1949" [later to be described as "the 1967 lines"].[24] Second, shortly after the Six Day War, the IDF prepared a document for Prime Minister Levi Eshkol advocating that a Palestinian state be established in the territories on the West Bank once a peace agreement was signed. Clearly, it is not the military's role to define such quintessentially political goals.

Within the military, the body responsible for strategic and political planning is the Planning and Policy Directorate. It began as a smaller branch within the operations division and was focused purely on military-planning issues. In 1969, under the command of Avraham ("Abrasha") Tamir, its role expanded to cover strategic planning, not just from a military perspective but from an overall national perspective as well, including the political and economic aspects of security.[25] This unit gradually expanded until it acquired the status of an independent branch of the General Staff in 1974, headed by an officer with the rank of major general. Following Shimon Peres's entrance into the Defense Ministry that same year, the planning division became a joint unit of the military and the Defense Ministry, and its head, Tamir, became subordinate both to the CGS and the defense minister. This strengthened the planning division and legitimized its penetration into distinctly civilian and political realms.

After the Yom Kippur War, the officers and experts of the Planning and Policy Directorate participated in the talks that led to two disengagement agreements: one between Israel and Egypt, and another between Israel and Syria. Their main work was to prepare security arrangements and maps of new deployments in the Sinai and Golan Heights. Later, the Planning and Policy Directorate also participated in devising the 1975 interim agreement with Egypt, and the following year it formulated a plan for an overall peace settlement. Indeed, when the Begin government began peace talks with Egypt in 1977, Tamir and the Planning and Policy Directorate formed the government's principal staff in preparations for the talks. And prior to the first Camp David conference in September 1978, Tamir headed the interministerial committee that prepared the working papers for the conference; he also participated in the delegation itself. This pattern was repeated in the peace talks between Israel and Lebanon in 1983—talks that led to the signing of an agreement, albeit one that was never implemented.[26]

The Tradition of Diplomacy in Uniform

IDF officers have been involved in cease-fire—as well as diplomatic—negotiations since the War of Independence. At the beginning of 1949, IDF officers were members of the Israeli delegation to the armistice talks in Rhodes. The director of the Foreign Ministry, Walter Eytan, headed the Israeli delegation, but the primary participants were Generals Yigael Yadin, who negotiated with the Egyptians and was assisted by the young Yitzhak Rabin; Mordechai Maklef, who negotiated with the Syrians; and Moshe Dayan, who negotiated with the Jordanians. Seven years later, at the end of the Sinai Campaign, IDF units were not positioned opposite Egyptian units but faced UN soldiers. As a result, IDF officers conducted negotiations with UN officers concerning the military's withdrawal from the area. A similar situation occurred after the Six Day War. The positions of the IDF's units were determined by the results of battles, so they largely followed natural contours, such as the Suez Canal and the Jordan

River. But in some zones their positions needed to be determined through negotiations with UN officers.

At the end of the Yom Kippur War, meanwhile, the negotiations between the Israeli and Egyptian militaries led to images still engraved in Israel's collective memory. In a military tent at the 101-kilometer point along the road between the Suez Canal and Cairo, CGS David Elazar and DMI Aharon Yariv participated in talks with the Egyptian delegation headed by Gen. Abdel Ghani al-Gamasy. While the talks mainly covered disengagement arrangements, Elazar and al-Gamasy signed the agreements and were responsible for their implementation. Similarly, in June 1974, the agreement that led to disengagement with Syria in the Golan Heights was signed by IDF generals Herzl Shafir and Dov Sion and their Syrian counterparts in Geneva after long negotiations between the two governments and with the very active involvement of U.S. secretary of state Henry Kissinger. It was therefore quite natural that when the new peace chapter began in the 1990s, military officers, particularly from the Planning and Policy Directorate, would participate in diplomacy. In this period, however, unlike earlier ones, there was another reason for their involvement—namely, the structural weakness of the government and the organizational culture of Israel's political system.

Israel's coalition government is in many respects a federation of ministers who run their ministries with a high degree of autonomy. The prime minister's office has little influence over the various ministries, and central bodies with broad responsibility for cabinet ministries are relatively weak. With no civilian bodies capable of doing systematic integrative planning work, this structure is particularly detrimental to long-term national planning, strategic thinking, and evaluation. Such structural weaknesses have been compounded by the unwillingness of politicians to make clear decisions on territorial issues, even in the course of peace talks. And the unwillingness of prime ministers and defense ministers to reveal their true attitudes or to even leave traces of their real views on paper—ostensibly to avoid giving the adversary an advantage in negotiations, but in fact to avoid exposure to public criticism at home—has placed the Planning and Policy Directorate in a "strange and difficult situation." As Maj. Gen. Shlomo Yanai, former head of the directorate, remarked, "We were asked to draw up strategic plans in the course of peace talks without the political echelon being prepared to tell us explicitly what its territorial policy was.

In fact, there was no open dialogue with us. We were forced to estimate, to guess, to make predictions of the leaders' intentions. We also knew that if a political problem arose they would disclaim responsibility for the papers we had prepared."[27] Such a situation occurred more than once.

In the 1990s, the personality and work style of Prime Minister Rabin also influenced the level of military involvement in political affairs. Rabin, a chief of general staff turned politician, liked the work style of the IDF officer corps staff, which was accustomed to undertaking special missions and therefore displayed flexibility, dedication, and a can-do spirit. He preferred this to the slow by-the-book manner of the government bureaucracy. He was also concerned about what he called "leaking sickness," which he described as a disease of politicians, and feared that personal political considerations could harm prospects for peace. Because of this, Rabin chose to utilize the military as a staff unit during the peace process. Unlike politicians, who were in constant competition with one another, and those operating in the government, who had to cope with its unwieldy procedures, the young military officers Rabin worked with were relatively unencumbered. They admired Rabin, referring to him as "Mr. Security"; they willingly submitted to his personal authority and were loyal to him in a way that is less common in civilian life. (A similar situation existed in the 1999 government of Ehud Barak, who also felt comfortable with the military; he had moved almost directly from the military to the prime minister's office. Because of his suspicious nature and his centralized working style, Barak relied greatly on the special team he set up for himself, which was composed principally of people from the armed services whom he knew and trusted.)

Shortly after Benjamin Netanyahu replaced Peres as prime minister in 1996, it became clear just how involved the military had become in political affairs and how dependent the political leadership had become on the military—for information and intelligence assessments, for political and strategic planning, and for the practical know-how that the IDF commanders acquired in the territories. It also became clear how dependent political leaders were on other elements of the defense system, primarily the General Security Service (GSS, or, as it later became known, the Israel Security Agency, or ISA) and to a lesser extent the Mossad. Netanyahu rose to power as an opponent of the Oslo Accords and sought to "stop the process of Israel's giving up its strategic assets." From the start he had a critical attitude toward the military. He did not like its senior officers' involvement in political matters, and he believed that IDF commanders should not rub shoulders at diplomatic meetings and cocktail parties with Israel's adversaries, individuals with whom they might have to meet later on the battlefield.

Thus, tension existed between the prime minister and the senior command as soon as Netanyahu took office, and it grew when he announced that only civilians would conduct political negotiations. However, not many months passed before he came to understand that without the military he lacked the knowledge, tools, and ability to conduct political-security negotiations with key parties, including the United States, and he had no choice but to bring the officers back into the fold. This is exactly how operations have remained ever since, under both Barak and Sharon. But, in such circumstances during the 1990s, how did the military use its political tools?

4

The Modus Operandi of the Military

Policy Planning

Among officers, the highest-ranking person who interacts most with civilian officials is the CGS. Aside from this individual, there are about a half-dozen major generals holding key positions, including the deputy CGS, the commanders of the MID, the Planning and Policy Directorate, and the Operations Directorate, and the head of Central Command (sometimes also the Northern Command); underneath them are about a dozen brigadier generals.[1] In this chapter, I will describe how the two main policymaking divisions of the military's General Headquarters (GH)—the MID and the Planning and Policy Directorate—have operated since the beginning of the peace process in the early 1990s. The role of the CGS calls for a separate analysis, which I will present later in this volume.

The beginning of the Oslo process was exceptional in the history of international relations. It was a private initiative of then deputy finance minister Yossi Beilin, who arranged for a group of academic associates to meet secretly with representatives of the PLO for five months, without the knowledge of the foreign minister or prime minister and in violation of government policy. After the negotiations progressed, they were made known to the senior political leaders, who gave their approval; Uri Savir, director general of the Foreign Ministry, entered the picture in May 1993. Even after Rabin, then the prime minister and defense minister, authorized the talks to continue at a more official level, he left the IDF out of the process and did not even report the existence of the secret negotiations to Barak, then IDF CGS. Rabin did this for several reasons. He later explained that the agreement at that stage dealt with general topics, which he described as "ideological and political," most of them concerned with mutual recognition. He therefore believed that there was no need for experts of any kind and that it was better for as few people as possible to be privy to the negotiations.[2] Internal political considerations, however, may have played a more important role in his decision.

Throughout the entire negotiating process, until the clandestine signing of the agreement on August 19, 1993, Rabin worried that the talks would fail. He preferred a process that would allow him to disclaim responsibility for the initiative, so that it would then be identified with his partner and political rival, Shimon Peres, if it did indeed fail. Rabin also thought that IDF officers were liable to significantly decrease the pace of the talks and to publicly reveal the existence of the talks, which would have likely led to their cessation.[3] It is possible that there was another factor influencing Rabin as well: he may have worried that military officers involved in the peace talks would have demanded detailed outlines of security arrangements.

Ultimately, the IDF's exclusion from the talks led CGS Barak to assume a critical stance toward their outcome. Barak asked Rabin for permission to present his personal viewpoint, ex officio, during a cabinet meeting, and Rabin allowed him to do so despite opposition from some ministers. Barak charged that the Oslo agreement was like "Swiss cheese," arguing that the absence of military experts resulted in numerous "security loopholes" that could harm Israel in the future. But there was also another reason for the military's criticism of the Oslo process. The IDF believed that Israel should first start negotiations with the Syrians rather than the Palestinians. According to Barak, Syria constituted a real threat to Israel's security: it was at the head of the Arab "refusal front" and it constituted the core of the eastern front. Additionally, a peace treaty with Syria would weaken the Palestinians and enable Israel to reach an agreement that required far fewer concessions on its part.[4] Barak's criticism of the Oslo Accords, regarding their content, significance, and the way in which they were achieved, would eventually lead him to take a step that seemed puzzling to many: he publicly confronted Rabin, his political patron who had brought him into the government. When the 1995 interim agreement, known as Oslo B, was submitted for government approval, Barak, then the minister of internal affairs, voted against it. He expressed concern that Israel would lose most of its territorial assets, which he thought should be retained for exchange in a final peace treaty.[5]

Nevertheless, the military became a major player in the process, more so than even in the past. After the signing of the Oslo Accords on September 13, 1993, Rabin set up the staff that coordinated the negotiations on implementation and appointed Deputy CGS Amnon Shahak to head it. Also, two subcommittees were formed, each led by major generals: Uzi Dayan, head of the Planning and Policy Directorate, would lead the military team, and Danny Rothchild, coordinator of activities in the territories (and later his successors, Gady Zohar and Oren Shachor), would lead the team on civilian affairs. Even the working group's legal advice would be given by a retired officer who had served for many years as head of the IDF's international law division, Col. Joel Singer.

The extensive preparatory work, occupying dozens of experts and clerks, including senior officers in the reserves, was done at the Planning and Policy Directorate, which also recruited civilians for this purpose. The Planning and Policy Directorate formulated position papers that were brought to the CGS for his approval. In turn, the staff recommendations were then presented to the political echelon. Every Friday, the negotiating team met with Rabin in his office at the Defense Ministry, and he would determine their next assignments. After some time there was a change at the top of the Israeli delegation, and the director general of the Foreign Ministry, Uri Savir, replaced Shahak—who had been newly appointed CGS—in the talks preceding the signing of Oslo B in September 1995.

While Foreign Ministry personnel played a role in the stage between the signing of the Declaration of Principles in 1993 and Oslo B in 1995, they certainly were not the only party involved. As Carmi Gilon, a future head of the ISA, stated, "with all due respect to the political work done by Uri Savir and Joel Singer [of the Foreign Ministry] on our side, and Abu Alla on the Palestinian side, who created the framework for the agreement, the content was filled in by the military and the ISA."[6] There appears to be more than a grain of truth in this statement. This is particularly relevant to later stages of the process, as this pattern continued until the last stage of the peace talks at the end of the 1990s.

For example, even after the interim agreement and prior to the signing of the Hebron agreement on January 15, 1997, the civilian arm remained weak, and there were increasing problems of coordination between the civilian representatives and the military representatives within the relevant bodies. The IDF expressed its concern about the economic committee, a committee that worked almost exclusively with civilians, citing its "dangerous neglect of security considerations." Similarly, the Planning and Policy Directorate "identified vast damage that could have been caused the state had the military officers not been sufficiently alert and had they not compelled the Finance Ministry, through the prime minister, to cooperate fully and to subordinate the economic agreement to the military agreement."[7]

Tasked by the military with preparing for the talks, the Planning and Policy Directorate coordinated all staff work, collected data on the various subjects of the negotiations, and developed position papers on topics ranging from border security to water-sharing and economic arrangements. Professionals in the Planning and Policy Directorate also coordinated the work of civil servants in other ministries and enlisted civilian experts who were either called for reserve duty or were employed by the directorate as contractors. The heads of the directorate played a major role in meetings with the defense minister and the prime minister; at these meetings, Israeli positions on the various issues were determined. In addition, the directorate commanders participated in the delegations to the talks, in most cases as heads of the subcommittee on security.

Following his election as prime minister, Barak, who preferred to have operations centralized under his command, established in his private office a special "peace directorate" that was supposed to direct the staff work of the negotiations. Like most of the newly elected prime minister's bureaus, this directorate, headed by Col. Shaul Arieli, was mainly staffed with active and retired officers. However, the military, from the CGS to the lower ranks of the Planning and Policy Directorate, did not believe that a foreign body, operating from the prime minister's office and not an integral part of the military structure, should be permitted to infiltrate the military's sphere of activity. Arieli responded by stating, "The fact that we employed civilians in the 'Peace Directorate' could improve the papers being written there, allowing them to present not only the security interest."[8] The result was constant clashes and power struggles between the peace directorate and the military, with the military holding the upper hand.

The military's main advantage was in its control of information. When Arieli was asked to prepare for the prime minister maps of the territories in question, a task the civilian administration did not have the capability to perform, he requested them from the military, but the officers refused to provide them. This incited a long and tedious battle, and in the end Arieli managed to obtain the material, but the struggle caused his relationships with colleagues at General Staff headquarters to deteriorate. Eighteen months later, the military succeeded in breaking up the special team that the prime minister had brought together. In January 2001 the peace directorate fell apart, and Arieli resigned.

But the military's extensive involvement in the peace negotiations distorted the Planning and Policy Directorate's work priorities throughout the 1990s. This matter was examined by the state comptroller, who discussed it at length, quite critically, in his annual report published in September 2001. Its focus on political issues—expressed by the growth of the strategic division within the Planning and Policy Directorate—prevented the directorate from fulfilling the primary function for which it had been established, he believed. That function was to serve as the planning headquarters for the IDF, in other words, to serve the General Staff in planning the growth and organization of military strength. However, the comptroller charged, "as a result of the growing investment in finding the necessary response to the political echelon for the needs of the peace process . . . the area of military strategy has not received adequate attention in recent years."[9]

Decision Making at the Government Level

At IDF headquarters in Tel Aviv, dozens of officers and civilians in the Planning and Policy Directorate pored over the material that served the decision makers, while the top brass participated in the political forums where decisions were actually made, working with both the prime minister's small, informal team of confidants and the cabinet, particularly a subcommittee of the cabinet known as the "security cabinet" or "kitchen cabinet." Interactions between the different team members in these meetings, whether military officers or civil servants, were generally quite informal.

This is typical of Israeli culture. Personality played a large role in the debates and discussions, and opinions expressed were not strictly correlated to institutional affiliation.

Despite the heavy influence of the IDF, the prime minister, as the ultimate representative of the political echelon, had complete authority to make final policy decisions. This indicates the special character of the political-military partnership. No one questioned, for example, whether the political level had the right to make the formal decisions. But this is not to say the military did not have a major impact on those decisions. Consider what happened after the Hebron Massacre, the killing of Palestinian worshipers by Baruch Goldstein at the Tomb of the Patriarchs on February 25, 1994. Yair Hirschfeld and Uri Savir suggested to Peres and Rabin that they take advantage of this opportunity and evacuate the Jewish settlers from the heart of the crowded Muslim city. Peres refused but did agree to evacuate Tel Rumeida, a segment of the settlement that had been causing problems for the government for quite a while. Peres even told Hirschfeld and Savir that Rabin had given his permission for this mission. But senior officers in the IDF, who were supposed to command the evacuation, flatly refused to cooperate and eventually convinced Rabin to disassociate from the plan.[10]

Four years later, consultations over the Hebron Accord took place at the prime minister's office, and the question arose as to whether Shuhada Street should be a one-way or a two-way road. This question was of major importance: its resolution would affect the status of the settlers living inside the Jewish compound in the heart of the city once Israel transferred authority to the Palestinians. The civilians on the team had difficulties discussing this issue. The only participant who had command of the subject was the head of the Planning and Policy Directorate, Maj. Gen. Shaul Mofaz. After all, he had formerly served as head of the Judea and Samaria zone and later as head of the Central Command.[11]

Martin Indyk, former U.S. ambassador to Israel, was deeply involved in the deliberations concerning the Oslo Accords and described an event that also illustrates the Israeli military's central role in decision making:

> A few minutes before the sides met to sign the Oslo Accords at the White House in September 1995, Ilan Biran, the commander of the Central Command, entered the president's room and launched into a stormy debate with Prime Minister Rabin. The commander argued that

Rabin must not agree to the new deployment lines in Hebron that were included in the agreement that he was about to sign. Rabin embarked on a long, vociferous debate with the general, while the rest of us, including the president, had to wait until the two had finished. . . . We were astonished. In our wildest dreams we could not have imagined that such a situation could occur between any prime minister and one of his generals. And all this at the White House, in front of the president of the United States. It was totally unbelievable.[12]

The advantage that military officers have over civilians is reflected not only in joint civilian-military bodies but also in pure civilian frameworks such as the cabinet. During the 1990s, a tradition had developed wherein whenever the CGS participated in cabinet meetings, he was accompanied by a group of senior officers. This was noteworthy because the heads of other organizations—such as the Mossad and the ISA, not to mention the Foreign Ministry and other civilian institutions—were prohibited from bringing in their own teams. "It infuriated us," lamented Arieli. "The IDF's narrative and positions were presented at cabinet meetings in great detail, and no other narratives were given anywhere near as generous a hearing."[13]

Dan Meridor added that "when a group of half-a-dozen generals participates in a cabinet meeting, they come with materials prepared in advance, after conducting a thorough staff work, often presenting a unified opinion, argued in an authoritarian and doubtless tone. The ministers would listen to them with no means to analyze the officers' opinion, to verify the material presented to them, or to set alternative policies. Representatives from other civilian bodies would not appear at all at these cabinet meetings, and the ministers were unable to critically examine what was presented."[14]

Participation in the Talks

Generals took part not only in the making of policy decisions but also in negotiations themselves. This aroused considerable public controversy. The bitterest dispute erupted when Rabin named Deputy CGS Shahak as head of the Israeli delegation to the talks with the Palestinians. The critics argued that IDF officers should not be involved in a political process that was at the heart of the most controversial political issue in Israel. Such involvement, they claimed, had an adverse effect on the

IDF's status as an apolitical national body. In addition, they argued that the officers' participation in the peace talks would come at the expense of training and preparations for war. On a more general level, the critics asserted that the social ties the officers would form with the Palestinian leaders would dull their alertness to the danger awaiting them from the enemy.

Rabin rejected these arguments outright and claimed that IDF involvement in diplomatic negotiations had been occurring since 1949. His controversial decision resulted in a photograph that would become a symbol of the peace talks. It showed Shahak, dressed in mufti, and his Palestinian counterpart, Abu Mazen, strolling like old friends along the shore of the Red Sea. In a media-saturated society with an enormously powerful visual culture, this picture stood in sharp contrast to the first iconic image of the peace process—the picture of Rabin shaking hands with Arafat on the lawn of the White House. There, Rabin's body language had conveyed his hesitation, skepticism, and even revulsion. But the photo of Shahak and Abu Mazen radiated deep friendship. More troubling to some was that the Israeli in the photo was not a civilian but a man who stood at the head of Israel's war machine.

Framing Public Discourse

One of the important levers the IDF has in influencing the decision-making process is its ability to shape public opinion. The Israeli public, whose level of confidence in its leaders is not high, prefers the assessments of professional officers to politicians in security-related matters. It perceives their analysis as apolitical and non-ideological. That is one of the reasons why all the political parties in Israel make great efforts to use reserve officers, who enjoy public prestige, in their campaigns. In the 1999 elections, for example, it was not the Labor Party's Central Committee that determined its policy vis-à-vis the Palestinians, but rather a group of generals who had only recently retired from the IDF. And when Prime Minister Barak left for the Camp David negotiations in the summer of 2000, he left behind a team of spokesmen and spin doctors, composed mainly of retired generals, who were meant to reassure the Israeli public that the far-reaching concessions he was going to make would not compromise Israel's security.

The Israeli military has great advantages, more than any other public institution, in shaping public opinion: the media in Israel is ready to
impose great constraints and limitations on itself when security issues are
concerned; the military has an almost complete monopoly on supplying
information; and the military also has a vast capacity to manipulate journalists and media outlets. All of these factors make military correspondents and analysts less critical than journalists covering other subjects.
Some of these correspondents and analysts, particularly those of the two
national television channels, behave more as spokesmen for the military
establishment than as representatives of the public.[15] Additionally, the
IDF's senior officers are well aware that politicians in all political camps
need their professional expertise and popularity to influence public opinion. This had been true for many years but intensified in the 1990s. Until
then, the military had been a sacrosanct institution, but during that
decade the media and society at large increasingly criticized it. As a result,
the IDF became more aware of the importance of public relations and
political packaging.[16]

The IDF's need to create a more positive image of itself grew with
the change in the nature of the conflict and with growing criticism, both
abroad and in Israel, of Israel's activities in the territories. During the
1990s the IDF also recognized that a new era was dawning, an era in
which images disseminated throughout the world by photojournalists,
and especially by television cameras, could determine the outcome of a
military operation no less than an army unit in the field. The military
understood that it had to develop a new marketing policy and utilize
public relations strategies to achieve its aims; it had to combat adversarial
opinions not only worldwide but also within Israel itself. As a result, the
IDF adopted the principles of "permanent campaign," regularly providing
political assessments to military correspondents, opinion leaders, and senior journalists. For example, with the beginning of the peace process in the
early 1990s, military officers frequently spoke to journalists on the record
and used off-the-record briefings as well to disseminate their views. In
this way, they greatly influenced the attitudes of the media, shaped public
attitudes toward the peace process, and indirectly influenced the decision
makers. This helps explain why initially there was broad public support
for the peace process and why most Israelis were very optimistic about
the probability that peace would actually be achieved.

As time passed, however, the peace process collapsed, and in September 2000 the second intifada broke out. The media was harshly criticized for having unquestioningly accepted the narrative the government and military had presented in recent years. The media was also chastised for not having presented the opinions of those against the Oslo Accords or the views of those who doubted the Palestinians' real intentions to reach a peace accord. In fact, the violent outburst in September 2000 and the subsequent attacks from suicide bombers led the media at large to accept this criticism. Consequently, the media embraced a very negative attitude toward the Oslo process and enthusiastically supported the views of the nationalists and the hard-liners, reflecting the opinions of the majority in the military and the public. But by doing so it repeated the same mistake it had committed at the beginning of the 1990s—it principally conveyed the narrative of one side only. Once again, hegemonic forces, military and civilian alike, were given the platform. But this time their narrative was not one of peace and reconciliation but one of mistrust toward the Palestinians that called for crushing them in war.

All through the 1990s, as long as the attitudes of the military and political echelons were compatible, the military's news management did not provoke any criticism. As we will see, only later, when a gap between the government and the IDF emerged and the latter continued to try to sell its positions to the public to influence policymaking, were its actions criticized. In 2000 the liberal daily *Ha'aretz* commented in an editorial, "It is intolerable that the IDF approaches the public directly in order to mobilize support for its positions and puts direct and public pressure on the Cabinet."[17] *Ha'aretz,* though, was a lonely voice.

The Officers: Hard-Liners and Accommodationists

According to the political-military partnership model, there is not a division between officers and civilians within the political-military elite, but rather a division between two groups, each one consisting of officers and civilians. In fact, a close examination of the actions taken by IDF officers during the 1990s does reveal an internal split between hard-line and accommodationist officers. The two groups held different opinions regarding several issues, including—most significantly—the basic assumptions of the peace process.

Although the IDF's top leadership had supported the peace process since the early days of the 1990s, certain generals in the General Staff were highly critical of the initiative. Compared to the accommodationists, who believed that peace with the Palestinians could be achieved and maintained, these hard-liners were in the minority. Yet this group included officers in high positions, such as Maj. Gen. Ya'akov Amidror, who served as head of the research division of the MID in the early 1990s, and Amos Gilead, who headed the division later on. Both of them believed that Arafat's peace policy was a political tactic designed to gain territory and that he had no real intention of ending the Palestinians' armed struggle against Israel. With regard to the terms of the settlement, Amidror and Gilead asserted that the PLO had no intention of changing its basic conditions for peace: that Israel must withdraw from all the territories occupied in 1967; that a Palestinian state must be established with East Jerusalem as its capital; and that Palestinian refugees must have the right of return. They believed that the PLO would not stop using violence against Israel during the course of the talks, even though it had done so while negotiating the Oslo Accords. They warned that after the Palestinians gained independence on the West Bank and Gaza Strip, they would pursue an irredentist policy against Israel.

Officers also differed in their behavior and style during the negotiations. In the Israeli deliberations that preceded the negotiations, the accommodationists showed a greater openness toward discussing the distress of the Palestinians and were willing to consider their needs and find answers to their demands. During actual negotiations with the Palestinians, these officers tried to build trusting relationships with their partners, occasionally showed empathy toward their colleagues sitting on the other side of the negotiating table, and proposed middle-ground suggestions. The officers of this compromising group came from different military backgrounds, but almost all of them shared past professional relationships with Palestinians. Standing out among them were officers who had worked as coordinators of operations in the territories—such as Danny Rothchild, Ya'akov Orr, and Oren Shachor—and, surprisingly, those responsible for security and the prevention of terrorism, such as the heads of the ISA. In fact, this latter group, which included Ya'akov Peri, Carmi Gilon, Yossi Ginossar, Israel Hasson, and others, had the deepest understanding of the Palestinians' needs and was most willing to respond to their requests.[18]

There were also other officers, ultimately categorized as accommodationists, whose positions were shaped throughout the negotiations and
as a result of the process itself. Sitting together around a table for many
hours of negotiations gave them a broader perspective of the Palestinians'
needs, interests, and attitudes. In fact, over the course of the talks, trust—
even forms of friendship—developed among certain Israeli and Palestinian
negotiators who had come from military backgrounds: for example, Shahak
and Maj. Gen. Dayan befriended Muhammad Dahlan and Jibril Rajoub,
who both led Palestinian security organizations. Their style, if not their
military experience, created a common language: "Their common control
of the language of force, tempered by human empathy, was what made
the relations between them so special and gave them the added value that
is so necessary at critical moments in the process."[19]

Meanwhile, the hard-liners who opposed compromise all shared the
basic assumption that the Palestinians were unwilling to begin anew in
their relations with Israel and that the Palestinians would neither recognize it nor live peacefully at its side. These hard-liners also did not believe
that any of Israel's compromises, renunciations, and understandings would
be mutually rewarded by the Palestinians. Because of these beliefs, the
hard-liners presented worst-case scenarios, overrated the dangers that might
follow each step of the negotiation, and constantly presented the down-
side of the process during internal discussions. This was true whether discussing water and infrastructure matters, transport routes, the size of the
areas to be evacuated, the nature of the relationship between the two
states, or, above all, the territorial issue.

The most significant expression of their attitude was their constant
demand for high-security arrangements, both for the interim and final
stages of the process. For example, while all the Israeli negotiators shared
the conviction that the Palestinian state should be demilitarized and have
no real military force beyond one for symbolic purposes only and that Israel
should supervise Palestinian air space, the hard-liners also demanded that
Israel be allowed to keep certain military bases and strategic areas within
the Palestinian state, even though this demand would substantially curtail
the sovereignty of the new state. It is no wonder, then, that the Palestinians utterly rejected this demand. This, in turn, strengthened the suspicions of the hard-liners that the Palestinians did not really have serious
intentions of making peace, and a vicious circle was created.

Another example of a dispute between the hard-liners and accommodationists involved a discussion about the nature of final borders. Since 1967 a consensus had emerged in Israel that whatever the eastern border of Israel might be, its security line would be the Jordan River. This strategic line was to prevent foreign armies from reaching the west bank of the Jordan River. As the peace talks proceeded, a question arouse regarding the exact character of this security line. It could take different forms: the terrain along the river could be under Israeli sovereignty, or it could be protected by IDF troops without belonging to Israel. Alternately, Israel could lease the area until a legal agreement granting the area a special status could be reached, or until different security arrangements could be properly considered, such as the deployment of international forces to the area. While the IDF held a strict stance regarding this issue throughout the 1990s, even in the advanced stages of the peace talks at Camp David, the accommodationists claimed that it was essentially a political issue and not for the military to decide. The hard-line officers argued that Israel's security needs should not be guaranteed solely by technical arrangements and that the area should be under full Israeli sovereignty. Ultimately, Barak changed overnight the stance Israel had adhered to for more than three decades; he dropped the demand for sovereignty. By doing so, he showed that a determined prime minister is able—with the wave of a hand—to do away with a principle that the IDF had considered an unassailable axiom.

The dispute between the accommodationists and the hard-liners over the border issue also manifested itself with what was known as Israel's "interests map." In this instance, Prime Minister Netanyahu, like those before him, did not want to address the territorial question or draw maps that might be interpreted as offering territorial renunciations. He bypassed this political obstacle by asking the Planning and Policy Directorate to present the government with a list of "security needs" translated into territorial terms. The military took advantage of this general request and inflated the list of security needs to such an extent that it almost made the principle of withdrawal from the territories empty.

While over the five years of negotiations many matters that at first seemed to be of vital security suddenly became less relevant, the main point regarding the security interests map is this: since all Israeli governments avoided creating a clear military policy toward resolving the Israeli-

Palestinian conflict, evading in particular the territorial question, it was left to the IDF to devise the maps for the desired agreements. As a result, government policy did not guide the military; rather, military interests and a strict military outlook controlled the design of the political plan. In turn, demographic, economic, human, moral, religious, and other interests were marginalized, receiving, at most, a bit of attention from the accommodationist officers.

Though two schools did exist within the IDF during the first half of the 1990s, as they did within the civilian sector, the majority of military officers supported reconciliation with the Palestinians. This was true both while Rabin and Peres were in office and even later once Netanyahu took over. But these military officers soon realized that the vision of Netanyahu was very different from their own, making a clash between the IDF and the prime minister inevitable.

5

The "Democratic Putsch" of 1999

The Ascendance of IDF Officers in Israeli Politics

Benjamin Netanyahu's rise to power in 1996 led to an unprecedented problem for the IDF. In contrast to the IDF's upper echelons, which had supported the peace process from the beginning of the 1990s, the new prime minister vigorously opposed the Oslo Accords. Whereas the military viewed the Palestinian Authority as an interlocutor for an agreement and territorial compromise as a condition necessary for the peace process to continue, Netanyahu opposed a compromise based on the land-for-peace principle. He had even announced in the run-up to the elections that, as prime minister, he would not shake Arafat's hand. This was the first time in Israel's history that the IDF's upper echelons and the country's political leadership were so deeply divided over Israel's security requirements.

Netanyahu's conceptual framework for understanding the Middle East was derived from the Cold War perspective, and he made no secret of his agreement with Huntington's "clash of civilizations" thesis. Applying the thesis to the Middle East, he believed that Islamic culture perceived the Judeo-Christian West as an enemy and that Israel was on the front line against Islamic civilization. Thus, he held that it was incumbent upon Israel to retain control, to the extent possible, of its strategic assets, that is, its military might and the territories in its possession. Gestures that for many appeared to indicate a willingness on the part of the Arabs, and of the Palestinians in particular, to compromise with Israel were perceived

77

by Netanyahu and his political partners as deceptions, in line with their *marhalya* (salami tactic) approach, a piece-by-piece strategy of gaining territory and advantage in the Palestinian's continuing war of liberation from the Jewish state.

Thus, Netanyahu and his followers interpreted each instance of territorial compromise as diminishing Israel's security. In place of the Oslo process, which had the goal of "normalization of relations," Netanyahu sought to create a relationship with the Palestinians based on what he called "the creation of external constraints on [Arab] adventurism, manifest in a balance of power . . . a balance of deterrence, surplus force, security arrangements, and security areas." He argued that "in the absence of genuine democracies in our midst, normalization of relations—which is a very important and very desirable goal—cannot be a substitute for a balance of power."[1]

Therefore, Netanyahu, along with a significant number of ministers in his new government, were dismissive of the military's approach to the peace process. In their minds, the IDF's position derived from its inability to professionally handle the challenges it had been assigned and from its inability to quell the insurgent warfare against Israel's presence in the occupied territories and southern Lebanon. They also believed that the military's upper echelons had adopted the policy positions of the Labor Party due to the military elite's close social relationship with that party. Netanyahu and certain cabinet ministers did not confine such criticism to closed quarters.

In addition, Netanyahu perceived the IDF's support for the peace process and active participation in negotiations as negative and dangerous. Military officers should devote their time to preparing for military engagement with the enemy on the battlefield, he frequently said, and they should not interact with the enemy in diplomatic negotiations or at cocktail parties. So strong was Netanyahu's wish to sever the IDF officers' political influence, he attempted to effect a revolution in the government's working arrangements at his first cabinet meeting as prime minister. After the top ranks of the General Staff had presented their positions, he asked them to leave the room so that the politicians could discuss the subject and make decisions. However, this practice did not last long.[2]

The IDF's supreme commanders rejected this criticism by Netanyahu; some even described it as "witch hunt."[3] They did not see themselves as having a particular ideological preference or as being supportive of a specific political party. They viewed themselves as professionals, stating that their opinion that the peace agreement was the best solution to Israel's security problem was based on experience and knowledge. Maj. Gen. Matan Vilnay, head of the Southern Command who implemented the Oslo agreement in the Gaza Strip, wrote in his diary on the eve of the agreement's signing that the intifada, "a popular uprising which had erupted with the difficult conditions of life in Gaza as its background, combined with nationalist, social, and economic pressures, has shown the limitations of the IDF's power. It has also shown that defeating terrorism militarily is insufficient, that the roots of terrorism must be addressed in order for terrorism not to reemerge."[4]

What appeared to the government to be a dispute based on two different political perspectives was seen by the IDF as structural tension between their organization, which operated on professional considerations, and a political leadership, which operated on the basis of an ideological framework. IDF officers did not hesitate to express their opinion about the situation, at times using particularly sharp language.[5] During an annual meeting of high-ranking IDF officers in May 1997, many officers, wounded by politicians' sharp accusations that they had failed in the territories and Lebanon, in turn accused the politicians of assigning it impossible missions.[6]

But relations between the political and military echelons might not have continued on a collision course had it not been for an additional factor. In Netanyahu's populist worldview, the IDF elite was part of Israel's hegemonic bloc, which he, as a representative of the counter-hegemonic bloc, saw as a bitter political enemy.[7] From his perspective, Israeli society was divided between "the elites"—which included the Labor Party, professionals, and the Left in general—and "the people," which included all the groups excluded from power and from decision making, groups that he represented and brought to power. The fact that the hegemonic bloc supported the peace process widened the gap between the two sides.

All of this resulted not only in differences of opinion regarding Israel's security but also in cold and tense relations between the two blocs. Maj. Gen. Oren Shachor, the coordinator of operations in the territories, expressed not only his belief but also that of his IDF colleagues when he said: "Netanyahu and his people call IDF officers 'servants of the Left,' and judge them as guilty to begin with, as people all of whose actions are suspect. All the prime ministers in the past embraced the IDF, since it is the foundation on which the country is based. That was not the sentiment with Netanyahu's government."[8]

The military also criticized Netanyahu's conduct as prime minister. The IDF's top officers did not respect Netanyahu's leadership abilities; and, after a few clashes with him, their assessment of both his leadership and professional abilities became very negative. "Not balanced" and "folds under pressure" were just two of their common characterizations of him. They also saw him as untrustworthy and unreliable, as someone who dodges responsibility but is quick to saddle others with it and to ascribe blame. Such evaluations of Netanyahu intensified as the number of clashes between the military and political echelons multiplied.

Netanyahu, for his part, thought that it fell on him to deal with yet another problem, CGS Shahak, Rabin's onetime protégé who saw himself as the bearer of Rabin's legacy. What concerned Netanyahu was not only Shahak's political position regarding Israel's security and his involvement in the peace negotiations, but also his popularity with the public. Netanyahu assumed that Shahak would begin a political career after his release from the military and thus become Netanyahu's most formidable political rival. To fend off such an eventuality, Netanyahu sought to undermine Shahak's popular support.

Only a short time after Netanyahu's rise to power did it become evident that the military and the civilian leader to whom it answered were on a collision course. The questions were: How quickly would the collision take place? With what force would the collision occur? And what would the consequences be? As it turned out, the actual collision was swift, drastic, and unprecedented in its results. On the eve of the 1999 elections, the military elite mobilized to aid the opposition parties. This was not an attempted putsch. Those who rolled up their sleeves were not uniformed military personnel, who are prohibited from acting on behalf of political parties, but retired and reserve officers. Still, these men had only very recently left the military, and they shared the opinion of their colleagues still in service. In the summer of 1999, no fewer than one hundred high-ranking reserve officers joined the election campaign with the aim of removing Netanyahu from office. It was no mere coincidence that their candidates for prime minister were reserve officers themselves.

Though the officers, for their part, explained that their behavior was grounded in their fundamental disagreement with Netanyahu's national-security perspective, it would be a mistake to ignore the additional motivation that lay behind their actions: the officers embodied the interests and the spirit of the IDF as an organization, which found itself in a position of acute conflict with the prime minister, and they expressed their desire to maintain the institution's status. The officers were involved in a power struggle in which the goal was to preserve the IDF's position within Israel's body politic.

Before describing the development of Netanyahu's relationship with the IDF's upper echelons during the course of his two years in office, and the "democratic putsch" that brought his demise, I will first examine the historical involvement of military officers in politics in Israel.

Generals in Politics: From Co-optation to Subversion

Political leaders often come from the military. This is the case not only in developing countries, in which the military, or a clique of its officers, might seize control over political institutions, but also in long-established democracies, where retired generals trickle from the military into parliamentary political parties and government. Israel, though a stable parliamentary democracy, is an exceptional case when compared with other democracies in this regard.

In Israel the trickle from the military to politics has been a flood. In each of the sixteen parliamentary elections held in Israel since the founding of the state in 1948, a sizable number of reserve officers entered the Knesset; their allegiances were all across the political spectrum, though they were especially represented in the left wing of the parliamentary chamber. Since the 1960s, on average, 10 percent of Israel's Knesset members have been high-ranking reserve officers.[9] Further, about 20 percent of cabinet ministers are generally high-ranking reserve officers, and of the three most important offices—prime minister, defense minister, and foreign minister—at least one (usually two) has been occupied by a former career officer, such as in the governments of both Ehud Barak and Ariel Sharon.[10]

This phenomenon—the overrepresentation of career officers in the Israeli body politic—was for years given a structural-functionalist explanation. This explanation referred to the "second career" norm, common in the IDF, whereby an officer's military career typically ends when he is young (in his forties), and he then is compelled to begin a civilian career. In fact, in each of the final years of the 1990s, well over one thousand officers inundated the job market, among which dozens were officers of high rank (the IDF has approximately 20 major generals, 120 brigadier generals, and 1,000 colonels). The functionalist explanation emphasizes the need for military expertise in Israel's high political echelons: since Israel's political leadership deals first and foremost with national-security matters, it is necessary that people possessing knowledge and expertise in this area be among the country's decision makers.

Scholars of the conservative school of civil-military relations, who emphasize the permeable boundaries between the IDF and civilian society, have pointed to this as a logical extension of the civilian character of the IDF.[11] Conversely, at the other end of the academic spectrum, radical scholars, who claim that Israel is a militaristic society, have pointed to the political careers of high-ranking officers as an expression of Israeli militarism.[12] No matter how this phenomenon is interpreted, the participation of a large number of former officers in politics is yet another manifestation of the political-military partnership in Israel.

Even with this long-standing tradition of partnership, the 1999 democratic putsch was a unique event in Israel's history. In the first fifty years of Israel's existence, there were two paths for entry into politics. The first path—one that existed from the state's founding until the 1970s—saw young generals enter into politics as protégés of veteran political leaders. This kept in line with the co-opting style of the political elite that controlled political mobility. Thus, for example, in 1959 David Ben-Gurion added retiring CGS Moshe Dayan to the Mapai (Labor) Party list for the Knesset. Similarly, in 1973 Golda Meir brought over to the Labor Party retiring chiefs of staff Chaim Barlev and Yitzhak Rabin, and in 1969 Likud leader Menachem Begin brought to his party the head of the air force, Maj. Gen. Ezer Weizman. Dozens of other high-ranking officers also embarked on political careers through this co-opting practice. In the 1980s, a second pattern of generals entering politics developed, a pattern of entrepreneurship. While some officers did follow the old path, joining existing political parties, entrepreneurial individuals founded new political movements and parties and even changed the existing political map. For example, in 1973 Maj. Gen. Ariel Sharon founded a new political party, Shlomtzion; soon after, he became the motivating force that united it with other like-minded parties, forming the Likud.[13]

In 1999, however, the pattern was entirely different. A large number of generals justified their involvement in political life neither as an attempt to support the existing leadership, nor even as an attempt to revitalize the political system, but rather as a struggle against the existing political leadership. The officers explained that they were entering political life to rescue Israel from its incumbent ruling political leadership, which they believed posed a threat to the country. To pursue this goal, a large group of generals formed a coalition called One Israel and supported the Labor Party leader, former CGS Barak. Just before the elections, Barak was joined by Deputy CGS Maj. Gen. (res.) Matan Vilnay, Maj. Gen. Oren Shachor, and a large group of other high-ranking officers. Some of them ran in the primaries for the party's Knesset list, and some of them did get onto the list, joining other high-ranking officers—such as Brig. Gen. Ephraim Sneh and Brig. Gen. Benjamin ("Fouad") Ben-Eliezer—who had served in the previous Knesset. A large number of them volunteered to work at campaign headquarters, and after the elections a number of reserve officers either got positions in the prime minister's bureau (a ministry in its own right) or in the prime minister's private office itself, while other reserve officers got prized positions in public service.

A second group of reserve officers founded a new party, the Center Party. It was headed by Maj. Gen. Yitzhak Mordecai, who, as defense minister, had resigned from Netanyahu's government on the eve of elections; recently retired CGS Shahak; and a large group of high-ranking officers. Three of the eight candidates at the top of the Center Party's electoral list were senior reserve officers. Other high-ranking officers joined other political parties, all of which opposed Netanyahu's government.

Netanyahu and the IDF: What Started the Deterioration?

The public criticism that government ministers leveled against the IDF's conduct in southern Lebanon was one of the first causes of the decline in relations between the government and the military. While the government criticized the IDF for its failure to eradicate Hizbullah's guerilla warfare and terrorism, the IDF claimed that the government had given it an impossible mission. These deep differences of opinion were aired publicly in *Ma'ariv,* which published an exchange between former CGS and government minister Rafael Eitan and CGS Shahak in October 1997.

Eitan argued, "These words [i.e., that there is no military solution to the Lebanon problem, only a political solution] are likely to be interpreted as pressure by the military on the government, as though the IDF is tossing the problem over to the political branch and saying 'solve it . . . do as you wish, we have no solution.' Such words must not be heard coming from the mouths of military people." To this, CGS Shahak replied, "I think the claim that the military is tossing problems over to the political branch is untrue. . . . it is incumbent upon the military to examine and recommend to the political echelon what it [the military] thinks is right to do with respect to the use of its power." Shahak added,

> In the Lebanon War, you will not reach a situation in which the other side will cease its activities. These being the facts, it is very good that the military is saying so to the political branch. Look what happened when we reached Beirut—it [the war in Lebanon in the summer of 1982] did not end and we withdrew from there. And [as for] the intifada—it was possible for it to have continued [an additional] eight years. I ask: why did it end? And in my opinion, it would not have ended [had there not been a political agreement reached with the PLO] but would, rather, have lengthened the list of graves on our side and theirs, and perhaps would even have worsened. In the case of guerilla warfare and in the intifada, it should be understood that it is the political echelon's responsibility to take the bull by the horns and to deal with the peace process.[14]

Disagreements about the war in Lebanon were not the only source of tension between the military and the prime minister; tension followed as well from Netanyahu's belief in the need for an ironfisted policy toward terror organizations and guerilla attacks in general. The public got a small glimpse of this during the 1999 election campaigns, when Mordecai ran against Netanyahu for prime minister. He publicly accused Netanyahu of frequently initiating "aggressive and irresponsible" military operations and "pursuing policy which would lead to the destruction of relations between Israel and its neighbors, to the point of harming [Israel's] national interest."[15]

Criticism of Netanyahu's defense policy was also being voiced behind closed doors at high-ranking officers' bureaus. After his release from IDF service, Deputy CGS Vilnay revealed, "Netanyahu's way was not my way. . . . He was disappointing as a prime minister. I was disturbed by his lack of understanding with regard to things he had to do. My main criticism of him is of his nonimplementation of what was agreed to with Arafat."[16] Officers were also critical of Netanyahu for not always telling the truth. In the language of Mordecai, "The prime minister is deceiving members of his government and giving them distorted information." Indeed, the period from the end of 1997 to the beginning of 1998 was one of the low points of the military-government relationship.

During the course of discussions about the second phase of the Oslo Accords, which included a proposed withdrawal of Israeli troops from Hebron, the prime minister requested that the recently appointed head of the Planning and Policy Directorate, Shlomo Yanai, prepare a detailed agreement for security cooperation between the IDF and the Palestinian Authority. The document was prepared, and Yanai flew with the prime minister to London to present it to U.S. secretary of state Madeleine Albright. Before showing her the document, Yanai received comments on it from a CIA representative, presented it to Netanyahu, and received Netanyahu's support and approval. On Netanyahu's and Yanai's return from Europe, the document was debated by the Israeli "security cabinet" (a smaller forum than the full cabinet), and the more militant among the government ministers sharply criticized the paper. The prime minister reacted by disparaging the document he had earlier approved not only in the closed forum of the security cabinet meeting but also in comments leaked to the press; he called it a "sloppy working paper" prepared for him by the military, claiming he had completely rejected it. The prime minister, who then withdrew from the agreement he had made with Albright at their meeting in London, simply turned the IDF into a scapegoat. This greatly offended the upper echelons of the IDF's General Staff, who were used to Rabin's fatherly working style; Rabin had always said "the responsibility is mine."

The "defense establishment"—a term the media often used when the chief of general staff's office was their source—quickly leaked its own views to the press, declaring its outrage at the criticisms leveled against the IDF. "The political echelon is cynically and evilly using the defense establishment. We weren't the ones who requested the 'security document'; it was designed all along for political purposes and approved by the political echelon."[17] Two days later, these opaque matters became

clearer to the public when Ben Caspit, *Ma'ariv*'s political affairs correspondent, wrote an explanation of how the "deterioration in relations
between Netanyahu and the defense establishment" had developed.

Additionally, the CGS did not accept the attacks on the IDF, especially those on the new major general he had appointed to head the Planning and Policy Directorate, who had left the security cabinet meeting
humiliated. The IDF spokesman published an announcement condemn-
ing "Major General Yanai's anonymous attackers." "Those attacking
Major General Yanai are wrong themselves and are misleading others,"
the announcement read. The IDF spokesman later explained that, of
course, he was not referring to the prime minister. But, in fact, all those
who saw the announcement knew just the opposite to be true.

Whereas in the situation with Yanai the scales of public opinion
tilted against Netanyahu, in the incident involving Maj. Gen. Oren Shachor the scales tilted in Netanyahu's favor. This latter episode erupted in
November 1996, when an Israeli paparazzi-style photojournalist caught
Shachor, coordinator of IDF operations in the occupied territories, entering the house of opposition leader Shimon Peres late at night and leaving
after an hour and a half. It emerged that Shachor was in the habit of holding one-on-one meetings with Peres, Peres's senior aides, and MK Yossi
Sarid, the head of Meretz (another opposition party), and that he was
doing so without the knowledge and approval of the CGS, the defense
minister, or the prime minister. This was in clear violation of IDF regulations, which ban such contact. Shachor tried to justify these meetings as
"social conversations," but it was clear that the major general, who headed
the civilian committee in talks with the Palestinian Authority, was in-
forming the opposition leaders about how those talks were developing.

This affair provoked great outrage from the government and its supporters in the Knesset. Shachor was accused of illegal activity, and ministers
called for his dismissal from the IDF, while Labor Party Knesset members
defended him. The prime minister and defense minister ultimately allowed
Shachor to remain in his position as coordinator of operations in the occupied territories, but they suspended him from his position as chairman of
the civilian committee for negotiations with the Palestinians, removing
him from the talks. "I think that the IDF's generals, its commanders, and
the IDF generally must make an effort to be thoroughly nonpolitical, as
regards both direct and indirect involvement," said Defense Minister

Mordecai. He explained the suspension by stating, "The IDF must zealously be kept out of political debates."[18] It was clear, however, that Shachor's suspension was also a message to the entire officer corps, indicating that a new policy had been adopted vis-à-vis the Palestinians. Soon thereafter Shachor requested a discharge from the IDF, and he left the military.

But, from the moment he exchanged his uniform for civilian clothes, Shachor began attacking Netanyahu and his government's policies. He claimed to speak "in the name of the generals who cannot speak and in whose back Netanyahu is shooting." He added that "there is an atmosphere of acute paranoia and witch hunting on the part of the prime minister, directed at the IDF's high echelons."[19] Announcing that he would run on the Knesset Labor list, Shachor explained that "[the behavior of] Netanyahu pushed both [Shahak] and me into politics . . . I, like [Shahak], see a threat in Netanyahu." Shachor did not conceal his political views and his disagreements with government policy either. "I already understood when I was a military man that Netanyahu was dangerous to Israel," he said in a January 1999 interview. "A [future] Palestinian state is a fact. The only question is whether it will be imposed upon us or whether we will deal with it through negotiations. My fear is that if Netanyahu will be in power in May 1999, and we do not see a Palestinian state as a fact, there will be a violent confrontation with the Palestinians in the territories, and this could destabilize the whole region, shaking the fragile membrane of which the peace with Egypt and Jordan consists."[20]

Two months after Shachor left the IDF, Brig. Gen. (res.) David Agmon, who had served for a few months as the head of the prime minister's bureau, also resigned. Upon leaving office, he made a restrained public comment: "I left the prime minister's office worried."[21] But, off the record, he, too, spoke very harshly about Netanyahu, as did other high-ranking officers.

Netanyahu and Shahak Clash

Soon after Netanyahu took office, he displayed a chilly demeanor toward CGS Shahak and unstable relations evolved between the two. For example, Netanyahu ended a long-standing tradition of the prime minister meeting one-on-one with the CGS each week. Indeed, from time to time the prime minister and CGS were in full-fledged conflict. In one instance,

Netanyahu silenced Shahak in the middle of a cabinet briefing, stating, "It was not the CGS's role to provide political analyses."[22] Netanyahu's actions—and his general pattern of behavior—created an uproar, making front-page news. "Outrage in the IDF: CGS Silenced by Netanyahu" read the headline in *Yedioth Ahronoth*, a newspaper read by nearly 70 percent of Israelis.[23]

The prime minister's and CGS's bureaus both hastened to explain the above incident, each from its own perspective, though the political branch has an advantage over the military, as the latter is barred, according to standard procedure, from arguing with its civilian superiors. In light of the prime minister's office's success at spinning the incident in the media, Shahak wrote to Netanyahu twice in the course of that week, accusing him of publicizing an incorrect and misleading account of the cabinet meeting, and then leaked the letters to the press. Shortly thereafter, *Yedioth Ahronoth* ran a cover story by military correspondent Alex Fishman, the headline for which read, "New Low in the Strained Relations between the Prime Minister and the CGS in the Wake of the Silencing Incident. The CGS Accuses the Prime Minister of Untrustworthiness." *Ha'aretz,* meanwhile, reported,

> The IDF spokesman refused to comment yesterday, but senior people at the IDF leveled strong criticism at Netanyahu and his helpers, their attitude toward the CGS, and, most importantly, their credibility. "Not one word from the mouths of those people should be believed," a military source said, referring to Netanyahu's office. The response from senior people in the Likud: "It is very serious when letters against the prime minister are leaked to the press. This move has a strong political smell to it. The CGS is harming the IDF and turning it into his personal political toy."

The conflict with Netanyahu was one of the reasons Shahak ultimately decided to join the political arena; he wanted, in his own words, "to continue Rabin's interrupted enterprise."[24] But Netanyahu suspected Shahak's political motivations even before the general had seriously thought of becoming a politician and went on the offensive. Knowing that the popularity and prestige of the CGS derives from his nonpartisan image, Netanyahu decided to strike Shahak's Achilles' heel: he did not praise the CGS in public, as Israeli prime ministers always do, but instead described him as a leftist. This was a real blow to Shahak. From the moment he decided to enter politics, he was forced to spend the bulk of his energy trying to remove this leftist label, which had stuck to him very quickly. As a result, he even rejected Barak's invitation to join him and be the number two candidate on the One Israel Party list for the Knesset. Instead of joining Barak, Shahak—as noted above—formed a new party with Mordecai and other former high-ranking officers called (what else?) the Center Party.

In the end, the reserve and retired IDF officers successfully mobilized against Netanyahu in the elections. Their involvement was not, of course, the only reason for the Likud leader's dramatic electoral demise. Netanyahu also lost the confidence of the right flank of his government. The media mobilized against him as well, not so much because of his policies but more so because of his character and behavior. But the assistance of the military establishment, through the actions of reserve and retired officers, helped the campaign against Netanyahu a great deal. As expected, the IDF's most senior officers did not conceal their delight at Barak's victory over Netanyahu. During the IDF reception for the newly elected prime minister, Barak even went so far as to say that he had been more excited to visit the General Staff's conference room in Tel Aviv than he had been to enter the prime minister's office in Jerusalem, because among the General Staff he felt as though he had "come home."[25]

In addition to being prime minister, Barak also took on the role of defense minister, as so many Israeli prime ministers had done in the past. His decisive victory in the elections was not the only factor that led to this decision; he was also prompted by his desire to involve deeply the military in the peace process. He explicitly stated this fact: "I insisted on being defense minister, because I was anxious about strong opposition from the military to agreements with Syria and the Palestinians, and I wanted to ensure that, under my direct supervision, the military would support the [peace] process and would be a full partner." But there was also the political factor: "I was also anxious about the dynamic that might form between three people, if the defense minister and the CGS formed a majority against me."[26]

The General Staff's major generals were no less excited at the reception for Barak than was the new prime minister himself. Their emissaries to the power halls, the many dozens of officers who had only recently exchanged their uniforms for civilian clothes, had succeeded in joining civilian political forces. Further, they had brought about the downfall of the Netanyahu government and returned one of their own to the prime minister's office, thus sending a clear message to the politicians about the generals' centrality to Israeli politics. Indeed, the Barak government included no small number of former major generals and brigadier generals, including Ben-Eliezer and Sneh.[27] No less important was that key positions in the new administration—particularly those that required close contact with the prime minister—were given to high-ranking retired officers. In fact, Barak gave them the responsibility of moving the peace process with the Palestinians and with Syria forward, the two main agenda items he set for his government. He wished to continue the historic transformation begun by Rabin in the early 1990s.

Soon after Barak's term in office began, the peace engine moved back into high gear, with the IDF's upper echelons helping Barak in his work. And, without the burden of having a defense minister who might be a barrier between him and the CGS, he was able to work closely with CGS Shaul Mofaz, whose views toward the peace process aligned with the his own. In fact, Mofaz enthusiastically referred to himself as the man who would be "Israel's first peacetime CGS." No one, however, asked, if the generals supported the peace process even to the point of influencing the general elections, albeit democratically and legitimately, might they not also show the same forcefulness if the government's peace policies suddenly became unappealing to them? This, of course, is what came to happen sixteen months after Barak took office.

6

The IDF Confronts
a New Intifada

Barak and the IDF Disagree

Throughout the euphoric days of the peace negotiations, there were officers within the military's General Staff who were not too happy with the
policies of the government. These officers never stopped questioning
whether Arafat actually intended to reach a peace accord with Israel, and
they voiced their opinion to the new prime minister. The most senior in
this group, Maj. Gen. Amos Gilead, missed no opportunity to express his
negative opinion of Arafat. "There is no chance we can reach an agreement with him," he said repeatedly. "We should not make compromises.
After each one he will demand ever more." Barak listened but deferred
responding to this view.[1] Although the IDF as an institution continued
to support the peace process, the hard-liners' position was further
strengthened by a number of events that began in 1996; these events eventually altered the balance of power between the two schools within the
General Staff.

The first and most important episode occurred in September 1996,
when there was a deadly response to the opening of an ancient Hasmonaean tunnel in the midst of the Muslim quarter of Jerusalem's Old City.
The Palestinians reacted to this unilateral Israeli step, seen as an attempt
to undermine the Muslim nature of the quarter, with a wave of violence
that left eleven Israelis dead. What most shocked Israelis was that the
Palestinian police helped the rioting citizens; the police, in fact, fought

IDF soldiers using weapons Israel had given them. The research division of the MID likely retorted to its professional rivals with the words, "We told you so" and referred to a document it presented a year earlier that stated, "Arafat is preparing a round of riots because he does not want to finalize the Hebron agreement, and he hopes to attain further political goals through the riots, such as a commitment to implement more withdrawals after the Hebron agreement."[2]

Another event that occurred in 1996 also had a far-reaching effect on military thinking. In the spring of that year, the IDF launched the "Grapes of Wrath" operation in southern Lebanon, aimed at eliminating the threat of Katyusha rockets and mortar shells being fired into Israeli territory. This was an operation in the style of future wars, using assault helicopters, mini–remotely piloted vehicles (MRPVs), mobile artillery, and smart ammunition. All this was designed to avoid exposing the IDF soldiers to friction and burnout. The operation went well until IDF shells were mistakenly fired on a UN base in Kana, Lebanon, killing more than one hundred civilians, including women and children. This turned everything upside down. Israel was widely accused of slaughtering innocents and lost favor in international public opinion. Prime Minister Peres was forced to stop the operation, which came to be viewed as a clear failure.

Though close cooperation between the United States and Israel continued in the second half of the 1990s, Washington placed constraints on Israel's acquisition of weapons and on its development of some military capabilities. "Contrary to the sense of security that the tight cooperation with our strategic ally had given us—which made it easier for us to give up the Sinai in the framework of the peace treaty with Egypt—we understood that now things were different, and that we would not be able to receive from the U.S. all of the weapons systems we had asked for," said Major General Almog, who was involved in the strategic dialogue with the United States at the time.[3]

Problems at the daily operational level compounded the difficulties the IDF was experiencing in the strategic sphere. The ongoing war in Lebanon and the continual terrorist attacks in the territories and in Israel proper made it clear to many IDF strategists that the peace process would not provide a sustainable solution to Israel's worsening security problems. These strategists were particularly worried that the IDF could not win in these conflicts. The IDF was restrained by political pressures—as the Kana case demonstrated—and its scope of action was restricted because of coverage by the international media. It knew any mistake at the tactical level, such as a misfired artillery shell or a soldier breaking the rules for opening fire, could have severe strategic and political implications. All of this was happening at a time when civilian society was growing increasingly tired of the ongoing conflict and wanted to return to normal life and when its traditionally supportive and admiring attitude toward the IDF and military service was changing. As a result, the self-confidence that had enabled the IDF's General Staff to promote negotiations with the Palestinians was eroding.

Nevertheless, the IDF's basic strategy of supporting the peace accords, which was developed in the beginning of the 1990s, had not yet been obliterated. The IDF recommended shifting the focus: postpone the negotiations with the Palestinians and renew negotiations with Syria. In fact, when Barak had served as CGS under Rabin, he had expressed a preference for negotiating with Syria first. The Supreme Command became encouraged by the fact that Barak, soon after taking his post as prime minister, began changing the late Rabin's line of policy and started negotiating with Israel's northern neighbor. This course of action lasted for ten months, during which the Israeli and Syrian sides became closer than ever before, to the discontent of Arafat and the Palestinians. After some initial probing in the autumn, the Israelis and Syrians began negotiations with the Washington Talks on December 15, 1999. But the whole process eventually collapsed after a failed summit between U.S. president Bill Clinton and Syrian president Hafez al-Assad in Geneva in March 2000. Israel, the United States, and to a large extent the international public blamed Assad for the failure of the negotiations. According to this interpretation, the fatally ill Assad was eager to pass his throne to his politically inexperienced son. But, fearful of the Western influence on Syria that might follow a peace accord with Israel, he eventually decided to preserve his totalitarian regime.[4]

In the IDF command, however, some, including CGS Mofaz, had a different interpretation for why the negotiations failed, although the difference of opinion between Mofaz and Barak over policies vis-à-vis Syria remained mostly hidden, known only to their confidants. To Mofaz and other officers, Barak's firm refusal of Assad's demand for an Israeli withdrawal from a very narrow strip of land along the eastern shore of the Lake of Galilee was unjustified. Barak had already indicated he would move away from previous Israeli policies and withdraw from all of the Golan Heights. His insistence on not complying with Assad's latter demand resulted from his belief that he would not be able to gain public support for such a far-reaching step. To the opposing IDF officers, this seemed a misguided political calculation and not an appropriate stand for a high-level statesman. To them this was "a victory of internal political considerations over considerations of security and the state."[5]

While Barak and Mofaz had at first agreed about the peace process with the Palestinians, their growing dispute became public when the two differed on policies concerning Lebanon. During his election campaign, Barak had announced that as prime minister he would take the IDF out of Lebanon within a year. This move had been planned to be carried out as part of a peace agreement with Syria. However, Hizbullah attacks led to a continuing blood drain of IDF personnel throughout 1999, and public pressure to retreat from Lebanon increased. Barak, realizing that he would not be able to achieve an accord with Syria, decided to act unilaterally. Mofaz and most of the General Staff officers rejected this move, estimating that Palestinian organizations in southern Lebanon would continue their attacks on Israel's northern frontier once Israel retreated from the security zone. They also predicted that Hizbullah would regard this move as a cowardly Israeli retreat and see its own violent actions as having led to this victory, thus weakening Israel's deterrence power.

In fact, Barak was not the first prime minister to broach the subject of withdrawal from southern Lebanon. His predecessor, Netanyahu, had also suggested withdrawal, but Mofaz had managed to successfully scuttle his initiatives.[6] Indeed, Mofaz, "who did not distinguish between a uniform and a homogeneous opinion, used to force uniform stands on the Supreme Command and was discontent when other opinions were expressed."[7] Though he initially managed to keep from the public the views of some IDF officers who believed that a unilateral withdrawal would be a better option than staying in southern Lebanon, as the public pressure to withdraw grew stronger, these opinions started to come to light. Eventually Barak set a date for retreat and announced it to the IDF. Mofaz and many other officers in the General Staff reacted furiously.

Following Barak's order to prepare for a withdrawal, Mofaz issued a statement saying that the IDF would obey this command, adding that "the IDF does not choose its own missions." This statement was an expression of the instrumental approach, according to which the military carries out the government's decisions. Barak and others, however, understood the statement's real meaning very well. As Maj. Gen. Uzi Dayan later articulated, "Allegedly, this declaration is the ultimate proof of the military's compliance with the decisions taken by the political sphere. However, it can also be seen in a different light, as the shedding off of responsibility. This declaration would enable the military to blame the politicians for any future failure or negative implications of the withdrawal."[8] Dayan added, "The appropriate state of affairs should be that military personnel participate in the decision-making process, when dealing with relevant issues. But once these decisions are made, the IDF should carry out its missions as if it has chosen them itself."[9]

The prime minister and the CGS also had differences of opinion about the point to which Israel should withdraw. The military wanted a line that would be easy to defend and that would give it control of the terrain, and therefore it demanded that the new line pass through southern Lebanon in certain areas. Barak recognized that the withdrawal would fulfill certain aims, such as bringing about an increase in international support for Israel and giving legitimacy to military responses to Hizbullah if the group continued attacking Israel from southern Lebanon. But he believed these aims could only be accomplished if the IDF were stationed on the recognized international border. This, in fact, is the line to which Israel ultimately withdrew, and the United Nations confirmed the border, giving its blessing to the move.

The withdrawal, which was accomplished the night of May 22–23, 2000, was carried out without casualties, despite the skeptics' predictions, and was presented to the public as a successful operation. The IDF, however, perceived it as a fatal error, a panicked retreat that was forced on the military. From 2000 onward, the withdrawal from Lebanon, a collective traumatic experience for the IDF, would have far-reaching consequences on the military's morale, strategic thinking, and operational mode.

Even though the pessimistic assessments regarding Hizbullah's anticipated behavior were proved wrong and the border remained relatively calm, this did nothing to improve relations between Barak and Mofaz. In

Barak's view, Mofaz's mistaken assessment harmed his personal prestige and that of his supporters in the Supreme Command, while Mofaz and most of his generals continued to perceive the withdrawal from southern Lebanon as a weakening of Israel's deterrent posture. Hizbullah, meanwhile, portrayed the withdrawal as a heroic victory. Many in Israel believed—and this was the prevailing opinion within the IDF—that this claim would only strengthen the Palestinians' notion that they could similarly drive Israel out of the West Bank. The perceived need to restore Israel's deterrent power in its enemies' eyes, and, equally, to restore the honor of the military in the eyes of the Israeli public, would hereafter considerably impact Israel's military policy toward the Palestinians.

The Way to Peace Leads to War

This series of events somewhat diminished the enthusiasm for the peace negotiations that the General Staff had felt at the beginning of the 1990s. Though the generals still supported the talks and participated in the negotiations, and though the skeptics on the General Staff were still in the minority, the IDF began to prepare itself for the possibility that conflict would resume, assessing that the next confrontation would be more violent than the first intifada, when the Palestinians' weapons had consisted mainly of stones.

Following the first intifada, IDF planners reached the conclusion that an irresolute policy and the absence of a sharp response in the initial days of unrest were perceived by the insurgents as weakness on Israel's part, encouraging them to continue the fighting. For this reason, the IDF devised a much more resolute and extensive response to suppress a future insurgency from the outset. This response was based on a simple premise: an intense show of strength immediately following a spate of violence would make the insurgents realize the heavy price they would pay if their hostilities continued; it was assumed, then, this would cool their ardor at once.

Based on operational lessons learned from the first intifada and the events of the Hasmonaean tunnel, therefore, the IDF formed a new strategy for managing low-intensity conflict known as "thorny field": the military would act only if the talks broke down and the peace process came to a standstill. This highly detailed plan accounted for every contingency, outlining courses of action for everyone from the soldiers standing at checkpoints to the highest-level politicians. The IDF prepared thoroughly for the possibility that it would have to implement this plan. Boogy Ya'alon, the head of Central Command who was deeply involved in the construction of this strategy, had no doubt that such a moment would arrive in the not-too-distant future.

In the summer of 2000, President Clinton's second term was coming to an end, and Barak was in a hurry to reach an overall peace agreement that would bring the conflict to a close. To this end, Barak urged Clinton to convene a peace conference at Camp David. On the eve of the conference, Gilead, as head of the MID research division, presented the prime minister with an unequivocal assessment of Arafat. He had not for one moment changed his opinion of him.

In Gilead's estimation, Arafat had far more in mind than obtaining his basic goals: a Palestinian state within the 1967 borders with Jerusalem (El-Kuds) as its capital, sovereignty over the Temple Mount (al-Haram al-Sharif), and the right of return for Palestinian refugees. The establishment of a Palestinian state, according to Gilead's assessment, was just the first stage in Arafat's plan. He believed that the veteran Palestinian leader's insistence on the Palestinian refugees' right of return to Israel stemmed from Arafat's intention to use them as a time bomb against Israel. Thus, Gilead warned, unlike President Sadat or King Hussein of Jordan, Arafat never intended to accede to the existence of the Jewish state. On the eve of the summit, Gilead proclaimed that Arafat would not conclude a deal with Barak at Camp David and that he had already laid the groundwork for a military confrontation that would start immediately after the summit's collapse.[10]

This was not the only assessment Barak received from his intelligence experts. The ISA, the Planning and Policy Directorate, and the head of the MID, Maj. Gen. Amos Malka, were more sanguine. Malka estimated that Arafat would not compromise on his basic demands, but that he nevertheless was interested in reaching an agreement at the summit.[11] Even more interesting was the position of Col. Ephraim Lavie, the head of the Palestinian desk in the MID's research division, who was considered to be very knowledgeable about Palestinian society and its organizations.

Prior to the summit, Lavie explained why Arafat could not possibly be expected to agree to Barak's demand, that is, to sign an agreement at Camp David that would "put an end to the conflict" and commit the Palestinians to renounce all their claims vis-à-vis Israel. This demand, explained Lavie, required the Palestinians to discuss the results not only of the 1967 war but also of the 1948–49 war. The representative bodies of the Palestinian national movement authorized the leadership to talk about the former but not the latter, and without a change in principle in the movement's political bodies even Arafat could not reach such a radical agreement at the summit.[12]

But Barak, a capable man with unbounded self-confidence, rejected the assessments presented by Gilead and Malka, not to speak of Lavie's intricate analysis. Motivated by a sense of historic mission and seeing himself as a leader of the magnitude of Israel's founder, David Ben-Gurion, Barak believed in his ability to cut the Gordian knot and do the unbelievable: he would persuade Arafat and the Palestinian delegation to put an end to the hundred-year dispute at one short summit conference. This was hubris par excellence.[13]

The ultimate failure of the Camp David talks engendered a shift in the attitudes of the IDF leadership. The intensity of the violence at the beginning of the second intifada and the actual participation of the Palestinian police and other security organizations in it—for example, on the first day a Palestinian policeman shot his Israeli partner in a joint patrol unit—led increasing numbers of officers from the accommodationist school to join the ranks of the hard-liners. Stated officers at the outbreak of violence, "It is a good thing that we prepared for this possibility and responded at once according to our contingency plan."[14]

While many within the IDF ranks saw Arafat as the cause of the violence, the Palestinians blamed Israel for the outbreak of the intifada. According to the Palestinians, the intifada was a spontaneous popular uprising in reaction to Sharon's visit to the Temple Mount on September 28, 2000. However, such an interpretation is wrong. The intifada was conceived long before Sharon's visit to the Temple Mount. While this event served as a catalyst, the intifada would have broken out with or without Sharon's action. But what the IDF officers had failed to realize was that their high level of preparedness for the riots and their aggressive response

—carried out according to prearranged plans—would not quench the fire burning through the streets of the territories. Rather, "thorny field" only served to fan the flames. Eventually, some in the IDF publicly admitted this, including senior officers who had been involved in the early responses to the intifada. According to Brig. Gen. (res.) Zvi Fogel, who was the operation's branch officer in the Central Command, the IDF was so well prepared, had created such high expectations in its soldiers and officers, and had such a low response threshold, that it seemed as if the military was waiting for an excuse to open fire. "I think," said Fogel in retrospect, "that our actions accelerated the Palestinians' massive use of weapons."[15]

During the first weeks of the riots, the IDF's heavy fire resulted in dozens of Palestinian casualties, while only a few Israelis were wounded; in fact, for each Israeli casualty, fifteen Palestinians were hurt. The IDF was pleased with the overall results, and Mofaz even took pride in a phone call he received from a worried Palestinian leader, Muhammad Dahlan, who asked, "Why is it that only we get killed and you don't?"[16] It later emerged that in the first days of the intifada the IDF fired missiles of various types and no less than one million rounds of ammunition in the territories. Officers in Central Command said this was an astronomical figure that testified to what happened in the field.[17] Shlomo Ben-Ami, foreign minister in Barak's government, carried out a postmortem on the conduct of the military at the beginning of the intifada and was critical of the IDF response. He compared what happened in those early days to a spring that had been stretched and suddenly released. "Sometimes," he added, "the dynamics of the IDF response far exceeded what had been authorized."[18]

What Mofaz had not taken into account was the possibility that such a huge blow to the Palestinians would have negative consequences and lead to a result that was the opposite of what he had anticipated. When the intifada broke out, it bore the character of a popular uprising, like the first intifada, with masses of people going out into the streets. Yet only two months later, after the harsh measures used by the IDF, the uprising changed its character and became a full-blown armed struggle. Palestinian Authority security forces and Islamist and radical groups moved to the front lines, while Arafat maneuvered between them. But, as the balance of blood continued to favor heavily the Israelis, the Palestinians reintroduced their ultimate weapon in January 2001: human bombs—suicidal terrorists —in the midst of the Israeli heartland.

If nothing else, the intifada, in which some of Israel's own Arab citizens took part (police shot and killed thirteen of them), strengthened the belief that "there is no one to talk to," a view Barak and others had disseminated immediately following the failure of Camp David. (Even President Clinton supported this perspective.) As Israeli military leaders began to echo this sentiment following the outbreak of the intifada, it gained currency and soon became the dominant Israeli view toward Arafat and the Palestinian leadership. According to Barak, Arafat had been "unmasked" and responsibility for the failure of Camp David and for the outbreak of the intifada lay with him. Barak stated that Arafat did not want and had never wanted to reach an agreement, because his ultimate goal was to establish a Palestinian state on the ruins of the state of Israel. Thus, at the end of 2000, Gilead could sit comfortably in his seat: the crusade that he had waged throughout the peace process against Arafat and against conciliation had finally succeeded. His point of view had become dominant not only within Israel's military elite but also within Israeli society itself.

The extent of Gilead's success only came to light four years later, when both Lavie and Malka, after their release from the IDF, revealed that Gilead's strategic assessment was not the only one that existed among MID officers. Lavie and Malka themselves had disagreed with the main thrust of Gilead's argument in position papers they presented to political leaders in 2001; both claimed that Gilead's assessments were not supported by intelligence material. For example, Lavie argued that although Arafat had exploited the violence for his own purposes, it had broken out from below, and that the insurgency was not continuing as an expression of his desire to destroy Israel but as a tactical move to gain more concessions from it.

However, the verbal assessments delivered by Gilead to the political leaders, along with his high status and the vast prestige he had accumulated, overshadowed the written positions of Lavie and Malka. More important, there was a strong correlation between Gilead's assessment of the situation and Barak's own political interests. The prime minister needed to explain why the talks at Camp David had failed and to justify to the public the many concessions he had been prepared to make there. His explanation was simple: by offering such far-reaching concessions, he was able to expose Arafat's true face as a man not interested in peace. Even though the Israelis and Palestinians grew closer on various positions at Camp David, Barak made no effort to cast the conclusion of the Camp David conference in a positive light or to present the outcome as an opportunity for further negotiations, as did senior Palestinian delegate Saab Arikat. Rather, Barak deliberately chose to present the "unmasking" thesis because it helped him politically.[19]

This particular spin soon had a critical impact on Israeli policy planning. After all, if the true intentions of Arafat and the Palestinian Authority had really been exposed and there was really nobody to talk to, there was absolutely no point in entering further talks with them or in trying to renew negotiations; all that remained to be done was to prepare for protracted conflict and a military victory. With Barak and Gilead as its champions, this belief remained the dominant one within the IDF during the first three years of the intifada. But Barak's relationship with Gilead and certain other members of the MID had other broad implications, too. Not only did it demonstrate the close links that have existed throughout the years between military intelligence and policymakers, but it also showed that military research personnel might promote policies based on erroneous assumptions, or—even worse—provide assessments based on political assumptions of the prime minister. As a result, some military officials have begun to express concern that intelligence assessments may be tailored to suit the needs and wishes of politicians.[20]

According to Amos Harel and Avi Isacharoff, "Malka and Lavie's words cast an unflattering light on the statesmen (Barak and later Sharon) and the top military echelon (Mofaz and Ya'alon), who heard from Gilead what they wanted to hear, namely corroboration of their 'conception.'" This analysis is supported by others, such as the former head of the navy and the ISA, Ami Ayalon, who said, "We imposed a certain picture of reality on the events and acted according to it. The defense establishment sold us a story, describing the intifada as a planned and coordinated move of the Palestinian leadership . . . and accordingly the IDF used snipers, backed up by legal approval granted on the basis of those intelligence descriptions, killing both armed men and civilians and escalating the conflict."[21]

Despite Barak's resolute stance against Arafat, calling him the ringleader of the intifada and demanding that he stop the uprising and order the Tanzim—the armed organization of Arafat's Fatah movement— to turn in its illegal arms, Barak had not yet lost hope that an agreement could be reached and gave his approval for a resumption of negotiations. According to Arikat, Israelis and Palestinians held no less than fifty-four meetings between the Camp David summit and the last conference at Taba,[22] which began on January 21, 2001, when members of the Israeli delegation that had gone to Camp David met with their Palestinian counterparts along the placid Red Sea shore. As these meetings took place while the intifada was raging, there was something bizarre about them, especially given Israel's earlier claims that it would not negotiate as long as violence continued. Barak made it clear that these were not formal talks and that whatever was agreed to would not be binding until all relevant issues had been resolved. He even disallowed the recording of the talk's protocol.

However, whereas the Camp David negotiations were conducted while Barak's government was a minority government lacking parliamentary support, the Taba talks were conducted by a caretaker government facing elections set to take place February 6. Further, all evidence indicated a landslide for the opposition. Therefore, the opposition parties charged that the government was conducting the negotiations at Taba for campaign purposes and that for this reason it would not hesitate to reach an agreement, even if this deeply jeopardized Israel's future. Additionally, the attorney general doubted whether a caretaker government was legally entitled to conduct such negotiations. And the public, disappointed by the Camp David talks and angered by the outbreak of the intifada, did not believe that the Palestinian Authority or its leaders wished to achieve any agreement.

Months later, Barak argued publicly that he had not expected the Taba talks to reach any conclusion and that his sole purpose had been to further expose Arafat's rigid, nonconciliatory stance. But that argument is easily refuted and indeed has been by some of the Israeli participants at the talks. Several of them even claimed that there had been progress on many of the issues left open at Camp David and that had there been more time, an agreement could have been reached.[23] Whatever the truth, the General Staff was vehemently opposed to the Taba talks and Mofaz clearly saw the very existence of them as a capitulation to Palestinian terror.

For his part, Barak did grow increasingly skeptical about an agreement ever being reached and ultimately instructed Ephraim Sneh, his deputy in the Defense Ministry, to draw up alternative plans.[24] For the first time since 1967, the possibility of Israel's withdrawal from the occupied territories without the framework of a peace agreement was broached. The purpose of this unilateral Israeli step, which included removal of Jewish settlements, would be to minimize friction between Israel and the Palestinians.[25] But such a strategy was anathema to the General Staff; they saw such an action as further submission to terrorists. Additionally, military strategists had concluded as early as September 2000 that "the conflict-resolution approach has been exhausted. From now on violence will dictate our adversaries' behavior and therefore ours as well."[26]

Did Barak Lose Control over the Military?

Between the outbreak of the intifada in late September 2000 and the conclusion of the Taba conference, which was followed by the fall of Barak's government four months later, an unhealthy relationship existed between the government and the military. On a structural level, the source of the trouble lay in the strained relations that started to develop between Barak and Mofaz as soon as Barak became prime minister. Barak's deep engagement in the peace negotiations resulted in his functioning only part-time as defense minister. This meant that Mofaz, who operated with a high degree of independence, virtually became acting defense minister. As a result, Mofaz's self-confidence increased. For example, on February 15, 2000, following a week of heavy fire in Lebanon, Mofaz informed the media that he would recommend that the cabinet implement a new policy in Lebanon that would include direct fire on Hizbullah positions located within villages. The cabinet ministers were furious with Mofaz. Following his announcement, Foreign Minister David Levy said that "it is improper for cabinet ministers to learn of the chief of staff's recommendations from the media."[27]

While friction between Mofaz and cabinet ministers grew, several disputes also raged between Mofaz and Barak during the course of that year. In one case, Mofaz opposed the appointment of Barak's candidate for the position of IDF chief rabbi, declaring, "I will not let politicians get involved in this matter."[28] A more severe incident occurred when Barak appointed Deputy CGS Uzi Dayan as the head of the National Security Council. Mofaz stood against the appointment of an acting officer close to the prime minister and sharply criticized his superior, surprising some of his own loyal colleagues in the General Staff with his comments. The prime minister responded harshly. A still deeper disagreement arose when Barak, in a casual remark made just before boarding a plane for the United States, told Mofaz about his decision to cut the defense budget (some say he wrote it on a crumpled piece of paper). This incident led Mofaz to feel increasingly insulted and angry, sentiments that had first arisen when Barak ordered Israel's withdrawal from southern Lebanon.

Indeed, the military and government were perhaps at greatest odds over defense policy. After the popular manifestation of the intifada dwindled in December 2000 and it assumed the appearance of an armed struggle conducted by the Palestinian authorities, the IDF's assessment was as follows: "This is not an Intifada, a peoples' uprising, but rather a campaign conducted from above by the PA. Therefore, containment will not do any longer, and there is a need to change the strategic approach and to put constant and uninterrupted pressure directly on the PA, so it confronts the terrorists."[29] But the government adopted a "dual-policy" approach; while it agreed with the IDF perception of *à la guerre comme à la guerre,* it attempted to continue negotiations with Arafat and the Palestinian Authority in the hope of reaching a settlement. The result was a policy that seemed to the military to be not only confused and incoherent but also wrong. As a close observer of the military noted, "It's a long time since there has been such a spirit of skepticism among the senior officers toward the politicians and the double message coming from the political level."[30]

Mofaz also had a very clear opinion not only of the appropriate attitude Israel should have concerning the Palestinian Authority, but also of the nature of any political solution in the future. In December 2000, when President Clinton publicly announced his parameters for a peace agreement, Mofaz voiced strong opposition to the proposal. In fact, during a consultation in the prime minister's bureau, he defined it as "a danger to the state." His remarks were so dramatic that Barak charged, "Shaul, you do not really think that Israel can't exist without ruling over the Palestinian people, but that's the conclusion that arises from your comments."[31]

While the CGS is expected to express his opinions in internal discussions, he is not expected to go public with them, especially when they differ from the policy of the prime minister and defense minister. But this did not stop news stories of the conflict between Barak and Mofaz from duly appearing in the press: "Senior officers in the IDF this week expressed surprise and criticism of the American proposal, which the government views favorably. In addition to the details of the agreement, the IDF has reservations about what appear to be exaggerated concessions to the Palestinians while the fighting in the territories still continues on a large scale."[32] This and other such news items made clear to all that Mofaz had blatantly deviated from proper protocol.

The IDF did not stop with general leaks, and, before the cabinet convened to discuss the Clinton plan, an article appeared in *Ha'aretz* describing in detail Mofaz's position on the subject and his opposition to eight substantial points in the proposal. "The IDF sees peace as important to Israel's security and supports continuation of the negotiations with the Palestinians," he told a *Ha'aretz* reporter, "but these security arrangements will destroy the peace agreement and present a significant threat to Israel."[33] At a government session, the CGS repeated this statement in such a severe tone that some of the participants later said that they were shocked. By most accounts, Mofaz had thrown down the gauntlet, defying the government and its head, challenging the president of the United States, whom the government saw as an incomparably faithful ally to Israel, and inviting public pressure to persuade the government to reject the Clinton plan.

As the intifada continued in late 2000, the friction between Barak and Mofaz only intensified.[34] While Barak's official policy focused generally on containment and reducing violence, the military, which spoke in the same terms, actively sought to suppress the insurgency. Without firm guidance from the government, commanders in the field enjoyed a high degree of freedom of action. This partially explains why operations varied from one sector to the next. For example, "The GOC southern commander, Yomtov Samia [who is responsible for the Gaza Strip], showed no hesitation in ordering the destruction of houses . . . and other aggressive actions, much more than in Judea and Samaria. It is not clear how many of these actions, and certainly their scope, had the full approval of the political echelon. To a Knesset member who came to visit the area and asked him about it, Samia replied simply: 'Nobody will tell me how to win.'"[35]

As the year 2000 drew to a close, the military increasingly perceived the government's decisions as being politically motivated because of the forthcoming elections; Barak clearly needed an agreement with the Palestinians to win reelection. But in conversations with journalists, politicians, and anyone else who would listen, the General Staff made no secret of its state of mind: "The IDF intends to win in this encounter. It is not ready to allow the political echelon, with its contradictory orders and other considerations, to dim its victory."[36] Deputy CGS Moshe Ya'alon even adopted a saying during this stage of the intifada: "The war is a wall, and it is impossible to win if holes are made in the wall." Defining the new insurgency as "the continuation of the War of Independence in 1948," he argued that it is impossible to win a war with your hands tied behind your back. [37]

Again and again, the cabinet ministers recognized that Barak's control over the military was growing increasingly tenuous. Cabinet Minister Shahak, who was asked by Barak to open a clandestine channel with the Palestinians to improve communication and to reduce tensions, realized that the military was not implementing his promises to Arafat. In one such instance, he promised Arafat that the Dahaniya airfield would be opened, only to realize that the Israeli army did not honor his pledge. The field was actually opened, but a roadblock had been installed a few miles away from it, and the local commander explained that it had been put there "for security reasons."[38] In another instance, Shahak informed the Palestinians, with the prime minister's consent, that tanks would be pulled back from a certain area, but they were not. Shahak and the entire cabinet realized that the IDF was also resisting any attempt to ease the economic sanctions on the Palestinians.

Additionally, Barak's personal assistant, Gilead Sher, describes in his memoirs many occasions in which the IDF deviated from instructions handed down from the political echelon and relates one instance in which instructions delivered to the military by the prime minister's military secretary simply vanished into thin air.[39] Others, too, noted this trend. For example, Deputy Defense Minister Ephraim Sneh, without mincing his words, wrote to Barak, "From the CGS to the last of the sergeants at the roadblocks, not one of them carries out your policy."[40] And Foreign Minister Ben-Ami asserted, "Barak's breadth of control over the chief of staff is very problematic. Mofaz did whatever he wanted, and Barak did not put him in his place." [41]

In a letter to the prime minister, Ben-Ami argued that the IDF was acting like a state within a state: "[The military,] together with others, is planning a move that is designed to prevent the last chance of a peace agreement [that is, President Clinton's initiative] and instead of this proposes military solutions which you know better than anyone are not viable. Apart from bombing them with fighter planes, the IDF has tried everything. What other means can be offered? . . . I'm sorry to tell you this, but in an enlightened country the PM would not overlook such behavior on the part of the military, expressing public protests and appealing directly to public opinion against government policy."[42] Says Shaul Arieli, "After elections had been declared and it was clear that Barak was going to lose, there was total collapse of the system. The IDF did exactly what it wanted, even if this totally contradicted the instructions of Deputy Defense Minister Sneh, or of Barak's military aide, or even of the prime minister himself. But Barak did not dare to confront the officers directly and spoke to them through his military aide."[43] Despite the many complaints of his ministers and the pleas of his assistants, including his military aide and Arieli, Barak refrained from asserting his authority over the military. In fact, he enabled the military to dictate some of Israel's more critical policies.

How much of Barak's behavior was a consequence of his being too weak to impose his will, or a result of possible agreement with the military's hard-line policies, is unclear. One feasible explanation is that Barak —who understood that the diplomatic option had been extinguished— hoped that a firm hand would return the Palestinians to the negotiating table, or at least improve his own political standing with the Israeli public. Or perhaps this was just the Pavlovian reaction of a military man who had been beaten and wanted revenge. Regardless, one thing was strikingly clear: the last several months of Barak's administration did not offer an ideal model of civil supervision over the military.

7

Sharon's Double-Headed Government

How to Deal with Arafat

The collapse of the peace dream and the outburst of violent attacks caused Barak to lose the election in a scorching defeat, with only 38 percent of the electorate voting for him. The fruits of victory were collected by another general, Ariel Sharon. A warrior who all his life had seen the Palestinian problem "through the sight of a gun," he received 62 percent of the votes. Sharon's assumption of the prime minister's office in February 2001 should, on the face of it, have created harmony between the military and the government, since Sharon never trusted Arafat, had opposed the Oslo Accords, and saw the Palestinian Authority as responsible for the insurgency. However, during Sharon's first administration, relations between the political and military echelons continued at times to be quite tense. Three elements contributed to this: the government's fuzzy policy toward the Palestinians, the political makeup of the coalition government, and Sharon's own personality.[1]

Unlike his predecessor Barak, Sharon did not instruct the military to contain the Palestinian violence; he ordered them to put a complete stop to it. Though he saw the Palestinian Authority as an adversary, and not yet as an enemy, Sharon's policy was identical to that of the IDF's: he totally rejected Barak's position that negotiations should be conducted while the violent confrontation was going on; he avoided any contact with Arafat and wanted to hound him into a corner; and he believed that by using greater force he could put a stop to the Palestinian insurgency.[2] If he were to reach any kind of settlement with the Palestinians, clearly it would be very different from that proposed by the Barak government and from the spirit of Oslo.

Sharon expected the military to bring about an immediate improvement in the battlefield, but his rise to the premiership had led the Palestinians to redouble their actions. If previously they had exerted some limited restraint in the hope that it was still possible to reach an agreement, they now understood that there was no chance of a settlement, and in 2001 suicide bombers actively began to infiltrate civilian population centers inside the green line, the 1967 border between Israel and the West Bank. As a result, Sharon voiced dissatisfaction with the IDF's inability to lower the number of terrorist attacks and to reduce significantly the number of injured Israelis. He criticized the officers for their lack of professionalism and resourcefulness. "The military is not creative enough," he said. "The military's operations are cumbersome." He spoke nostalgically about IDF successes of bygone days, when he himself had been a young and adventurous commando officer.[3]

He also did not hesitate to castigate the most senior of them, including Maj. Gen. Itzik Eitan, the head of Central Command, and Maj. Gen. Doron Almog, the head of Southern Command. Sharon made clear he did not like the thinking or sophisticated language of the officer class and demanded strict, direct, and sharp action.[4] The officers were quick to respond to Sharon's criticisms: "What is considered 'cumbersome' is our effort to prevent casualties." To these words, they added cynically, "And this is in contrast to Sharon's own policy. When he was in uniform, he used to send the IDF on missions and then forget who told it to act and who approved the action plan, passing the responsibility for failure on to the forces and their commanders."[5]

Beyond their personal criticism of Sharon, the officers criticized him on two other fronts. On the one hand they argued that he did not understand the complexity of the conflict, that he aimed to reach a strategic outcome with tactical weapons, and that he thought that with a few more bombings they could bring the Palestinians to their knees. On the other hand they complained of the restrictions imposed on them, particularly the prohibition on entering the PA territories.[6] The harshest complaints came from the junior officers of field rank, among them several dozen battalion commanders (of the rank of lieutenant colonel) and the commanders of the regular brigades (colonels) who bore most of the burden. They wanted to press more aggressively into the areas controlled by the Palestinian Authority and complained about the political leadership—voicing the very same complaints that the military had voiced against Barak.[7]

But Sharon, as prime minister, was subject to his own political constraints. Several times Washington raised objections to specific operations or types of weapons used by the IDF, even demanding the cessation of steps after they had been taken. Equally constraining was the effect of the criticism voiced by the international media; the desire not to be caught by the international cameras also had to be taken into account when planning operations, influencing Israel's choice of weapons and its style of operations.[8] Added to this was pressure from the Labor Party, which still saw the Palestinian Authority as a potential partner for future talks, collectively causing Sharon to oscillate in setting his policies.

As a result, Sharon, like his predecessor, zigzagged between restraint and violent retaliation. All this added to the frustration of the senior commanders, who reiterated their complaint that the same politicians who did not let them act according to their professional judgment avoided responsibility themselves and blamed the military for not providing the population with security. Not content with criticizing the prime minister internally, Mofaz and his senior officers made a point of expressing their position in the media. They retained the freedom they had assumed for themselves during Barak's term of government to openly air their disputes with the political echelon. This recalled what Sher observed in his memoirs, "It seemed as if they claimed the right to conduct direct discourse with the public, as if it were their duty to report to society at large and not to the political echelon."[9] Indeed, the locus of civil authority, to which the military owes allegiance, is a critical criterion distinguishing legitimate political partnership from illegitimate and destructive intervention in a democratic regime.[10]

Even before Sharon took office, Mofaz used the media to advance his position on an issue that had been hotly debated by the military and government throughout 2000—whether to define Arafat and the Palestinian Authority explicitly as an enemy and to fight them as such, or to see them as only using violence temporarily as a tactic and therefore to continue negotiations with them during the military confrontations. Mofaz took advantage of the state of transition between the two administrations and on January 2, 2001, declared, "The Palestinian Authority is becoming a terrorist entity." This was a declaration with legal and operational significance: if the PA was indeed attacking Israel and its citizens, it should be fought steadfastly. In fact, Mofaz's statement was a kind of declaration of war, modified only by his use of the phrase "is becoming" rather than "has become."[11]

Voices warning that the CGS had overstepped his authority made little impression on either the military or civilians, the vast majority of whom supported Mofaz's hard-line policies and had become accustomed to the intermingling of the military and political spheres during the intifada. A growing majority preferred a clear-cut, military solution rather than a policy of "mixed signals," as former Likud defense minister Moshe Arens labeled the government's approach.[12] As to Arafat himself, Sharon and the IDF did not differ in their assessment of his role. The prime minister also endorsed the MID's assessment that Arafat directed not only the PA actions against the IDF and the settlers in the territories but also those of Hamas and the Islamic Jihad, who sent suicide bombers to attack citizens in Israel proper. As the young intelligence officer in charge of compiling the Palestinian leader's personal profile concluded, "Arafat prefers an eternal struggle with Israel over a realistic arrangement." This perspective informed IDF actions throughout the intifada.

However, during the first year of the intifada, there was another view held by some within the defense establishment. Throughout 2001 the ISA held that it was not right to lay all the blame on Arafat, because his control of the system was not complete. Therefore, he should still be seen as a partner to future negotiations, even while fighting continued. This view was shared to a certain extent by the Planning and Policy Directorate, as well as by some within the MID, but support for it was marginal compared to support for the dominant viewpoint. Indeed, toward the end of the year, the General Staff as a whole adopted the dominant perspective. At one point, DMI Malka expressed his opinion that Israel should "focus on the best possible management of the continuing confrontation with the PA." But Defense Minister Benjamin Ben-Eliezer disagreed with this opinion: "The question is not just how to manage the conflict, but how to get out of it. If we present the Palestinians with a serious and positive option, we might get a partner on the other side."[13]

Therefore, even in Sharon's government there were ministers, particularly from the Labor Party, who thought that at a certain stage there would be a need to continue to conduct negotiations with Arafat. But the military command, particularly Mofaz, his deputy Ya'alon, and the head of the MID's research division, Gilead, conducted a campaign to discredit Arafat. They pressed to destroy the Mukata'a, the PA's headquarters in Ramallah, and to expel Arafat from the territories, or at least to neutralize him politically. "Arafat is not built for an historical compromise with Israel. He is not built to achieve a political settlement in which he accepts Israel's existence as a Jewish state with secure borders for any length of time," Malka said on the eve of his retirement as DMI in January 2002. His successor, Maj. Gen. Aharon Zeevi-Farkash, spoke in a similar fashion: "Arafat has not made a strategic decision to come to an agreement; without terrorism he would not be on the map."[14] But Zeevi-Farkash also argued that "it will not be possible to come to an agreement with Arafat regarding the end of the conflict, even if Israel agrees to the right of return, to withdrawal to the 1967 borders, to the division of Jerusalem, and to hand over the holy places to Palestinian rule."[15]

Mofaz went even further, more than once making public statements in direct contradiction to his superiors. In April 2002, he said in a press conference, "The IDF stance, which I will present to the political echelon, is that PA chairman Yasser Arafat has to be expelled from the territories." Reporters hastened to point out that the CGS's statement contradicted the defense minister's position. Later, a source from "the office of the defense minister" responded to the CGS's comments with the words, "it seems that Mofaz is attempting to alter the government's decision."[16]

In fact, the IDF's hard-line approach toward Arafat did have many supporters among the cabinet ministers. But, as noted, Sharon was constrained by other factors and the government was forced to continuously debate what practical policies it should adopt. This was particularly true after heavy attacks on the Israeli population. Following each of these attacks, Mofaz suggested that the military strike a blow at Arafat, neutralize his political power, and expel him or even "exterminate" him. This approach was very close to Sharon's own wishes, but he could not follow through on them, largely because of Washington's adamant demand that Arafat not be physically harmed or expelled from the Mukata'a.

This did not prevent Mofaz from continuing his efforts to bring people around to his position, and he even presented it personally to U.S. national security adviser Condoleeza Rice during her visit to Israel. Ultimately, the capture of the arms ship *Karin A*—which was meant to supply Palestinian insurgents—revealed the extent of Arafat's direct involvement in terrorism and was the decisive event that led President George W. Bush to see the pressing need for change in the Palestinian Authority's leadership and structure and to agree to Arafat's political neutralization. Thus, Sharon and Mofaz were, at the end of the day, partially victorious in the stance they had taken toward Arafat for so long. He would be rendered "irrelevant" and be confined to the Mukata'a.

The IDF Fights the Foreign Ministry

Relations between the military and political echelons in Sharon's first government were complex because of the power structure at the top of the defense establishment, namely the division of civil responsibility for security between the prime minister and the defense minister, and the low personal prestige of the defense minister among the military corps. Under Barak, Mofaz had significant independence, but Barak's professional superiority, as the most highly decorated soldier in the IDF, was never questioned. Ben-Eliezer, however, did not possess similar credentials.

For the first time in Israel's history, the defense minister, although a retired senior officer, did not enjoy the admiration and respect of the senior command, as compared to, for example, Moshe Dayan, Weizman, and Rabin. Ben-Eliezer had not reached the rank of major general; the military posts that he had held did not include command of a corps, a territorial command, or leadership of an important division in the General Staff. His last military post was coordinator of activities in the territories. If that was not enough, above him was a prime minister who possessed an impressive military record of many years' standing. Sharon had a hands-on work style, and as defense minister in the war in Lebanon in 1982, he had, in fact, been a sort of "super chief of staff." As prime minister, Sharon clearly intended to be directly involved in the work of the military. Thus, a relatively weak defense minister had to operate between a very strong, political CGS and an authoritative prime minister, a recipe for problematic working relations.

The situation was complicated further by the presence of Foreign Minister Shimon Peres. Peres's stature led to a departure from the long-standing tradition in which the role of the foreign minister was secondary to that of the defense minister and even the finance minister. After all, the national unity government formed in 2001 was based on the partnership and mutual understanding of the veteran leaders of the Likud and Labor parties—Sharon and Peres. In 2001 both of them were in their seventies and both had much higher prestige than all other government ministers. As a result, Peres was Sharon's real partner. Unlike Ben-Eliezer, who, squeezed between the military and the prime minister, could only recommend an alternative policy, Peres was capable of leading a somewhat independent line to Sharon's policies. This led these two old rivals to publicly conduct acrimonious debates, which Israelis perceived as contests between two forces of equal status.

Such friction also existed between Peres and the IDF. The CGS, his deputy, and the senior staff perceived Peres as their number one rival in the decision-making community, "the man who made holes in the wall" and who prevented them from succeeding in the war against the insurgency. For example, officers complained time and again that they would put military pressure on Arafat and, as a result, would think that he was closer than ever to capitulation, "and then Peres rushed up with a stretcher to rescue him."[17] Concurrently, "highly placed sources" in the Foreign Ministry often accused the IDF of trying to torpedo attempts to reach a cease-fire with the Palestinian Authority: "The IDF has not internalized the fact that it is possible to reach a cease-fire by talking and not only by using force. . . . It is a pity that there are people in the IDF who are busy all day long leaking information and inciting opinion against the prime minister and the foreign minister. It's time they realized that there is a government in Jerusalem."[18] At one point the IDF even pressured the prime minister to allow Maj. Gen. Giora Eiland, head of the Planning and Policy Directorate, to accompany Peres to a meeting with Arafat to limit Peres's maneuvering in the talks.[19]

One of the sticking points between the foreign minister and the top IDF leaders concerned the weight that should be given to intelligence assessments. Peres, who had tended to be critical of intelligence assessments in the past, was even more critical after the summer of 2000. He and his people accused the MID of presenting exaggerated and one-sided

evaluations and indulging in political forecasts and "mental stagnation."
All this was in addition to criticizing the IDF's get-tough policy.[20] When
Uri Savir, Peres's faithful disciple, conducted negotiations with the Palestinians on behalf of the Rabin government, he refused to look at the intelligence reports presented to him by the officer who was assigned to
him. "They understand the Palestinians like I understand the Republic of
China," he said mockingly, reflecting the same state of mind as Peres.
"They quote all the curses that Arafat brings down on the Jews in conversations and they think, 'That's it, we've caught him.' If they recorded
what Ehud Barak says about his ministers in private conversations it
would not be much better."[21]

The Tail That Wags the Dog

Although the weakening of civil supervision over the military in the last
months of the Barak administration ended with the change of government, tension between the political and the military echelons continued
to exist, with the military demanding a strict implementation of what Gal
Hirsch, head of operations in Central Command, defined as "leverage."
The idea was simple: by exerting heavy pressure on the Palestinian Authority, whether through direct military actions against its security forces, or
through indirect pressure on the Palestinian population, the Palestinians
themselves—to ease the burden on their own lives—would rise up against
their leadership and compel Arafat to change his policy and stop the
armed struggle.[22] But as long as Sharon could not give the IDF free rein
to actualize this strategy—due to pressures from his coalition partners
and the constraints placed on him by the United States—relations between the political and the military echelons remained tense. All this, as I
will later show, would change after September 11, 2001, and much more
so in March 2002, when the IDF launched Operation Defensive Shield.
Although the relations between the government and military had improved relative to Barak's last months in office, incidents reflecting the
discordant relations between them continued for most of 2001.

While there has never been a distinguishable case of the IDF explicitly ignoring the decisions of the political leadership or disobeying
political orders, there have been cases, particularly during wartime, when
military activity went beyond the original instructions of the government,

or was not exactly in accordance with them, or when the IDF secured the approval of the political echelon only after operations were completed. Stories of field commanders who turned off their radio equipment to avoid receiving orders they did not want to hear are part of the IDF military tradition and have even involved Sharon and Barak.

Conforming with this tradition, the IDF allowed itself a broad scope in interpreting government policy in 2001; in the words of one observer who described the situation, "The military drags its feet when the orders are not to its liking."[23] Similar stories were confirmed by the head of the civil administration in the West Bank, Brig. Gen. Dov Tzadka, who also complained of other infringements, such as the IDF's "stripping policy"—the razing of houses and uprooting of trees to prevent Palestinians from using them as cover when firing on Israelis. "They are given explicit orders [not to do so]," said the senior officer, "but when I reach the place, I find the forces in a state of hyperactivity. The soldiers and the commanders get carried away." In a small society with a reserve military, an informal political culture, and an invasive media, the IDF's loose style of behavior has been easily exposed.[24]

In several cases the military publicly argued with its civilian superiors before actual policy decisions were made. In late 2001, for example, the IDF began incursions into the PA territories but was asked by the government to withdraw at the end of the operation. DMI Malka called a press conference in anticipation of the cabinet debate and warned that "if the IDF pulls out of area A, terror will return to the Israeli streets." This was just one of the many occasions in which the military appealed to the public for support to compel the government to make decisions the officers wanted.[25] Inevitably, the public's support of any military position was assured. Since the start of the intifada, opinion polls showed that most Israelis feared that either they or someone in their family would suffer from an act of terror. In April 2001, 83 percent stated this concern. This number did not change significantly over the ensuing years.[26] A March 2001 poll, meanwhile, found that no less than 72 percent of the population thought more force should be used against the Palestinians; 17 percent said that the current force used was sufficient; and only 7 percent said that less force should be used.[27]

As usual, only the liberal newspaper *Ha'aretz* published an editorial criticizing the DMI for the statements he made at the press conference:

In the stand taken by the IDF in recent days with regard to the pullout from A Areas, the military's senior officers have exceeded the limits of professional speech befitting military officers. It is hard to avoid the conclusion that the IDF is exerting pressure on the political echelon through closed-door briefings and through public appearances by the head of Military Intelligence, aimed at influencing the prime minister.

This is a blatant violation of democratic norms: the IDF is not a branch of government, and it is appointed to implement the security policy formulated by the government. There can be no tolerance for a situation in which the IDF appeals directly to the public, in order to enlist support for its stand, thus exerting public pressure directly on the cabinet.

It is unacceptable that in the public discourse and in the process of national decision making, the IDF has become an actor of its own. The IDF should always remain the executive arm of the government. The trend evident in the last few days, whereby the IDF's operational considerations have turned into a central factor in decisions regarding the state's relationship with the Palestinian people, is unacceptable as well.[28]

Aside from these frictions, which naturally were highlighted in the media, the relationship between the military and civilian echelons in the first two years of the intifada could be more accurately described as an ongoing negotiation. Although this was certainly not always the case, the military would generally submit for government approval a proposal for an aggressive action only to have the government approve just part of the plan. After a subsequent terrorist strike, however, especially a severe one, the government would fully approve the given plan.

Mofaz was largely responsible for the unhealthy relations between the military and the government. As far back as June 1999, following Hizbullah's shelling of northern Israel, Mofaz stated publicly that "Israel should respond to Katyusha shelling, and in previous cases the government did not permit us to respond." He was reprimanded for this statement by the then foreign minister, Ariel Sharon: "Your job is to implement government policy, not to set it." Then, a short time after his election as prime minister, Sharon accused Mofaz of briefing journalists on government policy and swaying them against it. Mofaz did not take this quietly. Rather, he presented a file of press clippings that he had saved, containing evidence that the political echelon had leaked information unfavorable to him. Later, in July 2001, the prime minister seethed with fury once again when he read in newspapers that the IDF was moving forces toward the West Bank but that it could not take additional action due to the limitations imposed on it by the political echelon.[29]

With these strained relations as a backdrop, two additional incidents that occurred in 2001 are particularly noteworthy. The first concerned the plan to construct a "security fence," or, as the Palestinians call it, "the wall." For a long time, the military-political leadership had been examining ways to prevent, or at least reduce, the infiltration of Palestinian terrorists into Israeli territory. Eventually, a plan was devised to create a buffer zone, an area along the green line that would contain a fence and alarm system that would block passage into Israel and be declared a closed military zone. Although the buffer-zone plan had questionable military advantages, it clearly had far-reaching political implications. First, its implementation would show that Israel had given up hope of reaching a mutual agreement with the Palestinian Authority. Second, the fence would create a security zone inside the territories, like the one in southern Lebanon, which had been a constant source of friction and had provoked harsh international criticism. And third, the project resurrected the old border that successive Israeli governments had tried to obliterate since 1967. Not surprisingly, both Peres and Sharon opposed the fence, albeit for diametrically opposed reasons.

But in September 2001, while visiting Russia, Sharon unexpectedly learned that Mofaz was about to hold a press conference to announce the buffer-zone plan. An enraged Sharon immediately ordered that the press conference be cancelled. He explained to the journalists traveling with him that Mofaz had forgotten who made policy in Israel: "We are a state with a military and not a military with a state. They should remember that there is a government in Jerusalem."[30] Upon his return to Israel, Sharon lashed out at a group of IDF officers during a cabinet meeting. "Next time you want to tell me something, call me at my ranch," he said, before adding his home phone number.[31]

Mofaz—Politician in Uniform

A short time after this, the second noteworthy incident of 2001 occurred. This was related to the government's "zipper policy," whereby IDF forces entered PA territories, sealed off towns and villages, and later lifted the blockades in exchange for a Palestinian commitment to stop violence. On

October 12, 2001, at a meeting of the cabinet subcommittee on security, Ben-Eliezer proposed that the IDF start easing the restrictions on the Palestinian population in places where the Palestinian Authority had fulfilled its commitment and quiet was being maintained. Mofaz at first objected to these steps, but at the end of the meeting the decision was made to implement them.

Eventually, this story reached the media, which reported that Mofaz categorically opposed all suggestions for easing restrictions. The IDF spokesman hastened to issue a correction, saying that Mofaz did not object to easing restrictions in civil matters, except in those cases—such as withdrawal from Hebron—"that might threaten security and would make it hard to protect Israeli citizens and IDF soldiers." Mofaz was trying to show that he was not intervening in civil matters, but the military spokesman's announcement aggravated the affair, since it seemed to accuse the government of neglecting the security of Israeli citizens and soldiers. Burning with anger, Ben-Eliezer wondered aloud whether the time had come to dismiss Mofaz. Sharon had a similar reaction, and at a cabinet meeting on October 14, he banged his fist on the table, stating, "This is an impossible situation. How can the chief of staff issue such a press release? It is unprecedented. Nothing like this has ever happened in Israel's history. What, is he planning a political career? Anywhere else he would have been fired." The cabinet incident was fully disclosed in the press the next day, yet, in the end, the only step taken against Mofaz was that Ben-Eliezer summoned him to his office and reprimanded him.

Sharon's remark about Mofaz's political ambitions touched on one of the main weaknesses of civil control of the IDF. When the military penetrated more deeply into the area of policymaking, it became increasingly infected by politics and thus became more and more politicized. The case of Mofaz recalls the story of Rafael Eitan, who was nominated CGS in April 1978 largely because he had been a professional soldier; taciturn and apolitical, he was ultimately transformed into one of the most political chiefs of staff Israel ever had. After more than two years as CGS, Mofaz, too, had become such a political figure that the entire political class took for granted he would one day enter politics. The only question that remained was what political party he would choose. This unknown gave him political leverage with both the prime minister and defense minister.

By the end of 2001, Mofaz's behavior hinted that he was preparing to build a future coalition with Sharon's most serious rival, Benjamin Netanyahu. Public opinion polls showed that Likud supporters preferred Netanyahu—who had positioned himself far to the right of the prime minister—over Sharon. If Mofaz joined Netanyahu, they would certainly make a winning team.[32] But Sharon knew that pushing Mofaz out of the military would only make him a national hero and strengthen him politically. As a result, the prime minister and defense minister had very little room to maneuver against their insolent CGS.

In Israel's hyperpoliticized culture, the behavior of other senior IDF officers was also interpreted as being politically motivated. Shifts in their position, from supporting the peace talks to wholeheartedly endorsing war with the Palestinian Authority, were perceived as toeing the Sharon government line. Those with a charitable view saw this merely as the IDF aligning itself with changes in government policy, while the more cynical saw it as an expression of the opportunistic nature of senior officers trying to further their own careers.

Indeed, as Mofaz's retirement approached, the respective political opinions of the two leading CGS candidates, Maj. Gen. Uzi Dayan, head of the National Security Council and former deputy CGS, and the incumbent deputy CGS, Moshe Ya'alon, factored into the decision of who would replace Mofaz. Whereas Dayan represented the moderate school of thought, which emphasized the need to negotiate a political resolution to the conflict with the Palestinians, Ya'alon represented the hard-line approach and demanded the uncompromising submission of the Palestinian Authority. Not surprisingly, as Mofaz's day of retirement neared, Ya'alon's chances of becoming the new CGS increased.

Shortly before Mofaz's term expired, criticism about the political character of his tenure grew. As one commentator charged in *Yedioth Ahronoth*, "In six weeks' time Shaul Mofaz will go home. At last. Four years too late. It would be hard to find a CGS from the past who inflicted such severe military and political damage as Lt. Gen. Mofaz inflicted on everything around him." After enumerating a half-dozen failures and faults in Mofaz's military career, the commentator added, "To his discredit, it will go on record that there has never been a CGS during whose term the IDF so much resembled the military arm of a political ideology rather than a national military."[33]

Never before had such harsh criticism of a serving CGS been published. This was partially a reflection of the new climate in which security —and even its supreme representative, the CGS—was no longer sacred territory. Such criticism, however, reflected only the opinions of the minority Left. Among the majority, Mofaz's militant views made him more and more popular. He himself well understood that taking such a hardline stance could be used as leverage for a successful political career, and some officers who worked with him admit in private that considerations of his future political career influenced his decisions, a claim that he naturally rejects.

Yet, it would be wrong to analyze Mofaz's politics as simply a manifestation of the political ambitions of an experienced officer. A deeper look leads to a more intricate conclusion: his behavior as CGS was a direct outcome of the counterinsurgency warfare that he conducted. This is what makes the Israeli situation so interesting, and why it offers such a compelling case study of political-military relations in present times. The friction between the political and the military echelons was unavoidable, as it derived from the very nature of a low-intensity conflict.

8

Political-Military Relations in Low-Intensity Conflict

The Concept of Low-Intensity Conflict

Historians of political-military relations know that in wartime these relations tend to become particularly intense, resulting in a greater degree of friction than under peaceful conditions. While this has not always been true in Israel—for example, during the sixteen months of the War of Attrition with Egypt (1969–70) relations between the military and government were generally harmonious—difficulties did develop during Israel's eighth war, the Al-Aqsa intifada.[1] The *type* of war Israel fought beginning in September 2000 was different than past wars—it was not a conventional war but a "war of the fourth generation," a low-intensity conflict (LIC).[2] Further, there was an additional unique element to this particular war: it was conducted in the midst of a political crisis that had effectively weakened the political echelon's authority over the IDF. The military, which was less than successful in accomplishing its designated task of providing security for the population, felt disrespected, wounded by what it saw as unfair criticism by the politicians, and at times even alienated from society.

The IDF had prepared extensively for the new insurgency following the lessons of the first Palestinian intifada in 1987. During the 1990s it developed not only a tactical solution but an entire new doctrine concerning what it termed "conflict other than war," "limited confrontation," and, later, "low-intensity conflict." This new conceptual framework was to

123

have a great impact not only on the nature of Israel's relations with the Palestinians but also on the relationship between the military and the political echelons in Israel itself. The military doctrine defined such confrontation as

> violent conflict short of actual war, in which the opposing sides utilize armed force as a means to attain political ends, though, at least to the same degree, they also use political means. This stands in contrast with war, or even limited war, in which the dominant consideration is military-operational, and political considerations are secondary or indirect.[3]

The IDF's training manuals, updated to reflect the new military doctrine, indicated that of two belligerent sides, the non-sovereign entity usually chooses LIC, primarily due to its military inferiority vis-à-vis its adversary. The main distinguishing feature of LIC, however, is that, in contrast with war, each belligerent's ultimate objective is not to achieve material goals—that is, to capture territory or to damage an adversary's military capabilities—but, rather, political goals—"to achieve a change of consciousness in an adversary's society, by an extended process of wearing the adversary down."[4]

At the outbreak of the intifada, IDF commanders explained to the political echelon not only the military principles of the new LIC doctrine they had formulated, but also the political principles the application of the new military doctrine would entail. The first conclusion of IDF commanders was that they should by no means confront LIC as they would a traditional war. Utilizing the full range of the IDF's military capabilities, as in a war, would require reconquering the territories, setting up a military authority in the occupied areas, and managing the lives of more than three million Palestinians, who would then almost certainly commence guerilla warfare. Even worse, such a military response would likely push the Arab states into a full-fledged war with Israel and lead to international intervention that would neutralize Israel's hegemonic position over the Palestinians. This was exactly the Palestinian goal, and it, therefore, needed to be prevented.

The second obvious conclusion was that unilateral withdrawal from the occupied territories was out of the question, because this would be interpreted by the adversaries as weakness on the part of the Israelis and would encourage them to keep up the aggression. This position was supported by the way in which Israel's withdrawal from southern Lebanon under the Barak government was interpreted by the military, and the determination that such a mistake should not be repeated. Though prior to the intifada the option of unilateral withdrawal had been dismissed by the entire political-military establishment and, indeed, by the Israeli political class, Barak put it back on the table when he suggested it as an option at the beginning of the intifada (although this was not known to the public at the time).

By the second year of the intifada, this proposal had gained some currency: unilateral withdrawal had come to be advocated not only by public figures from Israel's peace camp but also by some key military personalities. For instance, on February 18, 2002, the Council for Peace and Security—an organization with about one thousand reserve and retired high-ranking officers in its membership, including former chiefs of staff —endorsed unilateral withdrawal.

Though the high prestige of the council's members meant that the council's endorsement was a significant professional challenge to the IDF's General Staff, the latter nevertheless vigorously rejected the call for withdrawing from some of the territories or from the entire Gaza Strip, for the dismantling of about fifty settlements, and for allowing the immediate establishment of a Palestinian state. Such steps, the IDF's officers claimed, would amount to surrendering to terror and admitting that the Palestinians had won the conflict. According to IDF strategists, with neither a withdrawal nor a full-fledged war, the only means of attaining victory involved following the principles of an LIC: "there is no purely military solution to insurgency because it is not purely military action. Insurgency can be forestalled by political moves, but once started, policy must be harnessed together with the use of force, bolstered by economic steps, in order to restore order."[5] The strategists further stated that the purpose of the new LIC doctrine is

> to undermine the adversary's determination and to lead to the adversary's abandoning his objectives, through a cumulative process of inflicting physical, economic and psychological damage, [and] to lead the adversary to realize that his own armed engagement is hopeless. Israel's past wars were existential wars, and the way to deal with them was through deterrence and decision. LIC is, by contrast, a battle over consciousness, and the side that can exhaust its adversary will win by wearing down the adversary's resolve to pay the heavy price of a prolonged confrontation.[6]

IDF doctrine had, in the past, stated that, due to its enemies' quantitative and economic superiority, Israel could not afford involvement in a war of attrition. Consequently, the IDF had adopted principles of "blitz" combat. LIC, in contrast, was meant to wear down the adversary in a continuing process. "The current struggle is about endurance, and the challenge is in getting the most out of IDF force without wearing it down," said Maj. Gen. Yiftach Ron-Tal, commander of the army.[7]

Presenting the new doctrine to the officer corps, its framers introduced a new set of terms, some of which, such as "containment," did not yet have a Hebrew translation. There is no point in talking about overcoming or finishing off the intifada, stated the doctrine, because we have to conduct a policy of containment. Such a policy would rely on political, economic, perceptual, and propaganda initiatives alongside military ones. However, containment was only one aspect of the new doctrine; the other was attrition. Unlike past conflicts, the doctrine held, it is not possible to reach a swift and sharp decision in this type of warfare, and therefore the winner will be the one who forces the leadership and the society of the adversary to abandon the struggle. Such an outcome, it was noted, could take a long time.[8]

This new approach to handling LIC was not known to the public, or even to elected representatives, until some time after the intifada broke out. The result was that, during its first long months, the public discourse was filled with concepts taken from past wars. Even more problematic was that the dialogue between the military and its superior civilian echelon took place, at times, along two parallel lines. For this reason, the political right wing continued to demand that the IDF "crush" the intifada, utilize all its military might, penetrate deep into the territories, and "cleanse them once and for all." "Let the IDF win" was written on large banners waved in nationalist demonstrations; ironically, it was a slogan that IDF officers rejected. At the other end of the spectrum, critics from the left (dovish) wing of the political map claimed that what the IDF termed "limited conflict" was just the opposite; they accused the military of over-using force and of imposing aggressive, harsh measures on the Palestinians, which they saw as unjustified, ineffective, and even immoral. This policy, they argued, worked to the detriment of the civilian population by strengthening the Palestinians' desire for revenge and enlarging the pool of potential terrorists.

On March 19, 2001, soon after Sharon took office, his government approved the IDF's strategic plan of war against the intifada. As in the past, the political echelon did not oversee the preparation of the document; the IDF defined its objectives and brought them to the government for approval. The main tenets of the plan were

> to give Israeli citizens security and a sense of security; to put an end to Palestinian violence and prevent Palestinians from attaining objectives through violent means; to minimize the likelihood of the conflict's internationalization; to diminish the possibility of regional deterioration; and to keep the option open—when the time came, after Palestinian violence ended—to return to a negotiating track; but not to conduct negotiations under fire.[9]

The political-military elites shared the same war principles, but the friction between the political and the military echelons was unavoidable, as it derived from the very nature of an LIC. Had the cabinet members read the military manual prepared by the IDF strategists in early 2000, they would have been aware of the inevitability of disagreement. According to the designers of the doctrine, in an LIC there is a "close tie between military acts (including those at the tactical level) and political acts, and it incorporates civilian, political and military means." The doctrine explains that

> in contrast to war, and to the sorts of operations relevant to war, LIC is political in its conduct (not only in its objectives and constraints). Therefore, the modus operandi of military operations—including those of low level and limited scope—will, in LIC, be dictated, sometimes directly, by political considerations, while military-operational considerations will be of secondary importance.[10]

But who is in charge of military operations "of low level and limited scope"? Can the government, the prime minister, or the defense minister be responsible for such operations when every day dozens of them are conducted simultaneously, many of them bearing political significance? On the other hand, can military commanders, even in the lower ranks, refrain from taking political considerations into account?

The LIC doctrine that the military handed down to its officers tried to address these questions by offering the following answer: a continuing dialogue will occur between the military and political echelons during the confrontation—that is, the military echelons will be involved in the construction of the political environment. But to many officers, it was not clear what was meant by a "continuing dialogue" or how it should be conducted. "In conventional warfare," explained Maj. Gen. Giora Eiland, head of the Planning and Policy Directorate, "the aims are clear. They speak of surrender, of destruction, and so forth. The concepts are clear and definitive. In LIC things are much less clear, and therefore the political-military conceptual system does not allow for simple dialogue as in the past. On this point I once heard Shimon Peres say that in such a war 80 percent of the items discussed are in the grey area between political and military."[11]

In a situation where the characteristics of LIC called for a higher level of coordination, understanding, and cooperation between the military and government, the IDF leadership continued to face the traditional functioning style of Israel's political leaders, who issued obscure instructions, failed to give clear directives, and avoided presenting specific political goals. As a result, what had characterized Israel's policy vis-à-vis the occupied territories for decades became more acute in the LIC after 2000. This argument was reiterated by IDF officers every time they analyzed their relations with the civilian echelon. For example, one of the IDF's field commanders in south Lebanon and later in Gaza bitterly testified, "from my experience I have learnt that each time a complicated situation exists, the political echelon tends to evade the difficult strategic decision. Instead it puts the burden on the shoulders of the soldiers and their commanders in the field. This really disheartened me a lot."[12]

Yitzhak Eitan, former head of Central Command, reiterated this sentiment, stating, "That is the nature of political-military relations in Israel. We have never received clear directives. Everything needed to be explained and it took efforts to understand the instruction." CGS Ya'alon more bluntly and cynically said, "it is naïve to expect the political echelon to give a clear directive to the military echelon."[13] Given this foggy situation, it is no wonder that a brigade commander could say in an officers' gathering that "the policy of blockades and closures is the government's ingratiating itself in front of the Palestinians."[14]

Even low-ranking officers, who became accustomed to hearing their superiors argue with cabinet ministers, started addressing political issues more frequently and expressing their criticisms in public forums. But the arguments during the intifada concerned not only military decisions but also the division of responsibilities between the two echelons. Thus, members of the security cabinet complained that topics of fundamental importance were not submitted to them for decisions.[15] And the defense minister struggled with the prime minister regarding his authority to command the military, while the public complained more than ever that the military was interfering in issues that were outside of its responsibility.

Toward the end of 2001, the IDF realized that the "leverage strategy" and the belief that massive pressure on the Palestinians would bring them to call on their leaders to stop the armed struggle had failed. On October 16 Cabinet Minister Rechave'am Ze'evi was assassinated in his hotel in Jerusalem, and the military reached the conclusion that "the ongoing and systematic pressure did not bring any fruits; there is no one upon whom leverage can be used." The conclusion, therefore, was that Israel should no longer expect the Palestinian Authority to fight terror; Israel would have to take this task solely upon itself. Sharon, who knew by then that the United States had accepted Israel's resolute position against the Palestinian Authority and its leader and was not against Israel's direct confrontation with the Palestinian Authority, embraced fully this policy, thus opening the third chapter in the history of the intifada. As had happened many times in the past, the Palestinians themselves provided a convenient justification for this strategic change.

Operation Defensive Shield

The year 2002 began in a bleak atmosphere, caused by a sharp increase in Palestinian suicide bombing incidents and a deepening economic crisis. The intifada had begun to take its toll and national morale dropped. At year's end, the preceding twelve months were characterized as the most difficult in the state's history. The occupation of Ramallah at the beginning of March did not bring about a reduction in terrorist activity but caused just the opposite: by the end of that month, terrorist activity had increased. Then, a turning point in the war occurred.

On March 28, the first evening of Passover, a Palestinian suicide bomber killed 29 people and wounded 150 others at the Park Hotel in Netanya, a town on the Mediterranean shore. (A second suicide bomber changed his mind at the last moment and did not join in the attack. He was supposed to blow himself up when the rescue crews arrived in response to the first explosion.) The horrendous attack on families who had gathered to celebrate a religious holiday at a seaside resort brought the number of deaths in that month alone to 127. The government, aware of its failure to stop terror and sensitive to the decline in the national morale, approved the execution of the Planning and Policy Directorate's "red scenario," under which the IDF was ordered to enter the territories in the West Bank that had previously remained outside the military's range of operations, including refugee camps. In fact, it was to reoccupy all the territories in the West Bank that were until then under the control of the Palestinian Authority.

The declared aim of Operation Defensive Shield was "to systematically dismantle terror infrastructures in the entire region," to seize Palestinians involved in violent acts, to confiscate weapons, to find munitions factories, and to neutralize potential suicide bombers and capture their dispatchers. But the operation had other, unpublicized, aims as well. First, it put an end to the immunity from IDF retaliation that the Palestinian Authority had been granted in Area A, the area handed over following the Oslo Accords, and it gave the IDF freedom of action in any part of the West Bank or Gaza Strip and freedom to control any area without having to undertake civilian governing functions. Second, the operation was meant to rehabilitate the deterrent power of the IDF, which, by the military's own assessment, had been damaged by Israel's hasty withdrawal from southern Lebanon. Finally, as per the principles of LIC, the operation was intended to burden further the Palestinian population so that it would ultimately decide to stop the violence against Israel. Therefore, in addition to enacting direct military operations against armed men, the IDF carried out its operation by tightening the blockades on the cities and encircling the villages, isolating and separating them, and, as a result, paralyzing the Palestinian economy and social services. These measures dramatically affected the lives of the entire Palestinian population, not just the fighters or terrorists.

Such measures were also intended to help reverse a situation that the Oslo Accords had created. The two sides had agreed that in return for Israel's granting the Palestinian Authority political status, the latter would prevent violence against Israel. But, despite the terms of the agreement, the violence continued. Even if Israel could be blamed for not fulfilling all its commitments in the accords, the Palestinian Authority certainly could not escape blame for this severe transgression: contrary to the agreement, the

Palestinian Authority did very little, and sometimes nothing at all, to stop the bloodshed. In fact, the armed struggle and terrorism against Israel was nurtured by inciting statements made by Palestinian leaders against Israel and Jews and encouraged by the institutions of the Palestinian Authority.

Under the red scenario, therefore, the Israeli government would re- claim direct responsibility for its own security. For this reason, the IDF did not hit just the terror and opposition organizations but also the security organs of Fatah and the Palestinian Authority itself, such as the Tanzim. Some hoped that the operation would also bring about the collapse of the PA's civic institutions, with security concerns serving as the pretext for doing so. The following year, when Israel renewed negotiations with Muhammad Dahlan, the "strong man" in Gaza, and complained that he was not arresting armed Palestinians, he answered sarcastically, "Where shall I put them? You've destroyed our prisons."

The IDF's incursion into PA areas and reoccupation of the West Bank led to a wave of protests around the world. Much of this was in reaction to the extensive foreign media coverage—which at times, such as in the case of the "Jenin massacre," was influenced by biased information and anti-Israeli propaganda—that showed the vast destruction and brutality of the operation, as well as the hard-hit Palestinian civilians. The Israeli public, however, had a different perspective—90 percent, including 60 per- cent of the Left, supported the IDF's efforts.[16] The Israeli media reported the operation's achievements in detail, offering accounts about ammuni- tion and arms seizures, the arrests of activists from Palestinian organiza- tions, and the discovery of intelligence material that proved the Palestin- ian Authority had trained terrorists and directed terror operations.[17]

At year's end, the head of Israel's military operations, Maj. Gen. Dan Harel, presented an analysis of the data that, in his words, justified the IDF's actions. The reduced number of terror attacks was the most signif- icant measure in determining the operation's success: "In the quarter pre- ceding the operation, forty suicide attacks were recorded within the Green Line, whereas in the second quarter, after the operation, there were just 23; in the third quarter there were 17, and in the fourth 12. The number of terrorist strikes in the West Bank decreased by 75 percent." According to his testimony, control of the Palestinian areas had also brought an increase in intelligence information and in successful preemption of attacks: "Before the operation, the ratio between suicide strikes where the perpetrators reached their destination and those that were preempted was 2 to 3 successful bombers for each one arrested. After the operation, the ratio was reversed."[18]

Meanwhile, the adverse effects of the operation were not voiced in cabinet sessions and were quickly dismissed by the public. Such negative outcomes of the operation included the deepening hatred toward Israel in the Arab and Muslim world, the growing motivation among Palestinian youth to volunteer for suicide attacks and become *shahids* (martyrs), the political damage caused to Israel internationally, and the increasing ethical deterioration of Israeli society.

In retrospect, however, the operation had, in a dialectical way, quite a positive impact. It accelerated the change in consciousness that both societies likely had to undergo to realize that violence would not bring about their respective national goals. The Palestinian Authority realized that Israel would not fold because of violence and that Palestinian society was paying too heavy a price for the insurgency. Israeli society, for its part, realized that it could not eradicate the determination of the Palestinians and that the settlements—perceived as illegitimate by the world at large—were a thorn in the Palestinians' side and a source of continuing conflict. As a result, more and more people in Israel supported the dismantling of the settlements, and calls for a unilateral withdrawal from the territories grew in strength, though supporters of this strategy used a somewhat softer term for it, "separation."[19]

Finally, in October 2002, the Labor Party withdrew from the national unity government, leading to early elections. In January 2003, Labor went to the general elections as a party deeply divided. Unable to agree on a leader from within its ranks, Labor appointed an ex-general as its head, Maj. Gen. (res.) Amram Mitzna, the mayor of Haifa who had been the head of the Central Command when the first intifada broke out. But the election results were predictable. Reconciliatory Mitzna, who called for resuming negotiations with Arafat and withdrawal from Gaza, failed to save the party from defeat. With the entire peace camp in a state of collapse following the failure of the Camp David talks and the waves of Palestinian suicide attacks, Labor lost, falling to the lowest point in its history, securing only 19 of 120 Knesset seats. Thus, Sharon set up his second government without the Labor Party, forming a center-right coalition, and

Ben-Eliezer was replaced as defense minister by an up-and-coming politician who had just doffed his uniform—Shaul Mofaz.

Mofaz—a Cabinet Member

Mofaz was not the first CGS to land at the very top of the political hierarchy, but his entry was more discordant than those of his predecessors. Just before the election for the new Knesset, Mofaz joined the Likud Party list as an ally of the prime minister, who promised him the post of defense minister. This strengthened Sharon against Netanyahu within the party and improved his public standing in general. But in joining the Likud, Mofaz violated the law requiring one hundred days of cooling off between retiring from the military and joining a party list. Mofaz claimed that the cooling-off period had in fact elapsed, offering legal arguments that distinguished between his actual date of retirement and the vacation preceding it, and between the Jewish and civil calendars. Mofaz's arguments were unsuccessful, however, and the Supreme Court refused to grant him an appeal. Thus, Mofaz remained outside the parliamentary caucus, and Sharon appointed him as a cabinet minister even though Mofaz was not a Knesset member.

Mofaz's quick entry into politics after his military retirement confirmed the claims of those who had long held that as CGS he had not always acted solely out of professional considerations but had also acted out of partisan calculations to aid his future political career. To be sure, such behavior sets a negative precedent for young officers and could have a harmful impact on the IDF. If a CGS could have such motives, would a junior officer receiving orders from the CGS, or even from his commanding officer, not ask himself, "Are the orders professional and appropriate, or are they the consequence of partisan considerations and therefore meant to advance the civilian careers of my superiors when their military service ends?"

The Likud, of course, the political party in power in January 2003 and the major beneficiary of Mofaz's jump to full political life, did not see the need to debate the consequences of the former CGS's behavior. A suggestion by former defense minister Moshe Arens to prolong the waiting period for chiefs of general staff from one hundred days to one year was not even put on the party's agenda for discussion. Additionally, most of the public did not see Mofaz's action as improper at all. Many even believed he might one day take over leadership of the Likud Party once Sharon stepped down.

Mofaz's quick jump from military to government service was far from unique. For example, Brig. Gen. Ephraim Eitam, a retired senior reserve officer, joined the government shortly after leaving the military in 2001. In fact, he was invited by the leadership of the National Religious Party to stand as its head even before his military career was over. The party hoped that his popularity among youth in the National Religious camp would help to rehabilitate it. An erstwhile leftist, Eitam had had a change of heart during his military service and began to embrace clerical and nationalistic anti-Arab positions, such as calls for the transfer of Palestinians from the territories. While repeated requests to oust him from the military because of his open political activism were rejected by the CGS and defense minister, his advancement in the ranks was slowed and eventually stopped. Finally, he retired in January 2001 and in April 2002 joined Sharon's first government as a cabinet minister, led his party to the sixteenth Knesset elections in January 2003, and joined Sharon's second government soon after.

Many of the relationship problems between the government and the military that had plagued both Barak's government and Sharon's national unity government did not exist in the early part of Sharon's second government. By 2003, the scope of opinion at the top of the political-military establishment had narrowed. As a result, Sharon was able to exercise his full authority much more easily, especially because his defense minister served at his pleasure. At the same time, Mofaz's seniority over Ya'alon, who owed his new appointment as CGS to Mofaz, promised a smooth relationship between the defense minister and the CGS. Indeed, for several months there was harmony between the new government, the prime minister, and the defense minister and the military, the General Staff, and its new CGS.

However, there was no decrease in the IDF's level of involvement in political processes. On the contrary, military participation gained more legitimacy. Daily newspaper articles, in which the IDF presented its position on current political issues, were a common manifestation of this fact.

The IDF described its positions as if it were a political party or an independent political entity. Officers publicly expressed opinions before government meetings and in government meetings, and at times did not hesitate to criticize government decisions even after they had been made. On the other hand, there was no conceptual gap between the government and the military, and Sharon exerted considerable authority. This was manifested in the status achieved by the MID, which, with Sharon's encouragement, acquired added importance as a political-diplomatic arm of the government. For example, the MID was recruited to publish material —mostly incriminating Palestinian documents uncovered by the branch itself or by the ISA—and to become Israel's major public relations face against the Palestinians and neighboring Arab states.

However, this new role for the MID did cause discontentment among some officers in the intelligence branch; they claimed that such MID documents were written as propaganda materials and not as professional reports and complained that positive Arab démarches, such as the Saudi peace initiative, had been ignored. Further, they argued that the intelligence branch's involvement in such activities might harm its professional reputation internationally, especially if, rather than presenting facts and assessments to the political echelon, it became active in promoting government policy. But these complaints did not find sympathetic ears.[20]

While such complaints are notable, demonstrating that some intelligence officers held on to certain professional ideals, anyone arguing that the level of IDF involvement in politics today is no different than it was in previous years must be reminded both of the intelligence community's current open keenness for political activity and of the words of Aharon Yariv, who served as DMI in the 1970s and is to this day considered one of the most effective leaders to have held the position. Unlike many recent intelligence chiefs, Yariv went so far as to ask his prime minister, Golda Meir, to limit his participation in diplomatic negotiations: "I told her that it is unhealthy for the military and the intelligence branch. The very fact of personal ties with the political sphere and involvement in political and diplomatic activity is damaging our analytical potential—analysis being the very purpose of our work."[21]

In the end, the honeymoon of Ya'alon and Mofaz and the idyllic relations between the military and Sharon's government did not last long.

Toward the end of 2003, it was already clear that relations would deteriorate as they had in the early years of the intifada. Anyone familiar with
the immanent dilemmas of an LIC could have anticipated this. This was
due not only to personal friction that existed between the political and
military echelons but, more significantly, to differences of opinion regarding the policy to be pursued in the war.

9

The Tragedy
of CGS Ya'alon

Politics of a Nonpolitical Officer

Lt. Gen. Moshe Ya'alon, a capable, sincere, and exemplary soldier, succeeded Mofaz as CGS on June 8, 2002. Mofaz's final years as CGS coincided with the first two years of the Al-Aqsa intifada, his handling of which catapulted him into national stardom and the defense minister's office. In contrast to Mofaz, "Boogy" Ya'alon—like most IDF officers, he is better known by his nickname than his given name—did not want to use his stewardship of the military as a stepping-stone to a political career; in fact, he made an honest attempt to disengage the IDF from the partisan game. What he did not understand was that in an LIC that is an entirely impossible goal. Thus, Ya'alon in his role as CGS personified the full extent of the predicament the LIC caused the IDF: both Ya'alon and the IDF slid into the political morass, their relations with civilian society were compromised, and in the end Ya'alon was even "fired," leaving the military on June 1, 2005.[1]

Mofaz became a hero with the nationalist camp in Israel following the outbreak of the intifada because he supported a hard-line policy. If at the outset he was indeed motivated strictly by military considerations, as time went on it became increasingly apparent that he also wanted to be in step with public opinion, which would aid his political future.[2] He fostered a spirit of militancy in the IDF; at every meeting with officers and troops, he preached the sanctity of "victory as a value" and exhorted them to "seek contact [with the enemy]" and to "apply maximum firepower to destroy the objective." On one occasion, he even demanded that his men "bring him heads"; senior officers quickly explained to their subordinates that the CGS's remarks were not an actual order and that they must obey orders only from their direct commanders.[3]

When Ya'alon took up his new appointment, most commentators believed that there would be a diminishing of political activity in the CGS's office. A major general on the General Staff was quoted as saying, "No one will be able to say that Boogy is a political CGS. He'll speak out, but strictly on military and security matters. He's a classic public servant."[4] That assessment proved mistaken by the second day of Ya'alon's tenure, throughout which he witnessed recurring crises in his relations with the political echelon. Most of these crises came to attention because Ya'alon had a tendency to make political comments in public that were in opposition to the views of the government; many saw these pronouncements as intrusions on areas that were solely in the civilian domain.

In all such instances, Ya'alon contended that the media took his remarks out of context and distorted them, and in some cases he was right. But even if this were the case and Ya'alon truly lacked an understanding of the way the news media functioned, his own direct and open style contributed to the turmoil. Comments such as the following were common in the press: "Ya'alon is perceived by his superiors as a man who fearlessly states the truth as he sees it" and "The trouble with Ya'alon is that he is too honest, and states his truth, a harsh, unpalatable truth, jarring to some ears."[5]

When asked why he was not content with internal deliberations with his superiors and chose instead to openly disseminate his views, Ya'alon answered categorically that he was "the CGS of the people of Israel, and not just of the political echelon."[6] The need to influence the public, to educate it, has become all the more critical in light of the "perception warfare" that takes place in an LIC, he added. Indeed, Ya'alon behaved according to the perception—prevalent in the IDF—that the CGS had not only the right but also the authority to be a full partner in fashioning national policy. This was self-evident according to the principles of an LIC, which Ya'alon had played a major part in composing while at Central Command. In fact, as CGS he developed further this strategy, establishing a new brainstorming group that met weekly and became, in practical terms, more important than the regular General Staff meetings in consolidating a battle plan against the Palestinians, from both a military and political perspective.

Although his style was different than Mofaz's, Ya'alon's views toward the Palestinians essentially aligned with the General Staff's hard-line camp (though he never stopped advocating negotiations with Syria). He had long lost faith in Arafat's intention to honor the peace agreement with Israel. Shortly after his appointment as intelligence chief in 1995, Ya'alon had a meeting with Arafat in which he showed him a list of thirty-five people who were involved in terrorist activities, saying he wanted the Palestinian Authority to arrest them. Arafat promised to do so but did not. Ya'alon said the last straw was when he asked Arafat to arrest Muhammed "The Engineer" Dif, who had been involved in numerous terrorist acts against Israel. Arafat pretended he did not know who the man was. Ya'alon related, "'Muhammed who?' Arafat asked. And then I realized that the man is simply a liar."[7]

Ya'alon was also convinced that Arafat had full control over the Palestinian leadership, orchestrating the armed struggle from above. He therefore believed that the Palestinian compromise with Israel during the Oslo process was not genuine but rather a tactical move that comported with the PLO's "doctrine of stages." In Ya'alon's mind, the ultimate aim of the PLO leadership under Arafat had not changed. Even after an Israeli withdrawal from all the territories, he believed Palestinians would not accept the legitimacy of Israel as a Jewish state with which peaceful relations must be maintained. Such was the outlook that underpinned Ya'alon's thinking when he became head of the Central Command in 1998. Ya'alon immediately set about preparing the command for the violent confrontation he expected with the Palestinians, an expectation that materialized that September. The same month, Ya'alon was appointed deputy CGS.

Even though he did not entertain personal political ambitions, Ya'alon had followed a career path typical of politically oriented IDF officers. As many such officers did, he held posts that had a significant political element, commencing with a position in the Sayeret Matkal elite reconnaissance and commando unit. Eliot Cohen has already shown that officers in special units have a closer and more direct connection with the top political echelon than do those in other units.[8] This is definitely true with the IDF; many of its officers—such as Mordechai Gur, Ariel

Sharon, Ehud Barak, and Amnon Shahak—that served and grew up in these units eventually reached political positions.

As indicated, Ya'alon gained additional political experience as chief of the MID, head of Central Command, and deputy CGS. He was also influenced, like the entire generation of officers for whom the Yom Kippur War was a defining experience, by the idea that politicians tended to avoid making clear-cut decisions, pursuing unpopular policies, and initiating long-term resolutions and that, when they are criticized, politicians place responsibility, if not blame, on the IDF. Therefore, Ya'alon believed military officers must be more aware of and influential in the policymaking process.

Ya'alon's Concept of Low-Intensity Conflict

Shortly after his appointment as CGS, Ya'alon set forth his views on the Israeli-Palestinian dispute in an address to a national conference of rabbis: "The present Palestinian leadership does not recognize the existence of Israel. . . . The Palestinian danger to Israel constitutes a threat of cancerous dimensions and character that must be eliminated, must be fought to the death. . . . The Palestinians want to cause the Israeli public to lose its morale and to drag its political leadership into decisions like unilateral withdrawal from the territories, which would in effect be surrender to terrorism. . . . My concern is the staying power of Israeli society."[9]

Like Mofaz before him, Ya'alon sharply criticized the IDF withdrawal from southern Lebanon. In fact, the IDF heads believed that this unilateral act encouraged Arafat's strategic decision to continue to use violence and terrorism against Israel. Ya'alon held that the Palestinians interpreted the Israeli move as flight, indicating Israel's internal weakness and its inability to remain steadfast in a protracted struggle. Indeed, this was the idea behind Hizbullah leader Sheikh Hasan Nasrallah's spiderweb theory. Nasrallah believed that, with constant bloodshed, the staying power of Israeli society would decline, causing the bonds of societal solidarity to attenuate and to eventually disintegrate like a spiderweb. Therefore, in Ya'alon's view, Arafat and the Palestinians assumed that losses among Israeli civilians would set in motion processes similar to those that led to Israel's withdrawal from southern Lebanon. Thus, Ya'alon contended, in the war against the Palestinians in Judea, Samaria, and the Gaza Strip, Israel must attain a clear-cut, decisive victory. "We must win this conflict in such a way that the Palestinians will realize that they have no prospect of gaining anything by means of terror seared into their consciousness."[10]

Ya'alon had an unclouded view not only of the military tactics needed for the counterinsurgency war but also of the political strategy that should be used toward the Palestinian Authority. In his talk to the rabbis, he also called on the government to not digress from Bush's road map and to not forgo the demand to remove Arafat from leadership. He also urged the government to destroy terrorist infrastructure, to insist on the transparency of PA economic activities, and to refuse to reach an agreement until anti-Israel textbooks currently in use in PA schools were replaced and mosque sermons were censored.[11] Such comments demonstrate how the CGS had wholeheartedly embraced the principles of LIC. Although members of the government were already familiar with them, the general public was not. For instance, while the phrase "seared into their consciousness" was in use by the IDF's commanders, it had never before been heard by the general public. As a result, the backlash to Ya'alon's speech was not long in coming; his address brought about an avalanche of sharply critical pronouncements and articles. In particular, his use of the term "seared" reminded some of the numbers the Nazis seared on the arms of Jews in concentration camps.

The popular newspaper *Yedioth Ahronoth* published an article that was perhaps the most biting ever penned in Israel against a sitting CGS, let alone against one who had just taken up his post and had not even completed the traditional hundred-day grace period. Part of the article charged, "Moshe Ya'alon is a man of the extreme right. For years, he led us from hesitant hope to a bloody, hopeless hell of despicable terrorism and filthy occupation. Boogy takes pride in having 'seen what was coming,' but it was he who brought it about." Commenting on Ya'alon's reference to the Palestinians as a cancer, B. Michael, the columnist who penned the article, warned, "A Jew should not forget the people who termed his people 'a cancerous element.' He is expected to remember them day and night, to sear their horrible image in his mind and to strive wholeheartedly to have nothing to do with them." Michael then pointedly concluded, "The cancer that really threatens Israel is the cancer of the occupation and brutalization, the cancer of ignorant racism, the cancer of Neanderthal militarism, the cancer of narrow-mindedness and power-worship, the cancer of unthinking acquiescence in the foolish, empty-minded rule of officers, whose world consists of nothing but a hammer, so the whole world looks like a nail to them."[12]

Ha'aretz's sharp-tongued social critic Doron Rosenblum was no less acerbic: "In the 'voluntary putsch' atmosphere in which Israeli politics is currently wallowing, it seems that the sky is the limit in all that relates to the authority and status of the CGS and other commanders. Hardly a weekend passes when we are not ordered to sit at attention as some senior officer not only pretends to lay unchallengeable claim to define what our condition is, but also to legislate, to dictate how we should manage things, what we should write and what we should think."[13] Although subsequent difficulties would provoke a different response, when this first storm erupted, Sharon publicly supported the statements of his new CGS. "His statements were correct and genuine," Sharon said. "Criticism of him was motivated by political considerations. Had he said the opposite, he would have been praised by the Left."[14]

Ya'alon's roots in Kfar Haim, a working-class Haifa suburb that is traditionally a Labor movement stronghold, his membership in Kibbutz Grofit, and his social connections, intellectual mind, and personal style, had all engendered the image of a man who leaned to the Israeli Left. Further, his statement on the eve of the 1992 elections that Iran was interested in a change of government in Israel contributed to this belief, even though it was based on information he acquired as head of the MID and was not made because of partisan considerations. Nevertheless, it was perceived that he supported Peres, arousing the ire of the Right and enhancing his image as a man of the Left.

But as Ya'alon continued to make public statements such as the ones he made at the conference of rabbis, the Left came to see him as an apostate, as someone who had forsaken his political faith to become an honorary member of the nationalist camp. That, however, was a superficial analysis. Ya'alon's perspective of the Israeli-Palestinian conflict was a far cry from that held by the religious-nationalists; he had never supported the idea of Greater Israel—that is, he did not relate to the historical Land of Israel as God's gift to the Jewish people and did not impute sacred significance to territories. What he advocated was the LIC doctrine that the IDF had embraced, and he conducted himself in strict accordance with it.

In Ya'alon's view, all of Israeli society needed to show unity and determination to defeat the Palestinians, or, in the language of an LIC,

"To prove to the Palestinians that their use of violence will not lead to a change in the aim of [our] civilian society, but rather the reverse, will cause Palestinian society to pay so high a price that continuing the war is not worthwhile." Israel needed to come out of the current round of conflict a clear-cut winner, he believed, "to engender a change in the mindset of the opposing side." Such a change is attainable "only by wearing down the enemy through a wide arc of means, both civilian—including political, social, and economic—and military."[15] In fact, Ya'alon used the term "wall" as early as 2000 to refer to national unity and accused ministers of the Left in Barak's government and in Sharon's coalition of drilling holes in it. Additionally, Ya'alon opposed using "intifada" to describe the events then erupting because he did not view them as a spontaneous popular uprising; instead, he described them as a "continuation of the War of Independence of 1948."

While an LIC does not involve the totality of military force, it does involve a totality of a different sort. An LIC is not just a battle between armies but a conflict between two societies, involving the psyche, consciousness, and worldview of each. That is why those in the IDF who devised the doctrine of LIC called for a "unity of effort," which was meant to supersede the principle of "concentration of effort" that had characterized conventional wars of the past.[16] In an LIC, effort is not directed at the physical assets of the enemy but at its national and moral strength; the war effort is directed at a nation's consciousness, and it attempts to compromise the enemy's faith in its ability to attain its own war aims. Similarly, any hesitation, doubt, lack of unity, or indication of internal weakness on one's own part is liable to undermine one's faith in one's ability to attain one's aim and hence is liable to bring the enemy closer to victory.

For these reasons, those who direct an LIC cannot limit their efforts to the employment of military units only; they must operate throughout civilian society to foster unity of effort and unity regarding their aim. And that is why the IDF intensified its indoctrination effort in the media, endeavoring to narrow differences of opinion in civilian political life.[17] Ya'alon felt that the need to impart to the decision makers a mode of conduct for the LIC justified standing up to the political echelon, even though at the end of the day officers must accept the prerogatives of statesmen to make the final decisions.

This need for internal harmony and unity of effort explains why Ya'alon could not acquiesce to the Barak government's dual policy. For example, how could Israel fight the Palestinian Authority and at the same time view it as a partner in talks? How could it fight Arafat and concurrently negotiate with him? However, the LIC strategy pursued by the IDF—employing all available civilian, economic, and social levers to raise the price the Palestinian population had to pay for continuation of the conflict, so that civilians would put pressure on the militants to cease violent activities—contradicted the government's stated policy of only attacking those behind the armed struggle without harming innocent others.

Furthermore, Ya'alon's claim that victory in the conflict would depend on civilian factors was viewed by his critics as his interfering in a realm outside the purview of the military. After all, since when had the IDF been charged with forging and strengthening the spirit of the civilian population? And if the IDF embraced the principle of the unity of aim, did that not mean that anyone who disagreed with the policy of the military and the government could be charged with undermining national unity? This is what Rosenblum warned about when he wrote, "And anyone who thought that the political and public standing of the CGS got out of bounds during the tenure of Shaul Mofaz hasn't seen anything yet. . . . 'L'état, c'est moi' is what the new CGS claims, and with the astonishing claim that any criticism of him weakens Israel, he refutes in advance any legitimate, publicly expressed thought concerning his assessments."[18]

Ya'alon Demands a "Political Horizon"

By the summer of 2003, the IDF believed that its war plan was bearing fruit. Its physical presence in all of the Palestinian territories enabled it to move from defense to constant offense. The military and ISA reduced the number of Palestinian attacks and resulting casualties, senior Hamas figures fell in a long series of "targeted eliminations," U.S. pressure on the PA intensified, and even Europe attenuated its support for Arafat. On top of all this, there was a coalition victory over Iraq. It appeared that the war against the Palestinians was drawing to a close and that the CGS's forecast was on target—2003 would be "the year of decision."

In fact, the Palestinians and Israelis did reluctantly accept President Bush's road map, which called for a cessation of Palestinian violence, an

Israeli withdrawal to pre-intifada lines, the renewal of negotiations, and, eventually, the establishment of a Palestinian state. The Palestinian Authority signed a temporary cease-fire agreement (the *hudna*) with Palestinian militant organizations, and Arafat moved to the sidelines and appointed as prime minister Mahmud Abbas ("Abu Mazen"), a pragmatist who expressed reservations about the use of force. Abbas and his determined partner, Muhammad Dahlan, were expected to restrain Hamas, Islamic Jihad, and Tanzim terrorist activities; and it even seemed they might have the courage to confront them.

As a result, a wave of optimism swept the IDF command. Ya'alon felt these positive developments were attributable to the IDF's LIC strategy; at a meeting with troops, he remarked, "I told you that 2003 would be the year of decision, and it [these developments] is actually what I meant."[19] Ya'alon made no attempt to understate the great turnaround being witnessed. In his view, success in countering the intifada led to a turning point in the thinking of some in the Palestinian leadership, including Abu Mazen/Abbas. Ya'alon stated, "They internalized the insight that Israel is an established fact in the region and that it cannot be defeated by force. . . . Now the Palestinians are going to make the transition from 'a consciousness of struggle' to 'a consciousness of accommodation'"; he further believed any wrangling with Abbas would be over only the exact terms of accommodation.[20] Similarly, Ya'alon was quoted as saying, "There's a high probability that in the fullness of time, we will be able to look back on this period and say, 'These were the last days of violence.' I am not talking about victory. I am talking about [forcing a] decision to the conflict. When there is leadership [that is, Abbas] that mobilizes the street against terrorism, that is a decision."[21]

However, this "turning point"—some newspapers even referred to the intifada as "The Thousand-Day War," as if it had actually ended—proved to be short-lived. Less than two months later, everything unraveled again with a suicide bombing on a Jerusalem bus transporting Orthodox Jews to the Western Wall. Israel blamed Hamas, but it also blamed Arafat for constantly hindering his new prime minister from taking action against such groups. Indeed, it had been clear from day one that Arafat would not allow Abbas any opportunity for success. Arafat did not intend to renounce his status as unchallenged leader and believed that he could face up to the Israeli and U.S. pressure, as he had in the past, and continued to run a highly centralistic regime, maneuvering among the numerous forces within the Palestinian Authority. In this respect, Mahmud Abbas did not constitute a challenge to his leadership.

Nevertheless, the Israeli government was not free of responsibility for Abbas's failure. In the West Bank, the IDF and ISA continued to impose curfews and area quarantines, to make arrests, and to kill wanted activists. Abbas's requests that prisoners be freed were grudgingly and partially acceded to, while requests for freer movement and alleviation of economic restrictions were virtually ignored. The IDF did not evacuate cities in which violence had ceased, and populations that had opposed terrorism continued to groan under the yoke of occupation. Under such circumstances, Abbas had no chance of success and duly resigned, leading Arafat to appoint his close collaborator Ahmad Karia ("Abu Alla") to succeed Abbas. The return of Arafat to center stage after he had seemingly been terminally weakened led many to perceive him as a man with a thousand lives; his return, along with the abrogation of the *hudna* and resumption of violence, frustrated the IDF leadership, including Ya'alon. The hope of seeing the end of the intifada went up in smoke, portending more of the same for the foreseeable future.

As could be expected, the Left pointed the finger of blame at the Sharon government, claiming that this was the second time that Sharon and his ministers had missed an opportunity to come to an agreement with the Palestinians that would bring the intifada to an end. (The first time was when the IDF successfully carried out Operation Defensive Shield in April 2002; in that case, the government did not exploit the resulting situation to advance a political dialogue with the Palestinian Authority and the United States, which may have led to a prolonged period of quiet.) But, more significantly, the military also joined in criticizing Sharon. From the IDF officers' perspective, if the government had only helped the newly appointed Palestinian prime minister, he would have been able to consolidate his ministry, weaken Arafat, prolong the *hudna,* work against terrorism, and begin the new peaceful era that Ya'alon felt was struggling to dawn. However, the hard-line that Sharon and Mofaz pursued weakened Abbas and strengthened Arafat. As a result, the opportunity for a peace process had been missed.[22]

This criticism of government policy from the IDF reflected the new chasm between Ya'alon and Sharon toward the end of the intifada's third year. While both favored wielding a big stick, and while Ya'alon did not change his negative opinion of the Palestinian leadership, above all of Arafat, he also believed—even though he did not say so publicly—that it would be impossible to reach a *modus vivendi* without also offering a carrot. Additionally, by summer 2003, Ya'alon felt that the time had come to give the Palestinian people a sliver of hope and to make life easier for those not involved in violence. Such a sliver would include removing limitations on movement, withdrawing IDF units from cities where quiet had returned, and in general making everyday life easier, especially regarding employment; in brief, Ya'alon believed such moves would show the Palestinians that a cessation of violence has rewards.

Ya'alon wanted an improvement in the situation for a number of reasons and was worried about a deterioration in affairs if Israel did not change policy. Specifically, he was concerned that a prolonged curfew would seriously damage various areas of agriculture, such as the olive harvest, so important to the livelihood of those in the West Bank. And he feared the economic situation there would eventually lead to what he called "a humanitarian crisis." He also voiced concern that a continuation of indiscriminate pressure on the Palestinians would exacerbate hatred of Israel, provoke an expansion of the human reservoir of the terrorist organizations, and in the final analysis cause serious damage to Israeli security.

Ya'alon believed that two groups competed for power within the Palestinian leadership. The strategy of the first group, led by Arafat, was to withdraw from the two-state solution but to continue the resistance until the Palestinians gained a demographic advantage over the Jews within a single polity; according to Ya'alon, this group assumed Israel would then wither from within as a Jewish state. The other group, Ya'alon held, advocated ending the intifada and returning to the negotiation table. The latter group should be encouraged, Ya'alon stated, if not for its advocacy of the resumption of talks, then for its focus on alleviating the tension and easing the security burden. Ya'alon was worried that if Abu Alla stumbled, rendering Arafat sole ruler, the result would be the complete collapse of the Palestinian Authority and total anarchy. Abu Alla, therefore, needed to consolidate his position to improve the probability of reaching a *modus vivendi* based on compromise. Hence, Ya'alon concluded, Israel should make positive gestures toward Abu Alla.[23]

But Ya'alon's view clashed with another one espoused by the upper echelons of the security establishment, a view that was vigorously embraced by ISA chief Avi Dichter. According to this other view, the primary aim, virtually the only aim, of policy toward the Palestinians in the immediate period had to be the prevention of terrorist attacks, and the only way to attain that aim was through the continuation of current policies. Proponents of this view were concerned that despite the decline in the number of attacks, future attacks had the potential to be more dangerous; there was an especially great risk of a mega-incident, something that would undermine the relative stability attained at that time and, with it, Israel's ability to contain terrorism.[24] Ya'alon and other likeminded officers responded strongly to Dichter's line of reasoning by stating that steps to prevent the next attack were liable to bring about another two hundred attacks on Israel. They argued that someone has to put an end to the bloody cycle and, as the stronger side, Israel carries this responsibility. Israel has the power to restrain itself, to "swallow," and to set out in a different direction, they continued, stating flatly that Palestinian society will not surrender and that the more it bleeds, the more Israel will.

The matter was referred to Defense Minister Mofaz, who rejected Ya'alon's position and accepted the ISA's view, which was also supported by Mofaz's senior adviser, Amos Gilead. At one meeting, Mofaz, referring to Ya'alon, stated sharply, "There are officers here who care more about what happens to Palestinians. They talk all the time about what is good for the Palestinians. I care above all about what is good for Israelis."[25] Ya'alon appealed to the prime minister, telling him that Israel should not antagonize the Palestinians in Gaza, Jericho, and Bethlehem to the point where they lack hope. He described prevailing policy as "sacrificing strategic interests for tactical considerations," but the prime minister left decision making on the issue to Mofaz.[26]

Realizing that he was unable to get through to the political echelon, Ya'alon did as his predecessor had: he went public, expressing his concern that Israel might soon start "trudging just to remain in place."[27] On October 29, 2003, all three of Israel's leading dailies ran nearly identical headlines that essentially read: "Unease among Military; IDF: Government Policy Destructive."[28] The stories that day quoted "senior military sources" and, after the storm broke, the CGS, in his usual, straightforward way, stood by what he had said in his background briefing to the three papers.

Meanwhile, the reaction among government ministers toward Ya'alon was one of anger. As in past instances, they were more concerned with the intrusion of the military in politics than the nature of the words themselves (only a minority of officials actually addressed the content of Ya'alon's views). As expected, a few in opposition parties even praised the CGS. Amram Mitzna, who had earlier resigned from leadership of the Labor Party, wrote,

> The CGS's criticism of government policy is surprising not only in the way it was expressed, but also because the CGS has hitherto supported the same conception as, and faithfully carried out the instructions of, the political echelon. There is no doubt that the statements of the CGS— which exposed in the clearest manner the enormous gap between the conceptions according to which the IDF has hitherto operated and reality —mark a turning point.
>
> For the first time, the head of the military admits that the IDF cannot win, that government policy hurts security and causes irreversible damage to Israeli society, to the IDF, and to the country. . . . Even if the Israeli public is not grateful to the CGS for the great importance of what he has done, history will be. Unlike a prime minister who is removed from the people, who senses neither suffering nor deep despair, or a defense minister who mixes politics with security considerations—the CGS looks mothers in the eyes. He knows there is no justification for the death of their children at Netzarim [a settlement in the Gaza Strip]. He knows that their presence there does not contribute to security, and he is beginning to understand that we have no business there. The State of Israel can defeat Palestinian terrorism, but only if it pursues a peace process concurrently with the fighting.[29]

The Controversy over the Barrier

During the summer of 2003, other bones of contention between the military and the government sprung forth. One such issue related to the defense budget. Though the military and the treasury generally have a disagreement every year, with the treasury generally wanting to cut defense spending, the conflict between the two became particularly acute during Ya'alon's tenure as CGS. The finance minister sought to cut the state budget, both as an expression of his economic philosophy and as a means of counteracting reduced revenues resulting from an economic slump brought on by the intifada. The military, however, demanded a larger slice of the national financial pie, particularly in light of the continued fighting.

Compounding the problem, the military saw the budgetary battle itself as an indication of the government's and civilian society's lack of gratitude for its efforts, and as an indication of its slipping status. In fact, the military also lay blame on Defense Minister Mofaz. Rather than defending the interests of the military, he had agreed to the budget cuts out of personal and political considerations, so that he would keep on good terms with the finance minister and the prime minister.

Another controversy centered on the security fence. The military supported the erection of a barrier that would prevent entry of Palestinians into Israel from the territories and that would hinder potential suicide bombers. Sharon had long opposed the idea of a fence; specifically, he believed it would cut Israel off from the occupied territories, which he hoped to eventually annex to the Jewish state. However, as terrorist attacks continued, he had to bow to public opinion and ultimately agreed to the plan, demanding that the fence be erected as far as possible inside Palestinian territory. The settlers and the right wing of the government supported Sharon's position as the least execrable alternative. As a result, the fence—in part an eight-meter-high concrete wall—would stretch along a tortuous path of some nine hundred kilometers. In places it would skirt the Green Line, which itself is only some five hundred kilometers long, while elsewhere it would wind deep inside areas populated with Palestinians, creating enclaves and ghettos and leaving tens of thousands of Palestinians on the west side of the fence and isolated Jewish settlements on the east side. It became increasingly clear, as time went on, that erection of the fence would upset the lives of hundreds of thousands of Palestinians, leading to a burst of international criticism.

Even Ya'alon joined in criticizing the fence, albeit for somewhat different reasons. Ya'alon called it a "patchwork." His complaint was not about the fence itself, but rather, about the lack of planning in erecting the fence, whose course in places was determined in the aftermath of terrorist attacks and the ensuing spurts of activity. As a result, Ya'alon criticized the frequent alterations in the fence's route, its plethora of snake-like windings, and the fact that passage gates were not properly planned. Ya'alon also voiced opposition to the plan of the prime minister and defense minister to erect an eastern fence between the Jordan River and the Jordan Valley and a double fence around such populated areas as Qalqilya. In the CGS's assessment, these actions would exacerbate the pressure felt by the

West Bank population and intensify international pressure on Israel. Above all, though, he believed such moves conflicted with the fence's original purpose—to be a genuine security barrier. In brief, while the IDF had wanted a fence that would address Israel's security needs—to close the border with the territories and prevent the entry of potential suicide bombers—the fence ultimately was erected to answer the needs of the settlers and to realize political goals that only made the work of the military more difficult.[30]

Yet another disagreement between Ya'alon and the government concerned the question of Syria. The coalition victory over Iraq and the U.S. presence there had created a new geostrategic reality that seemed to lead to a change in policy in Damascus; Bashar al-Assad, the Syrian president, announced his willingness to open a new chapter in relations with Israel and resume peace negotiations without prior conditions. Various emissaries who met with him even reported that he had hinted that he would be more flexible than his father, Hafez al-Assad, had been. But the declarations from Damascus fell on deaf ears in Jerusalem. The government saw them as a public relations game and a political maneuver designed to bolster the shaky position of the Alawi minority regime in Syria in the eyes of Washington. Additionally, explained the prime minister's spokesmen, the government could not handle the disengagement plan in the south and, at the same time, the opening of negotiations that would necessitate territorial concessions in the north.

Ya'alon did not see eye-to-eye with this position, nor did Zeevi-Farkash, the head of the MID, who thought that the Syrian declarations were sincere. Ya'alon believed a peace treaty with Assad could be concluded in a very short time, as many of the principle points had already been agreed to by both sides in the past, and estimated that only good could come out of talks with Damascus. More important, such a treaty would radically improve Israel's strategic situation and be followed at once by peace with Lebanon. This, in turn, would significantly weaken Hizbullah, which had become the most agitating factor among Palestinians in the territories.[31]

Ya'alon did not consider his view toward Syria as appeasement. In fact, whenever there was a violation of the cease-fire along the northern borders, he insisted on a sharp military response. Yet, at the same time, he did not want Israel to be seen as intransigent, as spitting in the face of the Syrian ruler. Israel needed to avail itself of every opportunity for peace, he believed. In background discussions, Zeevi-Farkash claimed that he had been encouraged by Assad's decision to no longer insist on the preconditions laid out by his father, that is, Israeli withdrawal to the lines of June 4, 1967.

At a cabinet meeting in early January 2003, Sharon had a heated exchange with Zeevi-Farkash, as the latter set forth his views. Tensions resurfaced on subsequent occasions during internal discussions between the defense and political leadership. When the intelligence chief was asked if he would publicly air views explicitly opposed to government policy, he unhesitatingly replied, "The head of the Intelligence Directorate must convey his opinion to the Israeli public, without filters."[32] CGS Ya'alon also supported this position. While Ya'alon reiterated that the military would naturally accept any decision of the political echelon, he did not hide his own views about Syria.

As with most debates among Israel's political-military elite, in the case of what policy to pursue vis-à-vis Syria, each side counted both officers and civilians among its ranks. In this instance, Ya'alon had the support of Zeevi-Farkash, while the director general of the Mossad, Maj. Gen. (res.) Me'ir Dagan, and the director of the research division at the MID, Brig. Gen. Yossi Cooperwasser, aligned themselves with the prime minister and defense minister.[33] Thus, during the last months of Ya'alon's term of office as CGS, the Syria issue remained an open wound in the relationship between the Israeli government and military. More than a decade earlier, DMI Sagi told Prime Minister Shamir that Assad was a potentially serious negotiating partner, but the prime minister rejected Sagi's view. Several years later, the IDF leadership expressed similar displeasure when Barak decided to discontinue talks with Syria; they felt that reaching a peace agreement with Assad was possible and were even willing to pay the full territorial price for it.[34] So in the summer of 2004, Ya'alon and others saw the same scenario repeating itself. Indeed, the Syrian question continued to occupy Ya'alon until his last day in office. After leaving his post, he gave a rare interview to an Arab newspaper presenting his reasons for calling on reconciliation with Syria. As might be expected, he was viciously attacked by right-wing ministers and by members of the Knesset.[35]

In addition to Ya'alon's differences of opinion with Sharon over political issues, and his disagreement with Mofaz over internal military issues, bad blood existed between them on a more personal level. This only grew as Mofaz became increasingly aware that his influence over the military was limited. He had above him a prime minister who was an expert in military matters and who practiced a hands-on management style, while below him he had in Ya'alon a CGS who wanted to guard his kingdom from too much interference, just as Mofaz himself had done when he was CGS a few years earlier. But when Mofaz first moved to the office of defense minister, he had expected to be a kind of super-CGS. Instead, he found himself having much less sway than he had anticipated. His attempts to influence even the appointment of senior officers in the IDF were thwarted by Ya'alon, and relations between them deteriorated to the extent that they hardly spoke to each other. This set the background for Mofaz's decision in February 2005 to terminate Ya'alon's office as CGS.

Ya'alon and Mofaz were not the first chiefs of general staff who took part in critical decisions that shaped Israel's destiny. Indeed, the deep political involvement of IDF commanders is a structural element of Israel's politics. To better understand their role as political actors, a historical perspective is first needed.

10

The Chief of Staff as a Political Actor

The Distinctive Power of Israel's Chief of Staff

The political prowess of the CGS has been expressed not only in times of tension, such as war, but also during more relaxed periods, when the relations between the military and the political echelons have been more harmonious. Indeed, the CGS is one of the most powerful persons in Israel and possesses a capacity for political influence greater than that of his counterparts in other democracies. But what factors contribute to making his position so highly potent?

The first factor is the structure of Israel's defense system. For the most part, the three IDF branches are highly unified. The navy and air force have separate headquarters and different uniforms, but the General Staff serves as the operational directorate of all elements of the armed forces, and the CGS is the nation's senior officer and the supreme military commander for all the IDF. In this respect, the Israeli model is opposite that of the United States, the United Kingdom, and Germany; the Canadian command structure is the only Western command with more unity among its various branches. Furthermore, unlike many of its Western counterparts, the Israeli General Staff has two key responsibilities—building up forces and overseeing their operation. In other words, it has two roles, serving as a center for policymaking and as headquarters of the IDF's ground forces. Consequently, the CGS serves both as chief of the Defense Staff (comparable to the British chief of the Defence Staff or the U.S. chairman of the Joint Chiefs of Staff) and as leader of the ground forces.[1]

With the General Staff serving as a theater headquarters for all military operations, the CGS, in effect, oversees land and air operations as well as those in the four ground-force quadrants: north, center, south, and home front.[2] In addition to the high level of centralization within the IDF, there is one more structural characteristic of the whole defense structure that empowers the CGS: the absence of integration with civilian staff. There is no merging of civilian and military staffs that deal with similar tasks into one integrated civil-military staff.

While more and more countries have adopted an integrated structure of this kind, Israel has not. Due to the absence of such integration, defense functions are divided between military and civilian components, with the military component being the more powerful of the two. For example, the military generally determines, in effect, what the defense budget will be—although formally this matter should be in the hands of the Defense Ministry. "The military's domination in this important function is primarily a means by which the IDF preserves its preeminent position and maintains a high degree of influence and authority in areas that in most other countries are considered beyond the sphere of responsibility of the military."[3]

The military's great power is manifested in other functions as well, such as in intelligence, an area in which other countries—such as the United Kingdom, the United States, and Canada—intimately involve the civilian element. Also, the military's advantage over the Defense Ministry allows the CGS to have greater influence than the director general of the ministry or its political appointees, such as the deputy defense minister. Indeed, the CGS's power exceeds that of most government ministers. This is demonstrated, among other ways, by the fact that since 1967 the CGS has participated in cabinet meetings, not on an occasional basis (for example, as an expert when defense policy is being discussed) but on a permanent, regular basis as a nonvoting participant.

Aside from these structural elements, other factors that affect the power of the CGS and the military include the work habits of the IDF. High-ranking officers tend to micromanage subordinates, involving themselves in operational activities that do not require or justify high-ranking involvement. Therefore, the CGS will often personally visit sites of relatively small-scale terror attacks. The strengthening of the CGS's position also is reflected in the traditional career path to this post. In the past it was hard for a senior IDF officer to become CGS without first serving as the head of the Northern Command. The Syrian front was initially the area where one could gain experience in war preparations and, at times, in actual warfare management. But, once the Palestinian front became the major conflict zone for the IDF, the route to becoming CGS started passing through the Central Command and the MID. The political aspects of these two areas are broad and diverse, and those who hold posts within them therefore become prepared for and accustomed to involvement in the political process.

Compared with the CGS, whose power stems from the institutional structure of the defense establishment, those in the civilian arm are particularly weak.[4] This has been especially true since 1967, when the prime minister's and defense minister's functions were divided; the supervision of the defense establishment fell to both, and the CGS could thereafter maneuver between them, gaining a quasi-ministerial position. For example, in 1971, CGS Chaim Barlev opposed Defense Minister Dayan's proposed withdrawal from the Suez Canal. In this plan, the IDF would withdraw from the banks of the Suez in exchange for Egypt's opening of the canal to international vessel traffic. However, Prime Minister Meir opposed any movement of IDF forces from the armistice lines that had been determined after the Six Day War in 1967 and sought the General Staff's opinion. Barlev, who was politically close to Meir and a rival of Dayan, supplied Meir with the ammunition she needed. Armed with the General Staff's opposition to troop redeployment, Meir was able to reject Dayan's proposal. As prime minister, she could have rejected the proposal without Barlev's opinion, but it was much easier and more convenient for her to hide behind the IDF's view, which could be presented as "professional" rather than as political.

This pattern of relying on the military's professional assessments to better one's position in the political arena enabled politicians to appropriate for themselves some of the public legitimacy the military enjoys and, worse, to dodge responsibility when necessary by placing it on the military's shoulders. This also led to the military's having to manage, time and again, matters properly belonging in the political realm.

Until the mid-1970s, the Israeli constitution was ambiguous on the question of how the political echelon and the military should relate to each other and provided no guidance on how the cabinet, the prime minister, and the defense minister should interact. But after the Yom Kippur War and in light of the Agranat Commission's recommendations, the Knesset passed the Military Basic Law in 1975, which specifically addressed political-military relations. The law specified the military's subordination to the cabinet but left vague how the various civil actors—the prime minister, the defense minister, and the cabinet—should interact as a unified body. Additionally, the relationship between the CGS and his political supervisors remained unclear. For instance, could the defense minister order the dismissal of a senior military officer? This question was not just theoretical; it had previously arisen when Defense Minister Rabin ordered CGS Levy to fire Deputy CGS Amir Drori, and the CGS refused to do so. The two sides ultimately reached a compromise, and the constitutional dilemma remained unsolved.

The rules of the game, which allowed a CGS to approach the prime minister directly without the defense minister serving as an intermediary, also enabled chiefs of general staff who so desired to increase their political power. In many cases, chiefs of general staff were deliberately appointed because they were closer to the incumbent prime minister than to the defense minister. Often, the appointment itself of the CGS was meant to increase the prime minister's influence on defense matters, even though, formally, the CGS was subordinate to the defense minister.

On one occasion, the lack of constitutional clarity on this issue resulted in a case being brought to the halls of the Supreme Court. In 1979, a suit was filed that sought to classify as illegal the military administration's decision to appropriate land in the Palestinian village Hawaja and to use it to build the settlement Elon Moreh. Although CGS Rafael Eitan maintained that the land had been seized for security reasons, Defense Minister Ezer Weizman, while endorsing the decision, argued that the settlement had been established for blatant political reasons. The court agreed with the defense minister's assessment that the seizure was political, and it therefore judged that an illegal act had been committed—according to international law, privately held land can only be seized for security reasons. It also did not hesitate to note in the verdict that Eitan had not told the truth to the court.[5]

Eitan was not at all unsettled by the fact that in court he had presented an account of the land seizure that contradicted the assessment given by the minister to whom he was subordinate. Later, he explained, "Weizman understood the meaning of relations between the defense minister and the CGS to entail the CGS's subordinating his opinion to that of the defense minister in cases where there are disagreements and the one is unable to convince the other. This approach was not acceptable to me. The minister of defense is not the CGS's commander. The government is the CGS's commander, and the minister of defense is the government's representative. If there are differences of opinion, the CGS can, and in certain cases must, express his diverging opinion."[6]

Similarly, Cabinet Minister Dani Naveh commented on the dynamics among prime minister, defense minister, and CGS in Netanyahu's government:

> In Israel, where the prime minister devotes most of his time to foreign and defense matters, control of the security establishment is very useful to the prime minister, to his ability both to directly steer the security forces and the IDF and to rely on their fieldwork. The absence of dependence on a defense minister spares the prime minister a lot of headaches.
>
> In the negotiations with the Palestinians and the Syrians, the IDF and the security forces have a central role. A prime minister, who directly controls them, can navigate more easily in negotiations. Netanyahu needed Mordecai each time he wanted either to come down hard on the Palestinian Authorities, or, alternatively, to allow Arafat's helicopter a rare landing. The tension-filled personal relations between Netanyahu and Mordecai, and the [two men's mutual] suspicion, made things all the more difficult.[7]

The political nature of the CGS's role has intensified as well because of a pattern that has become established: when a CGS desires to enter the Knesset and the government, it is perceived as only natural that he should do so, and it is understood his chances of becoming prime minister are very good. Of the sixteen chiefs of General Staff Israel has had since 1948, only three chose not to enter public life; clearly, the prevailing norm is for a CGS to choose a political career. Even officers who are not especially political find that having reached so central a position in Israeli politics—having participated in decisions regarding the nation's most essential matters and having rubbed shoulders with government ministers and heads of state—makes it difficult, at the end of their military service, to withdraw from the political arena and into private life.

Therefore, the question should not be, will a given CGS make professional or political decisions? Rather, it should be, what political ideology will he follow in making his decisions? Is he a hard-liner, or does he have a more pragmatic outlook? Does he have any partisan preferences? Do his political decisions serve his plans for a future political career? In Mofaz's case, he caught the political virus only after serving as CGS for a while. In his first year as CGS, Mofaz, as before, kept his distance from the political echelon. During his second year, he started learning the political game and fell for it head over heels. This, in any event, has been the popular reading at General Headquarters ever since Sharon nominated him as defense minister.

Dayan Opposes Withdrawal from Sinai in 1957

Accounts of the involvement of chiefs of staff in political decisions throughout Israel's history could fill many pages and would fall outside the scope of the present volume. However, to gain perspective on the activities of the IDF chiefs of staff in the years since 1990, it is worth examining the historical role they have played in decisions regarding diplomatic negotiations and peace talks.

The first time Israel conquered territory beyond the armistice lines, which had been determined at the end of the War of Independence in 1949, was when it took over the Sinai peninsula in 1956. However, under the pressure of a U.S.-Soviet ultimatum, Prime Minister Ben-Gurion decided to withdraw hastily and unilaterally from the entire area and to redeploy to the international border. CGS Moshe Dayan strongly opposed withdrawing and tried to convince Ben-Gurion not to do so. Dayan was not content after discussing the matter with his superiors; he also engaged in parliamentary lobbying. To that end, with Ben-Gurion's consent, he addressed, in civilian clothes, the Mapai (later Labor) Party parliamentary group on November 14 and spoke for a full hour.

However, this case should be viewed in the context of its time. Dayan, a very politicized officer, served in an era when the IDF was still a "revolutionary army."[8] In other words, the boundaries between the military organization and the political field were still blurred. As a high-ranking officer, he also was put on Mapai's list for elections to the first Knesset in 1949, along with three other high-ranking officers on active duty (the law was later changed to prohibit uniformed military personnel from being on party lists). While still CGS, Dayan even engaged in intraparty activity.

Dayan's vigorous opposition to withdrawal from Sinai was not surprising. In fact, as CGS, he and his political ally, then Defense Ministry director Gen. Shimon Peres, were the decisive forces that influenced, encouraged, and motivated Ben-Gurion to go to war with Egypt. They feared that the Arabs would begin a second round of warfare against Israel and that, even if this did not take place, Israel would be compelled to sign a peace agreement that would establish the 1949 borders as permanent. A war initiated by Israel, they estimated, would enhance Israel's geostrategic position in advance of a peace agreement.[9]

For this reason, during his term as CGS, Dayan pursued a policy that was meant to hasten the start of a war. He was tireless in trying to convince Ben-Gurion of the war's necessity and deliberately escalated the IDF's level of retaliation to Arab attacks. Together with Peres, Dayan forged Israel's military alliance with France and the United Kingdom, actively participated in political and military negotiations with those two colonial powers, and prepared the military for war. As Golani stated, "This war, especially its Israeli angle, cannot be understood without a grasp of the role of the IDF and of the man in charge of it in the preparations for war."[10]

Dayan was not the only CGS opposed to withdrawal from Sinai. Whereas in 1957 Dayan opposed a withdrawal that required no concessions from the Egyptians, Mordechai Gur, the CGS who took office twenty years after him, even more vigorously opposed withdrawal, even though in this instance there was a precious remuneration for the withdrawal—a peace treaty with Egypt. Israel had conquered Sinai, along with the West Bank and the Golan Heights, in June 1967. After the Yom Kippur War in 1973, CGS Gur participated in the armistice talks that were held between Israel, Egypt, and Syria and proactively coordinated by U.S. secretary of state Henry Kissinger, who shuttled back and forth between the Arab capitals and Jerusalem.

Gur Opposes Withdrawal from Sinai in 1977

Gur reached the top of the IDF pyramid after the Yom Kippur War, when his predecessor David Elazar had to resign in the wake of the publication of the Agranat Commission's findings. Like all of the IDF's upper echelon, Gur was infuriated that the commission had exonerated the politicians of all responsibility for the "mishap" and had laid all of the blame on the IDF alone. Gur, an officer with a political character and political ambitions, was aware of the government's having been weakened as a result of the war. Golda Meir and her defense minister, Moshe Dayan, were on the verge of political collapse, so Gur assumed a very proactive political posture.

At a certain stage, Gur persisted in negotiations with Syria, even after Dayan had cut off contact and had stopped participating actively in diplomatic meetings. "I heard rebukes and criticisms [from Dayan] of my excessive interference and my ludicrous suggestions, which 'were embarrassing to put forward and which were devoid of national honor,'" wrote Gur in his diary.[11] On another occasion, in May 1974, Gur was summoned to Meir's office before a meeting with Kissinger began; in her well-known critical tone, she warned Gur, "To my mind, there is no more [for us] to concede, and I ask that you act accordingly."

Despite this, during the meeting with Kissinger, Gur raised new ideas, some of which were adopted, though Dayan charged that it was "shameful" to present them. The aspiring heirs to Golda Meir's position, Rabin and Igal Alon, for their part, commended Gur as they left the room. Young officer Gur took the lesson from this episode to heart; it showed him "the extent to which political considerations influenced experienced politicians' behavior and their opinions, even when the issues at hand were of fateful national significance."[12]

The crisis in the political echelon in the first months after the Yom Kippur War did not subside, even after Golda Meir's government resigned and was replaced by a new government composed of the Labor Party's younger generation. The split between the party's two subelites, who were almost equal in power, was apparent once again when the new prime minister, Yitzhak Rabin, had to cede the position of defense minister to his sworn rival, Shimon Peres. The dispute between Rabin and Peres persisted even while the armistice talks with Egypt were being held, and Gur did not hesitate to fill the vacuum that had been created.

Gur's diary entries from that period reveal a CGS with great self-confidence who did not see himself as having lesser stature—other than formally—than the people at the head of the political echelon. At one point, he wrote in his diary, "The defense minister was short tempered, and he expressed opposition to the very fact of the General Staff's involvement, which is to say the CGS's involvement, in the discussions about the fate of the agreement. He thought that the IDF, and especially the CGS, was spilling over from military-strategic advice and into political-military advice, and he was correct. The question is whether these two areas can be separated, especially in light of Israel's situation after the Yom Kippur War."[13]

Gur did not conceal his own opinion: the matter at hand lent itself not to formalistic-bureaucratic division but, rather, to the judgment of those directly involved, both on the political side and on the CGS's side. "I did not think for a minute that a minister's personal political considerations should influence either the IDF's positions or the CGS's duty to present them to the whole government."[14]

Gur's understanding of his role led him, in his first months in office as CGS in 1974, to support conciliatory positions that facilitated the signing of the interim agreements with Syria and Egypt. Three years afterward, the same understanding led him to espouse an opposite position, which, had it prevailed, would have prevented the signing of the peace treaty between Israel and Egypt.

This happened after the Labor Party's political crisis led, in the end, to the demise of the Rabin-Peres government. In May 1977, the Begin government rose to power, with Weizman serving as defense minister and Dayan as foreign minister. In secret talks that Begin and Dayan held with Egyptian president Anwar Sadat and his advisers, a process was begun that would lead to peace. As part of the negotiation, Israel agreed, in principle, to withdraw from the whole of Sinai in exchange for a peace treaty. The talks had been kept completely secret, even from CGS Gur, who continued to believe, throughout that whole year, that Egypt had not departed from its intentions to attack Israel once again and that it was looking for an excuse to restart the war. Gur presented his position, which was supported by the MID's assessments, over and over to the prime minister and the defense minister, but they completely rejected it.

As the romance with Egypt intensified, so too did Gur's opposition. He termed Israel's willingness to withdraw from all of Sinai in exchange for a peace treaty "an outrage," and after he saw that he was unable to stop negotiations and that President Sadat was about to visit the Knesset, Gur turned directly to the public. On November 15, 1977, *Yedioth Ahronoth* published an interview with Gur in which he said, "It should be clear to

President Sadat that if he is planning additional deception of the type he engaged in during the Yom Kippur War, his intentions are clear to us: we know that the Egyptian military is in the midst of preparations to commence war against Israel, toward the year 1978, notwithstanding Sadat's declaring his willingness to come to Jerusalem."[15]

While Gur presented a professional face, remaining nonpolitical, Defense Minister Weizman was livid. "Why did you do this?!" he asked his subordinate. Gur replied, "Because I believe that we are willfully getting into an exceedingly bad situation, which, from a national morale perspective, I could not allow. All the internal discussions we had were of no use, and I had no choice but to explode the matter publicly."[16] In turn, Weizman informed Gur that his term as CGS would end in January. "Suit yourself," replied Gur, "I'm willing to resign right away if that's what you want. I could either resign, or you could fire me, but I will not accept punishment. I'm not some low-ranking commander; I don't get punished." Weizman was required to attain authorization from the prime minister to fire the impertinent CGS, a dramatic step that had never before been taken in Israel. But Begin, who so esteemed IDF officers, would not authorize the firing, even though he shared Weizman's criticism of Gur, and so Gur remained in office.

After a few weeks, DMI Shlomo Gazit admitted his mistaken perspective about Egypt. "We developed a conception of war plans for Egypt, and did not see the prevalence of the trend and the desire for peace [which had formed] since the Yom Kippur War," Gazit later wrote. "It's possible that due to the trauma we had endured during the Yom Kippur War, it was difficult for us to believe that the Egyptians, led by Sadat, who had regained honor and prestige, would now be able to allow themselves to choose the path of peace."[17] But Gur continued to be far removed from this position regarding Sadat's intentions. "The CGS serves in a position which combines military and political considerations, and this occasionally forces him to deal with sensitive matters on the boundaries of both spheres."[18]

For this reason Gur tried to obstruct even the talks themselves. He opposed Begin's position of being receptive to the Egyptian demand that a comprehensive agreement be reached. At a cabinet meeting held on December 13, Gur expressed opposition to the proposals that had been approved by the prime minister that called for autonomy for the Palestinians in the occupied territories. He further suggested that Weizman was acting "out of a misunderstanding of the matters at hand, and out of an illusory analysis of the situation" and warned that these proposals would lead to the establishment of a Palestinian state, "which ought to be opposed to the utmost."

Gur interpreted the openness and eagerness that characterized the politicians in their dealings with the Egyptians as "drunkenness and political illusions, which had usurped the place of judgment and realistic political vision."[19] Opposing a comprehensive withdrawal from Sinai, he demanded that the IDF deploy on the line spanning across Jabel Hillel-Jabel Charim at a distance of fifty to seventy kilometers from the internationally determined border. In the end, the peace treaty with Egypt was signed, Gur retired, and, as had been anticipated, pursued a political career, this time without a uniform.

Following his shaky relationship with Gur, Weizman decided to appoint a CGS who was a professional officer with no interest in politics, and so he chose the head of the Northern Command, Rafael Eitan. But this reticent man soon changed his colors, in the same way that Mofaz would twenty years later, and became a hyperpolitical figure. Unlike his predecessor Gur, Eitan did not keep his political views to himself, freely sharing them with the public. In a book he published after retiring from service, Eitan describes the friction between himself and Weizman—who had been a super hawk during his military career but since 1977 had become the staunchest supporter of peace:

> Ezer never understood the Arabs' mentality. His basic approach was that concessions to the Arabs would soften their basic stance, would lead to a thawing of their hatred, and would encourage them to compromise with Israel and to abandon their dream of eliminating it. . . . He sought compromises in Judea and Samaria and believed that a soft-handed approach toward the Palestinians there would cause their hostility to dissipate, would pave the road to dialogue. . . .
>
> Ezer was detached from the Arab reality and erred in his illusions about concessions and reconciliation. My view is the opposite [of his]: concessions made to the Arabs are interpreted by them as signs of weakness and of weariness from the struggle. Such concessions teach them that their continued intransigence pays off, that they will gain the upper hand in the end. [Concessions lead the Arabs] to harden their position, and turn them into even more vigorous adversaries.[20]

The IDF's Support of Greater Israel

Dayan's opposition to withdrawal from Sinai in 1957 and Gur's opposition to the peace treaty with Egypt twenty years later are examples that are liable to create the impression that chiefs of staff have always opposed both peace agreements and the withdrawal of forces from occupied territories. However, there have been several cases in which military officers held the moderate view and advocated compromise, while civilians held hard-line positions. This has been true both before war and, in the case of troop withdrawal, after war. An example of the first case is CGS Dan Shomron's opposition to Israel's participating in the Gulf War in 1991. An example of the second case is CGS Moshe Levi's recommendation in 1984 that the IDF withdraw from Lebanon.

In the first case, Defense Minister Moshe Arens recommended that the IDF take direct action against Scud launchers in western Iraq to put an end to missile attacks on Israel. Prime Minister Shamir disagreed with Arens and decided to accept the U.S. request for restraint. He did not want to jeopardize the coalition forces' operations and had confidence in the U.S. Air Force's ability to find and destroy the launchers. As the missile attacks on Israel continued, however, the pressure from Arens for action intensified. Opposing Arens, and helping Shamir, was CGS Dan Shomron. His position, which was supported by a number of officers, including the DMI, strengthened Shamir's rejection of the defense minister's ongoing demand.

Unswayed, Arens wanted to examine further the possibility of military action and asked that the air force fly a plane over Jordan to see what the Jordanian reaction would be if Israel decided to send planes to Iraq. Shomron displayed a lack of enthusiasm to this request. "This is liable to lead to an unnecessary conflagration," he said. In an understatement, Arens summed up his defeat by Shomron in this duel: "I was frustrated with the slow pace with which the military responded to my demand for a flight over Jordan."[21]

In the second case, involving CGS Levi, the IDF actually supported a withdrawal of forces from conquered territory, whereas the political echelon opposed withdrawal. In this case, too, it was Arens who took a hard-line, whereas Levi took the more moderate line. In early 1984, the CGS understood that Israel's ongoing presence in Lebanon would lead to

military casualties without yielding any military advantages. He recommended a withdrawal from most of Lebanon (in the 1982 war, the IDF
reached Lebanon's capital, Beirut) and redeployment in the southern zone
of the country. However, the Shamir-Arens government opposed this. In
the end, redeployment did take place, but only after the Labor Party joined
the national unity government in 1985 and after vigorous lobbying by the
IDF, which used the media effectively in voicing its position.

These cases—and many others could be cited—demonstrate the
active political role the military maintains in decision making at the highest political-strategic level in Israel. Even more significant is that these
examples refute the claim that IDF positions on such topics as the occupied
territories and relations with the Palestinians and Arab states are purely
professional ones. What seems to be, or are claimed to be, objective professional considerations are, in many cases, subjective assessments, prod-
ucts of psychological and cultural factors.

This brings us back to Gur. Unlike other CGSs, such as Eitan,
whose ideological positions were well-known, Gur portrayed the image of
the professional officer. Nevertheless, while pretending to be nonpolitical,
Gur at times operated out of political, even ideological, considerations.
After leaving service, he revealed in his memoirs how deep his convictions
were. His attitude toward the peace process with Egypt did not simply
result from his desire to secure a wide defense perimeter for Israel; first
and foremost, it was a product of his perception of the Arab world and its
intentions, his conception of Israel's national priorities, and his interpretation of the Zionist vision.

Gur saw the occupied territories not only through the narrow lens
of security but also through the broad lens of politics and ideology. This
was made explicit in one of the documents he submitted to the defense
minister at the end of 1977. Weizman had asked Gur to draw up a map
that outlined what Israel's borders would be when comprehensive peace
was achieved with the Arab states, and Gur vigorously opposed doing so.
"In my judgment," Gur wrote at the time, "presenting a map with the final
borders will lead to a precipitous war between ourselves and the Arab
countries. . . . such a war would erupt in the midst of particularly disad-
vantageous conditions for Israel; it would be a hard war, and it would neither enhance our geopolitical position nor advance us toward attaining
our national objectives. I recommend that such a map not be drawn up."

Gur suggested, instead, that a decision regarding peace borders be postponed until a future point. "There is no chance of reaching an agreement with the Arab states on the basis of the current peace map. If we yield and accept narrower borders we are endangering the state. A return to 1967 borders appears to me to be impossible from our perspective, because it would imply willful military suicide." But, later in the document, it becomes clear that Gur opposed a withdrawal to 1967 borders not only for military reasons but also because of broader national, political, and ideological objectives, what he described as "the fulfillment of Zionist goals": "The purpose of the State of Israel and of World Zionism was and will be to gather the majority of the Jewish People in Israel. . . . [To that end] we must continue building an infrastructure of settlement, industry, government, and military in all the territories that we consider essential to implementing Zionism. As we build the infrastructure, the final borders will be better established and more accepted by all sides in the conflict, whether by agreement, or out of necessity."

In Gur's opinion, as matters stood at the end of the 1970s, the status quo was preferable to peace, not only for military reasons but for societal reasons as well. "The process of building Judea and Samaria is more important than signing a peace treaty," he wrote.[22] At a meeting in the defense minister's office, Gur argued,

> All of these steps are a function of a worldview—as long as war continues and there is tension, there exists a melting pot in Israeli society. Once war stops, so too will the melting. . . . In my opinion, the melting pot will end prematurely if there is peace now. We could have built much more and reached a final setting of borders and a definitive relationship dynamic between ourselves and the Arabs. . . . For me, immigration [by Jews to Israel] is a key question. . . . I attach great importance to the question, how can a war be utilized for national purposes, and it would be very good if we had wider breathing space.[23]

This worldview also casts a different light on Gur's behavior in the "Sebastia Affair" of 1975, when members of the Gush Emunim settlers group founded—for the first time and in an illegal manner—a settlement in Samaria. Prime Minister Rabin, who saw this as a challenge to his government, demanded that Gur disperse the settlers. But Gur objected on the grounds that doing so either would require the use of force and likely lead to bloodshed, or would result in soldiers refusing to follow their orders. Rabin yielded, the settlers won, and the incident is now con-sidered a watershed moment, establishing an important precedent for future Jewish settlements in the occupied territories. It exposed the gov-ernment's weakness and made clear to the settlers that through the use of force they would be able to impose their will on the government. This is, in fact, what they have done ever since.

What would have happened had Gur behaved differently? Did he really fear that using IDF soldiers would lead to genuine violence, or was this just an excuse to avoid a confrontation with the settlers, whom he saw as pioneers and as an example for the whole nation? What would have happened had Gur not been such a true believer in the "process of building Judea and Samaria"? Whatever his motivations were at the time, Rabin candidly admitted to me that he never forgave himself for having yielded to Gur on that day.

11

Is It a Just War?

A Mobilized Supreme Court

Democratic theory criticizes the military's overinvolvement in political affairs. Yet, while such intervention might be negative, as discussed earlier in this volume, intensive relations between the military and civilian society at large can also have positive implications. This is particularly so when commanders take into account civilians' dispositions and views and react to constraints stemming from the civil sector. But the analysis of the relations between generals and statesmen in Israel will not be complete without also looking closely at certain developments that resulted from the intifada and affected all Israelis.

The military's ability to win in an LIC is decisively influenced by civilian society, through both its identification with the war's goals and the legitimacy it grants the military, and its readiness to bear the burden of a lengthy struggle. This is particularly true in a nation in arms.[1] For this reason, intensive negotiations were conducted during the intifada between the military and many civilian institutions. The exchanges between the military and the Supreme Court were especially noteworthy and occurred with an intensity and frequency unparalleled in any of Israel's previous wars. On several occasions, the court was asked to deliberate on matters related to the war, whether concerning the legitimacy of certain uses of arms and operational methods, the conduct of soldiers in the territories, or the nature of the orders they received from their commanders.

The Supreme Court was forced to address the matters in question following injunctions put forward by civilian groups, Knesset members, human rights organizations, political groups, Palestinians injured by the IDF, and ordinary citizens. As a whole, the intifada influenced the court's position on the issue of balancing security needs and civil rights, and caused the court to retreat from the line it had followed the previous decade, one in which the court did not involve itself in questions related to the defense establishment.

Only in the mid-1990s did the Supreme Court actively begin to address military issues. In 1975, when it was first asked to deliberate on such matters, its then president, Meir Shamgar—a reserve brigadier general and former military advocate general—ruled that "issues related to the military's organization, structure, deployment, equipment and operations are not judgeable, as they do not fit the judicial system." The Supreme Court accepted this decision until 1996. In that year, the Supreme Court, headed by its president, Aharon Barak, ruled that "the CGS's judgment is not definitive" and that the Supreme Court is allowed to question the CGS's judgment by applying the test of reasonability. Moreover, it ruled that the court is entitled to nullify a decision by the CGS when it does not meet the latter test.[2] This transformation reflected the judicial activism policy advocated by Aharon Barak, and, furthermore, signaled the weakening of the military's autonomy and the growing incursion of civilian institutions into the military sphere.

In wartime, especially in the case of fourth-generation warfare, just as society tends to rally around the flag, so too does the judicial system tend to fall in line with the dictates of the political leadership. When the intifada started, then, the Supreme Court returned to its previous approach of relying on the positions presented by the professionals and the officials in charge of security. In only a few cases did it object to decisions of the defense establishment. One such objection occurred in the case of the security barrier, "the wall," erected in Palestinian territories in July 2004. In most cases, however, the judiciary reiterated the positions of the IDF and the security apparatus.

For that reason, the court allowed the destruction of houses belonging to the families of terrorists and granted legal sanction for "targeted assassinations" and other steps taken by the military that were challenged by civil rights organizations. This approach of the court was characterized, in rather poetic language, by Judge Mishael Heshin: "an act of war is responded to by an act, which is itself in essence an act of war, and in the way of war. I, as a judge, did not train my hands to do war and I do not know the ways of warriors."[3]

The dialogue between the military and the judicial system was just one element of the intensive exchange between the military and Israeli society in general, and the stance of the court reflected the prevailing atmosphere within Israel since the outbreak of violence. The confrontation with the Palestinians led to the intensification of patriotism in Israel, deepened the commitment to Zionism—the constitutive ethos of Israeli society—within the country, and led to a public circling of the wagons. [4] But, as the war dragged on, two issues arose that at first appeared to be marginal in nature but later emerged as broad social problems. A controversy developed regarding two dimensions of the war: both its *jus in bello*, the conduct of the fighting forces and their commanders, and its *jus ad bellum*, the legitimacy of the war itself. Specifically, there were four principal areas of concern: (1) the level of adherence to professional and military ethics; (2) the arms and means of warfare the military was permitted to use; (3) the methods, principles, and operational tactics of the military; and (4) the military's disposition toward the noncombatant civilian Palestinian population.

The IDF and Jus in Bello

The first type of criticism that some civilians have leveled against the military in the intifada has been voiced in past wars—namely, that members of the military are guilty of property destruction, looting, and vandalism. The difference in this war, however, is that such acts have been more widespread. In some cases the IDF has condemned the improper actions—in one case it even dismantled an entire military unit—but generally it has claimed that these phenomena are exceptional and contrary to the IDF's ethos.

The second type of criticism has been more complex and novel, and concerns the military's means of warfare. Throughout the war there have been claims that the military has been using weapons that are forbidden by international law and ethically illegitimate. One of the cases brought to the Supreme Court concerned the use of Fletch shells, which shoot a barrage of metal bullets that strike a large area around the target that is hit. The court allowed the use of Fletch shells, but its decision did not satisfy the critics. They claimed that the use of such a shell might well be justified on the conventional battlefield but not in the present conflict: if a shell does not hit its original target on the battlefield, it will only hit another enemy target; but if a shell is aimed at a terrorist in a populated area, many innocent civilians may be hurt or killed.[5]

Other complaints have been raised against the military's principles and methods of warfare. Many of these stemmed from the directives regarding when Israeli forces can open fire. Until the outbreak of the intifada, the authority of IDF soldiers to use live ammunition in the territories was regulated according to guidelines set forth in Israel's penal laws. Opening fire was allowed in two cases: when there was an immediate and genuine threat to life, and only when there was no other way of averting the threat; and in the course of arresting someone suspected of committing a serious crime. In this latter case, it was permissible to shoot at the legs, though only after giving a warning, shooting in the air, and confirming there was no danger that others might get hurt.

In the beginning, the IDF defined the intifada as "an armed conflict short of war," and thus it activated orders for opening fire that were tailored to limited confrontation. The new directives widened the circumstances in which it was permissible to open fire and gave the commanders in the conflict areas greater flexibility and leeway than in the past. Thereafter, soldiers were permitted to shoot suspects without warning, to use live rounds on stone throwers (in the past, only rubber bullets had been permitted), to shoot armed people even if they were not using their weapons, and to shoot those violating a curfew or trying to cross the security fence in the territories.[6]

Human rights organizations and reserve soldiers, as well as the media and politicians, challenged the IDF about some of its operational methods. Among these methods is the "human shield" tactic, whereby IDF soldiers stand Palestinian civilians between themselves and Palestinian fighters to decrease the risk to the soldiers. The "pressure-cooker" method—whereby instead of sending soldiers to break into a flat in which a suspect is hiding, the whole building is brought down by cannon shells or a bulldozer—was challenged as well. So was the "neighbor procedure," whereby soldiers force a Palestinian to enter a flat or building from which they have been fired upon to locate suspects, to clear suspected objects, or to find out if the flat has been booby-trapped.

Following an appeal by human rights organizations, the military initially committed itself to stopping the use of civilians as human shields against shooting and attacks, but ultimately it did not put an end to these practices. Even military commentators generally well respected by the IDF were driven to express disgust with the method:

> [It] denigrates the IDF. The IDF is a strong and experienced military, equipped with sophisticated arms, and it does not need methods which harm its reputation and the reputation of Israel. From a document issued by the military's legal division, it is clear that the use of a civilian as a living shield is a serious violation of the rules of engagement. This action is in fact a contravention of the moral code of the IDF, which was the result of a lot of work by the IDF's chief education officer in conjunction with academics and other civilians. The duty to uphold the moral code of the IDF does not depend on the moral conduct of Palestinian terrorists.[7]

Some of the IDF's operational methods became topics of discussion at cabinet meetings. Among them was the practice of "targeted preventions"—what the international media referred to as "targeted killings," "liquidations," or "extra-judicial assassinations"—actions meant to destroy specific targets, particularly armed Palestinians. The IDF introduced this method a few months after the start of the intifada in response to criticism in the international media about its wide-ranging operations in the territories. These new "surgical actions," which employed special units or were carried out by launching missiles from helicopters, were meant to minimize full-blown IDF incursions into the territories.

However, international criticism of Israel did not diminish as a result of the new method; rather, it increased, even within Israel itself, when the IDF started adding Palestinian political leaders, not only combatants, to its "bank of targets." Critics argued that the method only led the Palestinians to escalate their violent activity; this criticism intensified as a growing number of innocent civilians who happened to be physically close to targets were killed or injured.

In January 2001, human rights organizations—such as the Association for Civil Rights and the Committee for the Rule of Law and Human Rights of the Israeli Bar Association—demanded that the prime minister and the government's legal adviser immediately stop this strategy, "which consists of a liquidation policy that is in fact an illegal order."[8] Subsequently, three appeals concerning this issue were presented to the Supreme Court. The appeals came not from small, marginal organizations but from well-established groups. The court rejected the appeals, declaring that it would not interfere in the selection of fighting methods used by the security forces in its battle against terror. Furthermore, the court maintained that "the State of Israel no longer relates to the intifada as a popular uprising but rather as an armed confrontation."[9] Thus, the judicial system once again sided with the majority of the Israeli public and supported the IDF's position. Most Israelis saw the Palestinian political leadership as responsible for dispatching the terrorists, and therefore they believed the leadership's liquidation was well-justified—on both moral and tactical levels.

IDF's Spokesperson Loses Trust

The most common criticism within the *jus in bello* category was related to the IDF's abuse of the civilian Palestinian population. The curfew, siege, and closure imposed on the territories isolated Palestinian towns and villages from one another, made movement within the territories difficult, and paralyzed the economy. The result was an unemployment rate that tripled, reaching 40 percent in 2003 and leading to 60 percent of the Palestinian population living in poverty, with an income of $2.10 per capita per day. The hundreds of roadblocks that were placed in the West Bank and the tough policy imposed there turned into a focal point of daily friction for thousands of people. Cases of abuse and of injured civilians became a daily routine and suffering became the lot of thousands. Accounts of ambulances being prevented from crossing checkpoints— leading to the deaths of the sick or of pregnant women—ceased to be rare. The shooting of civilians who violated curfews—causing the deaths of both young and old—mass detentions, and the abuse of detainees all became routine as well.[10]

In contrast to what viewers saw on television in Arab states and even in the West, there was relatively little coverage of such scenes in the Israeli media. But the information was not completely hidden from Israelis, and it sometimes led to shocked reactions when it contained especially unsettling accounts of abuse, such as the case of the border patrol unit in Hebron that, for laughs, threw a Palestinian youth out of a speeding jeep, cracking his skull. Events that contained symbolic meanings were particularly shocking to the public, such as the incident in which soldiers inscribed numbers on detainees' arms, or forced a Palestinian youth to play the violin for their amusement.

These episodes were followed not only by a massive wave of verbal criticism but also by direct action from civilian groups. The public's language became harsher, and, for the first time in Israel's history, Israelis who were not from the fringe started accusing IDF soldiers of committing war crimes. Civilian groups, meanwhile, made appeals to the military, the courts, and the media, and, in some instances, introduced innovative means of checking the military's activities. For instance, in what was termed the "roadblock watch," civilian Israelis began to stand guard at IDF barriers in the territories, observing the actions of soldiers there and sometimes even helping Palestinians.

Another issue that certain civilian groups criticized was the lack of accountability for Palestinian deaths. Indeed, military prosecutors had less work in the second intifada than in the first intifada. A few months after hostilities began in 2000, the IDF explained the reasons for this: in the previous intifada, which lasted almost five years, a military police investigation was opened for each death case. As that intifada mainly involved public disorder, the military combated it with policing tools: the political situation was pre-autonomy; Israel controlled the whole area; and the judiciary addressing all death cases was the Israeli criminal law court. The second uprising, however, was defined as an armed confrontation. It was a war against terrorist groups. The enemy, therefore, was often unidentified. The relevant law for such a situation is international law, which details the regulations governing war. The end result was that, just as in full-scale wars, there were no investigations of each instance of an enemy death.[11]

Two years after the intifada began, the chief military prosecutor, Maj. Gen. Menachem Finkelstein, appeared before the Knesset's constitutional committee at a special hearing concerned with "preserving human rights in the context of a war on terror." In an effort to present the military's achievements in the judicial sphere, the general reported 360 investigations by the military police, mostly of conduct unbefitting soldiers at checkpoints. Most of the committee, like most of the Israeli public, saw the investigations as evidence of the IDF's status as the "most ethical military in the world." But one can interpret the data differently. As MK Zahava Gallon of the Meretz Party asked, "why, when there have been 2,000 cases of deaths of Palestinians, only 6 inducements for shooting were presented?" She concluded that "this is a sign of disregard for human life and it should be interpreted with all due alarm."[12]

The Israeli media has stood at the military and government's side in the war against the intifada, just as it has done in past national security crises, and it has accepted the narrative that the military and government presented about the war, interpreting the conflict with information supplied to them by IDF spokespersons. Reporters accepted the IDF's version of events and rejected—and in most cases ignored—Palestinian explanations or external viewpoints. International criticism was viewed as biased, stemming from prejudice against Israel or from anti-Semitism. Apart from *Ha'aretz* and a handful of journalists, the Israeli media solidly supported the Israeli government's position in the war.[13]

Yet, as months passed and the insurrection continued, there were an increased number of stories and reports that supported the criticisms leveled against IDF operations in the territories. The recurrent denial of such reports by the military spokespersons brought about a decline in the trust granted to them, not only by international journalists but also by Israeli journalists, the same ones who had earlier been criticized for not fulfilling their professional role and for allowing themselves to become mouthpieces of the military.[14] A particularly serious credibility crisis occurred in November 2003, when the media discovered that the IDF had given false information to military correspondents regarding the kind of ammunition used in a targeted assassination mission in the Gaza Strip.

The Debate over "Purity of Arms"

The LIC also reopened a debate over "purity of arms," an issue that over the years had gained full consensus and related to the illegitimacy of harming civilians during warfare. Since its establishment, the IDF used an intensive system of indoctrination, intended to teach its soldiers about purity of arms as a supreme value, an expression of a military that keeps high moral values. This indoctrination included stories about past military events involving the self-sacrifice of soldiers and officers hurt while defending Arab civilians.

Yet the intifada brought about a new situation in which harming innocent civilians during warfare became inevitable. This situation was compounded by the Palestinians' frequent use of civilians as human shields, their positioning of armed men among civilians, their use of ambulances to transfer armed personnel and weapons, and their firing from civilians' homes. For example, in the weeks before his killing by the IDF, Hamas leader Sheikh Ahmed Yassin, already aware of a death threat against him, made public appearances surrounded by an entourage of children. He was not the only one to use this technique.

The purity-of-arms issue became more acute in June 2001; this was when the policy of targeted killings was put into practice. The official IDF policy was to hit only those individuals characterized as "ticking bombs," meaning the targeted killings were not to be done as punishment or revenge but as a preventive measure against those who intended to act violently and harm Israelis. But what should be done when such an operation would have to be carried out among civilians, many of whom would inevitably be injured or killed if the action were taken? This question remained in the forefront of many minds, especially given such situations were quite common. Indeed, on June 25, 2003, the head of the air force told journalists that in more than a quarter of the "preventive" air strikes against terrorists, innocent civilians had also been killed or injured. Further, in more than 50 percent of the attempted targeted killings in densely populated areas, civilian bystanders were killed or injured.

The LIC caused the IDF to reestablish the criteria regarding the legitimacy of harming innocent civilians. Deputy CGS Ya'alon addressed this matter with great frankness after the killing of Palestinian leader Salah Shahada in July 2002 by a one-ton bomb that also caused the deaths of fifteen civilians, among them eleven children. Admitting that "lately we have made things easier for ourselves," he stated that "there was a discussion regarding whether we ought to hit [Shahada] when his daughters were with him, but we decided that no, we would not harm his daughters. We decided, though, that we would hit him even if his wife was with him."[15] The issue regarding innocent civilians became more acute when the IDF authorized the elimination not only of a "ticking bomb"—for example, someone on his way to an actual suicide or terror attack—but also of a "ticking infrastructure," referring to anyone who was known to collaborate in the violent struggle against Israel.

The IDF, and particularly the air force, made earnest endeavors to ensure the accuracy of their strikes and avoid injuring civilians. After all, even if the LIC had created new problems from the early days of the intifada, when armed fighters hid behind the masses of civilians demonstrating in the street and shot at IDF soldiers, the concept of purity of arms still influenced the IDF ethos. As a result of this impossible situation, criticism was hurled at the military command, not only by those who were concerned about the IDF's growing insensitivity to civilian life, but also by those who believed that it was not justified to risk the lives of IDF soldiers for the sake of maintaining purity of arms.

A classic example of this dilemma came in the summer of 2004 when a soldier, Moran Vardi, was killed while storming a house in Nablus in which a wanted man—an armed Palestinian—was hiding. The report that was presented to his family after his death revealed that the senior commanders had chosen not to fire a missile at the house and, instead, ordered the soldiers to break in, fearing that the missile would injure the civilians who were in the building. In a meeting with the bereaved parents, Maj. Gen. Israel Ziv, the head of the Operations Directorate, who was responsible for the procedures for opening fire, told them that firing a missile was not authorized because "the citizens of the adversary are no less important than IDF soldiers." A conservative commentator responded angrily to this, saying there was not even an apology or admission of error, or even the excuse of international pressure, but simply "an ideological argument of a sick morality."[16]

Attempts to keep innocent civilians away from harm were made more difficult by the military's growing use of helicopters in the densely populated Gaza Strip. These attacks led to the injury and death of many civilians to the great distress of some reserve air force pilots. After the killing of Shahada, Brig. Gen. Avi Dagan, commander of the reserve squadron, asked his colleagues to reconsider any command they received before executing it, in an effort to prevent actions taking place based on an illegal command. Others were spreading warnings that IDF officers might find themselves subpoenaed by the International Tribunal for War Crimes in the Hague.

In the face of such severe criticism, the IDF thought it crucial to defend its policy and its staff. An unsuccessful attempt was made by the air force commander, Maj. Gen. Dan Halutz, who tried to support his pilots by vigorously arguing, "There is no clean war. I don't know anyone who can handle a clean war. . . . Those who want to murder children in Israel should take into account that their own children might get killed. . . . The leftists who claim that the pilots are committing war crimes should be the ones to be judged." Asked how a pilot feels when he drops a bomb in a targeted assassination, he responded, "What do I feel when I drop a bomb? I feel a light bump in the plane, as a result of the release. A second later it passes, and that is all. That is what I feel."[17] His blunt words caused a surge of protest, and subsequently he apologized for the statement.[18]

When Halutz was later nominated for the post of deputy CGS, the human rights organizations Yesh Gvul and the Committee Against Torture filed a suit with the High Court of Justice to protest his appointment. "I have an uncomfortable feeling, to say the least, about Halutz's words," said Justice Edmond Levy, who headed the panel of judges, and asked Halutz to describe his code of morals. "I see myself not just as a moral and ethical person, but as someone who is imbued with the values of the IDF," replied Halutz in his statement to the court. "Sensitivity with regard to hurting innocent people is part of me." The court rejected the suit, although it declared that a person who sets an example to so many others should choose his words carefully before expressing himself so bluntly on the pages of the newspaper. The incident resurfaced early in 2005, when Halutz was proposed as a candidate to succeed Ya'alon as the IDF's eighteenth CGS, but this did not prevent his eventual appointment.[19]

In September 2003, the IDF presented a formal, codified position on its military values in a document titled "Moral Warfare," authored by the commander of the National Security College, Maj. Gen. Amos Yadlin, and by Prof. Asa Kasher, a philosopher specializing in ethics and morals who had earlier authored the IDF's *Ethical Code*. They wrote, "Our warfare values raise many hard dilemmas, which require complex solutions. The most outstanding example is that of the targeted prevention missions taking place where terrorists are found amongst civilians. We have a moral obligation to protect the citizens of Israel from those terrorists, as they present an immediate danger, but we are also obligated not to harm the innocent Palestinian civilians, as they are not in any way dangerous."[20]

Yadlin and Kasher defined the targeted prevention as "an act of defense against future danger, and not as retaliation for a past terror attack." It is morally legitimate to execute such an act against "ticking bombs," they wrote, that is, "people who are in the midst of an active process, which holds immediate danger to Israeli citizens, and [in which] there is no way to counteract their intentions other than by harming them."[21] They further argue that "a person is considered a 'ticking bomb' not only when he wears an explosive belt and is on his way to an Israeli site in order to activate his murderous attack, but also in the earlier stages of the active process—when he provides the logistics, arranges for the necessary equipment and means of transport, plans the procedure of the attack, etc."[22]

But to what extent, according to Yadlin and Kasher, is it permissible to harm civilians? They write, "The leading principle is that of military necessity. One should not risk harming those who are not involved in terror, and in case of military necessity to perform a mission that might endanger the human surroundings around a terrorists' core, it is our obligation to find the best way to decrease this danger." The principle of military need, they continue, asserts that "we are forced to come to terms with the damage inflicted on the human environment around the military actions' target . . . as much as there is full justification to the execution of this military action; otherwise we will not be able to provide the protection needed to the citizens of Israel, its soldiers included."[23]

Those in favor of the new policy claimed that the inevitable injuring and killing of civilians does not contradict the Fourth Geneva Convention, which established that in cases where fighters hide among the civilian population, the area where they are staying is not immune to attacks from the other side, and if civilians are killed, it is not the attacker that should be blamed for their deaths but those who hid among them.[24] Therefore, argued the supporters of the new policy, there was no need for a fundamental change in the moral behavior of the IDF; everything that it had done since the outbreak of the intifada, given the new conditions of counterterror warfare, followed the principle of military need.

But this position, although accepted by the military and the public, was also subject to opposing opinions. One such view held that defining the war against the Palestinians as "counterterror warfare" distorts reality, as many Palestinians are not involved in terrorism but in a legitimate resistance to the Israeli occupation. To the contrary, some argued, it is the Israelis who are breaking international law by establishing settlements in the territories. This criticism held that "the IDF soldiers know very well that 90 percent of the military action in the territories has nothing to do, even

indirectly, with preventing terror. The ethical code for the war against terror is actually the ethical code for the protection of the settlers."[25]

Israeli officers are generally sensitive to the military's public image
and are attentive to public debate on matters related to it. They became
ever more so throughout the intifada, when the IDF especially needed
the public's support. Indeed, since 2000, the military has been confronted
with perhaps the most severe legitimacy crisis it has ever experienced.
This crisis derived not only from the civilian population but also from
within the military itself.

12

Conscientious Objection

The Selective Conscientious Objectors

The criticism of the government's policy and of the IDF's conduct in the confrontation with the Palestinians led to a change in the nature of conscientious objection in Israel. Until the end of the 1970s, conscientious objection had been a marginal phenomenon, with objectors coming from small pacifist and leftist groups. But the 1967 rupture in the national consensus on security, the territories, and peace, followed by the political stalemate of the 1970s, ultimately established conscientious objection as a significant social phenomenon. The symbolic beginning of this dates to March 1978, when 348 reserve officers wrote a letter to Prime Minister Begin stating that "Israel's security depends on achieving peace tied to territorial concessions. Without the sense of a just path, motivation to enlist in the military will decrease among the nation's youth." The Peace Now movement was later launched by some of the signatories of that letter.

A little over a year later, on July 25, 1979, the first explicit, collective conscientious objection was declared in what is known as the "letter of the twelfth graders." In that letter, twenty-seven high school students announced to the defense minister that when the time came for their military drafting, they would refuse to serve in the occupied territories. They wrote that "service beyond the green line contradicts our political beliefs and our consciences. We will not accept the occupation, which turns us into oppressors and the Palestinians into oppressed."[1]

The twelfth graders' letter referred to the occupation in general. But during the Lebanon War in the summer of 1981, objection became concrete, focused, and selective. In the course of that conflict, a few hundred officers and soldiers formed the Yesh Gvul (meaning both "there is a limit" and "there is a border") movement to express their objection to serving in the war; 170 of them were prosecuted and sentenced to prison terms. This protest wave ebbed with the end of the war but resumed in 1987, with the eruption of the first intifada, during which 180 conscientious objectors were imprisoned. Between those two waves, dozens of conscientious objectors were tried in the courts. By the time the second intifada began, about 400 objectors had served sentences in military prisons.

The wave of objections during Israel's eighth war, however, was different from previous waves both quantitatively and qualitatively, that is, for what it expressed. Even though the number of objectors remained small relative to the overall force size, their protest expressed the growing problems between the IDF and civilian society. The wave began to build in January 2002, when fifty-one officers and reserve soldiers announced that they would refuse both to serve in the territories and to participate in the war against the Palestinians. The destruction of Palestinian houses in Rafiah and a targeted liquidation of a Palestinian leader, Raad Karmi—which interrupted a relative calm in the territories—provided the impetus for their protest, as explained in a letter they addressed to the minister of defense:

> We, reserve combat officers and soldiers of the Israel Defense Forces, who were raised upon the principles of Zionism, self-sacrifice and giving to the people of Israel and to the State of Israel . . . We hereby declare that we shall not continue to fight this War of the Settlements. We shall not continue to fight beyond the 1967 borders in order to dominate, expel, starve and humiliate an entire people. We hereby declare that we shall continue serving the Israel Defense Force in any mission that serves Israel's defense. The missions of occupation and oppression do not serve this purpose—and we shall take no part in them.[2]

The officers' letter received wide media coverage, and the number of those who signed their statement grew rapidly. In just two months, it reached 571. Some of the signers were prosecuted in military courts, and as of June 2005 about 250 had been tried and imprisoned. This was more than the number of soldiers tried during the Lebanon War and more than the number of objectors during the entire thirty years of occupation.

Still, the relatively small number enabled the IDF to claim that the refusal to serve was an insignificant issue. But even those who made that claim knew quite well that the objectors who were tried and imprisoned were just the tip of the iceberg. Underneath the surface, there was a huge mass of gray objection, of discontent in the civilian sector, especially in that segment from which the reserve forces were drawn.

The basic principle regarding the treatment of conscientious objectors, which had guided the IDF over the years—especially since the 1980s— was to minimize as much as possible the prominence of the problem, so as not to grant objectors a public forum for an ideological showdown. The IDF left the response to selective objection, which was mainly engaged in by reservists, to the discretion of the unit commanders, who tried to convince their soldiers to withdraw their stated objections or, when that failed, changed the nature of the objectors' service or exempted them altogether. This approach was taken as long as the objectors in question did not make their actions publicly known. It was possible because the IDF did not need so many recruits, and each time a reserve unit was called, many more draft letters were issued than personnel were needed. In the end, the military could do without those who were unable to serve for medical, family, or occupational reasons, as well as those who did not want to serve for reasons of conscience. Thus, objection was legitimized and became a gray area in military affairs without causing the IDF a significant problem.[3]

But when objection to service began to surface in January 2002, there was grave concern among the senior command. Mofaz remembered well how civilian criticism had influenced the Lebanon War in the 1980s. At that time, the protest waged by reserve soldiers, who were sick and tired of the continuing bloodshed in the Lebanese "quagmire," was an important factor influencing Israel's decision to retreat from the Shoof mountains in the center of the country and to take positions in the security strip near the Israeli border, in southern Lebanon. For this reason, the IDF avoided using reserve units in southern Lebanon over the next fifteen years, preferring to use young, conscripted soldiers, who were keen to participate in combat missions.

In 2002 Mofaz understood very well that if this refusal to fight Palestinian insurrection spread any further among the reserves, the IDF's ability to win the LIC would be significantly reduced, particularly in light of the social background of the objectors. In addition to Yesh Gvul—

which had continued its activity against the occupation since the war in Lebanon—new conscientious objector groups had sprung up, including Profil Hadash (New Profile), which supported objection as part of its fight against the "militarism of Israeli society," and a feminist group, which encouraged conscientious objection by women. The dominant group of objectors, however, was the one developed by the officers who wrote the letter to the minister of defense in January 2002. These objectors did not come, as past objectors had, from marginal groups or from the anti-establishment Left, but rather from social circles and groups considered mainstream in Israeli society. They belonged to centrist parties and to the upper social classes. They were graduates of prestigious schools and served in elite volunteer units. On the letter signers' website, they defined themselves as "Israelis. Zionists. Warriors. Objectors."[4]

The reasons for objection were also more poignant and varied than they had been in the past. The objectors' criticism of the IDF in reference to the war centered on two areas, *jus in bello* and *jus ad bellum*. Their *jus in bello* argument recalled philosopher John Rawls, who held that when a soldier is ordered to engage in certain illicit acts of war, he may refuse if he reasonably and conscientiously believes that the principles applying to the proper conduct of war are plainly being violated. Objectors believed that in such a situation, the soldier should be able to maintain that his natural duty is not to be made the agent of grave injustice and evil and that his obligation to justice and morality outweighs his duty to obey.[5]

Objectors' criticism of Israel's *jus ad bellum* was more severe, casting doubt on the legitimacy of the war itself. Suicide bombings had united Israeli society in patriotic sentiment but had also helped the government obscure the fact that, in Israel's eighth war, two struggles were combined: one involved fighting Palestinian terrorism aimed at innocent civilians inside Israel, and the other involved fighting the popular uprising in the territories against the ongoing occupation. While the fight against terror was considered by almost all Israelis to be legitimate and even morally imperative, the country was divided—although definitely not evenly—in its view of the IDF's suppression of the uprising.

Just as the intifada can be interpreted as an illegitimate use of violence, aimed at forcing Israel to pull out of the territories without negotiations and an agreed settlement, it can also be seen as a legitimate

national liberation struggle against the occupation and Jewish settlements. The objectors referred to the IDF's low-intensity conflict with the
Palestinians as the "War for Peace of the Settlements," which was meant
to evoke, sarcastically, the name Begin had given to the war in Lebanon.
Begin had called that war "The Peace of Galilee War," but many Israelis
perceived it to be an unjust war, intended to dictate by force a new political order in Lebanon.

Inevitably, the IDF attempted to undermine the objection phenomenon by presenting it as something that was driven more by political interests and goals than consciences. The military also tried, as it had in the
past, to solve the problem using a pragmatic policy that did not draw
unnecessary attention to it. "If they [the objectors] had not gone to the
media, this case would have been closed within the military," admitted
the IDF's chief education officer, Brig. Gen. Elazar Stern, "but because of
the media, it turns into incitement and our response must be very sharp."[6]
For that reason, when an objector publicized his act, the IDF did not hesitate to take public measures against him.

The more the objector conducted a noisy public campaign, the more
severely the IDF punished him, charging him repeatedly with insubordination if necessary. In January 2004, a military court sentenced five conscientious objectors to a year in prison, a sentence that had not been
equaled since 1981. In a few cases, objectors were sentenced to six, even
seven, consecutive prison terms. At the same time, the military continued
to try to downplay the importance of the phenomenon by not referring
objectors to military courts, defining it as a "discipline issue" handled by
an officer-judge, who was able to hand down sentences of up to thirty-
five days in a military prison.

While in the past the mainstream tended to react very negatively to
conscientious objectors, in this new era the objectors managed to gain some
support, albeit not on a very large scale, from the center of the political
map, including from those with high stature in the judicial system, academia, and even the security establishment. Prominent among the latter were
Maj. Gen. Ami Ayalon, former head of the navy and of the ISA; Ya'akov
Peri, former head of the ISA; and former attorney general Michael Ben-
Yair.[7] An article by Michael Ben-Yair captured the intensity of the public
debate surrounding the conscientious objection phenomenon:

The Six Day War was imposed on us, but the seventh day, which started on June 12, 1967, and continues to our day, has been our choice. We chose, ardently, to become a colonial society. The seventh day has transformed us from a moral society certain of the justice of its national revival, into a society oppressing another people and preventing it from realizing its legitimate national aspirations. . . . The intifada is the war of national liberation of the Palestinian people and history teaches us that nations are not willing to be ruled by other nations and that wars of national liberation end in victory.[8]

Ben-Yair recalled in detail the harsh testimonies that had been given regarding the IDF's conduct in the territories:

The killing of small children on the run; execution without trial of suspects who are not on the way to commit an act of terror; sieges, closures, and road blocks which turn the lives of millions into a nightmare. . . . Even if all this were a result of our self-defense, we would have been spared the need to defend ourselves in this manner if it were not for the occupation. Therefore, a black flag flies over these actions. . . .

The occupation undermines our moral justification and prevents peace and therefore it endangers the existence of the State of Israel. With this background in mind we have to examine the refusal of the reserve officers and soldiers to serve in the territories. According to the dictates of their consciences, they cannot be partners to such acts and therefore their refusal is justified and recognized in every democracy governed by the rule of law. In the judgment of history, their act of refusal will be marked as the action that returned the moral backbone to our society.[9]

The Refusniks and the Law

During the second intifada, only a minority of the Israeli public supported conscientious objection, as might be expected in a mobilized society in a time of war. In late 2003, between one-quarter and one-third of Israelis thought that refusal to serve in the territories was legitimate.[10] Those who opposed conscientious objection generally pointed to one of three major reasons for being against it.

First, conscientious objection during the intifada was selective, based largely on an ideological-political perspective rather than an overall objection to violence. The firm stance of the Supreme Court, which ruled in the 1980s against selective refusal, helped the IDF in its campaign against the conscientious objectors. In the 1980s the court said,

> Even in countries where there is a legal right for exemption from military service for conscientious reasons, this exemption does not exist unless the conscientious objection is to military service as such, for the objector believes in nonviolence as is and in general. But when the objection is not general, based on conscientious conviction regarding nonviolence, but a selective objection stemming usually from ideological-political reasons, not to act against a specific group or specific places, then this objection was not recognized. . . . Acknowledgment of selective objection hurts the democratic decision-making process, and it contains a real danger for discrimination in the draft.[11]

The second argument against the objectors was that refusal to serve during the intifada constituted not an ideological objection to a situation the conscience could not bear but was, rather, a political act meant to apply pressure to change an elected government's policy; as such, it stood in contradiction to the fundamental principles of accepting democratically made decisions. To be sure, the objectors had a political goal: to bring about a change in the government's policy toward the Palestinians.

The military also claimed that the objectors damaged the IDF's apolitical character. Military attorney Yuval Roitman warned,

> In selective objection there is a danger to the military's strength and to the stability of the society as a whole. The danger of dragging the military into the heart of political controversy lurks beneath the phenomenon of refusal to serve. That phenomenon has the potential of undermining the very foundation of the IDF as an apolitical and nonpartisan military under the authority of the government. Therefore, we should not accept selective objection that might create rifts in Israeli society and in the democratic regime reigning in the State of Israel.[12]

The objectors, for their part, used exactly the same argument to justify their actions. They refused to serve because they believed the IDF was failing to act as a nonpolitical body and instead was executing a particular party's policy. They protested against the politicization of the military and argued that the government was exploiting the military to achieve illegitimate political goals. "This is a war of deceit," one objector proclaimed, "an attempt to use the IDF in order to establish facts on the ground, and to achieve goals that it was not meant to pursue when it was founded as a military."[13]

The final argument against objection involved its illegality and the difference between conscientious objection and civil disobedience. Whereas the latter is a "politically motivated breach of law designed either to contribute directly to a change of law or to express one's protest against, and dissociation from, a law or public policy . . . the [former] is a breach of law for the reason that the agent is morally prohibited to obey it."[14]

When a group of law professors published an advertisement in which they expressed support for the right of soldiers to refuse to serve in the territories, Education Minister Limor Livnat issued a declaration stating that they should be prosecuted for incitement. Israeli criminal law defines incitement as occurring when three or more people express support for noncompliance with an order. The penalty for such an act is imprisonment for up to fifteen years (item 105 A2 of the ordinance of criminal law). Incitement to refuse to serve, or insubordination, can result in imprisonment for up to seven years (items 109–110 of the criminal law). Ultimately, no legal action was taken against the professors.

Reform of the Reserve Military

The mounting wave of objection resonated publicly and internationally, and it seemed that it would grow larger quickly and would harm the military. The IDF was also worried that it might strengthen the Palestinians' belief, which was at the core of the intifada, that Israeli society, when faced with a Palestinian attack, would not succeed in staying united and would crumble from within.

Over the course of the violent conflict, however, the power of the ideological mechanisms and the mobilization capability of Israeli society were not damaged. The horror scenes of suicide bombings in the heart of Israeli cities united Israelis around the IDF and the security forces, the last "personal insurance agents" available to them. The refusal phenomenon did not come out of a principled objection to military service as such; for some, it was not even the result of opposition to serving in the territories per se but opposition to the unjust nature of the fight against the Palestinian insurrection. The fact that the objectors identified with the IDF, believed in the Israeli security ethos, and felt pride in their military status and contribution to security, was so remarkable that one researcher called the wave of refusal "militaristic objection."[15]

Yet the IDF was unable to impede the evolution of the objection phenomenon, which until then had been largely alien to the Israeli world, and even more to the security culture. Beginning with the third year of the intifada, there were several qualitative leaps in the objections. For example, on September 9, 2003, the eve of the Jewish New Year, a group of twenty-seven pilots published in *Ha'aretz* a protest letter in the spirit of the letter of the original objecting officers. These pilots, who came from the heart of hearts of the security establishment, declared,

> We, pilots of the air force, raised on Zionist ideology, sacrifice, and giv-
> ing to the State of Israel, always served in the frontlines, ready to per-
> form any task, whether difficult or not, in order to defend the State of
> Israel and strengthen it. We, both veteran and active duty pilots, who
> served and still serve the State of Israel during long weeks every year,
> object to illegal and immoral attacks of the kind in which Israel is engag-
> ing in the territories. . . . We refuse to take part in the air force's attacks
> on civilian population areas . . . refuse to continue to harm innocent civil-
> ians. These acts are illegal and immoral, and are a direct consequence of
> a long occupation, which is corrupting the whole of Israeli society.[16]

The pilots' letter elicited greater shock than the officers' letter because it came from a group that was considered the elite of the IDF and of Israeli society, and it used language of a kind never used before in Israel by people of their status, accusing the IDF of performing illegal acts and war crimes. Israeli society found this very hard to accept. The Foreign Affairs and Defense Committee of the Knesset debated the issue, and a few Knesset members demanded the prosecution of the "traitors."[17]

Mofaz and Ya'alon reacted severely to the letter, responding with practical measures: the air force commander dismissed nine pilots from the group still serving in the reserves. In the media, many, including some who were left of the political center, severely attacked the pilots' action.[18] As with the officers' letter, the fact that the pilots' message commented directly on the occupation made it easy to argue that they were driven by political rather than moral interests, a claim that would have been harder to present if the pilots had written only about the immoral injuring and killing of civilians.

Three months after the publication of the pilots' letter, thirteen graduates of the IDF's elite unit sent letters to the defense minister, the CGS, and their commander. In it they wrote that they "can not be indifferent to the situation anymore. . . . We will not keep on giving our support to the oppression regime in the territories and to the deprivation of human rights of millions of Palestinians; we will not be used anymore as a defense shield for the settlements; we will not keep on corrupting our human spirit in the missions of the occupation army; we will not deny anymore our call as fighters for the Israeli *Defense* Army" [the emphasis appears in the original letter].

Their action was not novel; their terms and arguments had already appeared in the pilots' letter. The drama in this case was caused by the fact that these were graduates of the most prestigious unit in the IDF. Major figures such as Barak, Shahak, and Netanyahu had graduated from this unit, as had many other Israeli political and security elites. The public was shaken, and for several days the papers were filled with reports and opinions about the letter. Commentators on both sides did not miss a single chance to articulate every possible overstatement. "This place is on fire. We cannot keep on lying to ourselves. This is not some small burn caused by several wild weeds, this is a fire consuming the top of the sturdiest cedar trees," wrote one commentator on *Yedioth Ahronoth*'s front page. "We should condemn them, dismiss them, judge them," asserted Likud MK Ehud Yatom. But, in its editorial, the usually conservative and patriotic tabloid *Yedioth Ahronoth*, questioned, "Is it not about time to finally ask ourselves where is this occupation leading the IDF and the state?"[19]

While conscientious objection spread throughout the reserve units on a modest scale, there were also a few negligible refusal cases within the compulsory and professional military. Military authorities quickly took severe steps against the refuseniks, including the dismissal of pilots from the helicopter squadron and soldiers from the commando unit. Even so, it was no longer possible to diminish the extent of the phenomenon. Further, a large number of IDF reserves believed that the counterinsurgency war was not justifiable even though they themselves did not object to service. Among them were some who even demonstrated in Jerusalem against the war. While they explained that they opposed any kind of objection and were committed to serving in the reserve unit should their recruitment be necessary, they called for the IDF to withdraw from the territories.[20]

Ultimately, the IDF was hurt less by the refusal phenomenon than by a protest of a different kind: the complaint of reserve soldiers and officers that addressed neither the political nor the moral issues of the war but rather the unfair burden placed on them in fighting it. In the 1990s, reservists increasingly criticized the fact that only a minority of Israelis were required each year to stop their civilian way of life and serve in the military for forty-five days or more. This criticism intensified with the continuation of the intifada, which led to an extra burden for those reservists who were actually called up and who constituted less than 20 percent of the entire reserve force.

Many reserve soldiers' lack of willingness to serve arose not from conscience but from resentment. They believed that they were suckers, or "being 'Frier,'" to use a popular Israeli expression and that they were being taken advantage of and given an unequal and unfair share of the burden of reserve service. In fact, the motivation to serve in times of emergency, such as during Operation Defensive Shield, did not decrease. Most of those who were called reported for duty, but routine, nonemergency service in the territories was increasingly perceived as an unnecessary burden. Soldiers and officers who returned from reserve service told their friends, families, and the media about wasteful uses of time and resources and poor service conditions. In one case, a group of reserve officers from a unit in Netzarim, a settlement in the Gaza Strip, appeared on the cover of a weekly magazine after finishing their service and, while stating they would continue to report for duty in the future, called on the government to evacuate the settlement.[21]

This mounting criticism from reservists about the unjust division of the burden of service forced the IDF to rethink the structure of the whole reserve system. Indeed, the IDF set up a few more battalions from the regular forces in the territories to relieve the reserve units of routine security duties. Research on conscripts by military psychologists showed that they were motivated to serve in the territories and did not regard service in pacification missions negatively. The military also activated a plan for privatizing some of its functions, all with the purpose of decreasing, to a large extent, the drafting of reservists for routine security duties in the territories. And, in December 2003, the deputy CGS, Maj. Gen. Gabi Ashkenazi, and the IDF's chief reserve officer announced that in the future reserve soldiers would be called to duty only in times of emergency and would only be called for training once every three years. The plan was formally adopted in March 2004.

Such developments created a revolutionary change in the IDF's self-identity, since they meant a certain retreat from the nation-in-arms principle. Following the Six Day War, military commanders had decided not to create special units for the territories but to send conscripts and reserve forces instead, believing these units, even if they were less trained, would preserve a "civilian spirit" and preclude an "occupying military" mentality from developing. But the decision to create more permanent units for the territories, a significant departure from past policy, shows just how seriously the IDF took the reservists' complaints.

13

Who Won the Intifada?

Civilian Society Awakens

Toward the end of 2003, on top of the strain caused by some policy differences between the military and the political echelon, other events triggered friction in the relationship between the military and civilian society. There was a widespread feeling among the public that despite the success of the IDF and the ISA in dramatically reducing the number of terrorist attacks, neither the military nor the government had a fundamental solution, either military or political, to the ongoing conflict. Many individuals with considerable experience and high standing in the military and security fields also held such views. In December 2003, the director of the ISA himself added to this self-criticism, claiming that the defense community, including the ISA, did not "furnish the people of Israel the protective suit they deserved."[1]

The criticism was not based on moral considerations, as was the criticism of the conscientious objectors, but on considerations of a utilitarian nature. It underscored the fact that while harsh measures were necessary against insurrections, they also made the lives of hundreds of thousands of Palestinians intolerable, consequently deepening their hatred of Israel and making it longer-lasting. While the reoccupation of the West Bank and aggressive measures against the Palestinians had reduced the number of terrorist attacks, they had not provided anything approaching a fundamental solution to the underlying problem. In fact, they might even have aggravated it.

"The more hardship there is, the more strength the Hamas will gain. If the Palestinian street has nothing to lose, then we will lose. Instead of going to work, they will occupy themselves with preparing explosives and ambushes in Tel Aviv," said Maj. Gen. (res.) Ya'akov Orr, a former coordinator of operations in the territories.[2] Similarly, former minister and CGS Amnon Shahak warned, "IDF soldiers experience daily friction with hundreds, perhaps thousands, of Palestinians waiting at roadblocks. . . . This insufferable friction of Palestinians with IDF personnel creates potential new suicide bombers every day."[3]

In the latter half of the third year of the intifada, the political deadlock and the weakness of the parliamentary opposition led to various initiatives among individuals and groups in Israeli civil society. In November, for example, four former heads of the ISA, in a joint interview with *Yedioth Ahronoth,* characterized the government's policy as a policy of force that would not lead to an agreement with the Palestinians, stating firmly, "We are on the road to a catastrophe."[4]

While such critiques continued, proactive political initiatives were also formulated. Noteworthy among them was the plan of Maj. Gen. (res.) Ami Ayalon and Prof. Sari Nusseibeh of Al Quds University. Together they published a declaration calling for a historic compromise between the two peoples that involved mutual recognition and the willingness to establish a Palestinian state, with East Jerusalem as its capital, alongside an Israel within green-line borders, and that renounced the right of return of Palestinian refugees. In a mass campaign, more than three hundred thousand Israeli and Palestinian signatures were collected.[5]

The architect of the Oslo process, Yossi Beilin, and former Palestinian minister Yasser Abed Rabo led an even more noteworthy initiative. Throughout 2003, they had joint work teams draft a memorandum of understandings regarding a comprehensive and final settlement to the conflict. The document, which was signed in a festive and colorful ceremony in Geneva, Switzerland, on October 12, 2003, drew criticism from the Israeli government and its supporters, both for its substance and for the fact that an unauthorized group was conducting diplomatic negotiations. But it enabled the opposition in Israel to argue that there was a partner for talks and that there were substantive issues to discuss. The long slumber of the peace camp was finally over.[6]

Ya'alon realized that the atmosphere in Israeli society had evolved to a point where it would not indefinitely support the military's LIC and felt that the IDF had come to an unhealthy impasse in its relations with civilian society. In a lecture he delivered at the University of Haifa in the first week of January 2004, he referred to the potential decline of Israeli societal cohesion. Those who knew him well realized that his remarks "reflected only the tip of the iceberg of his concern and frustration, and those of his generals."[7]

What particularly concerned Ya'alon at that point in time was what he described as incitement against the IDF through an ongoing delegitimation campaign. "This is systemic malfunction, a destructive process, and it all adds up: conscientious objectors, demonstrators against the security fence, treasury officials with their media spins who agitate against their military, politicians on the Right and Left, the media." One can criticize the military, contended Ya'alon; that is well and good, "but one must keep a sense of proportion. You can't turn the IDF into a punching bag. That is annoying, dangerous, and destructive."

What especially irritated the CGS was that society's frustration and criticism of the IDF was on the rise even though progress was being made in the war against terrorism. For example, in 2003, 214 Israelis were killed in terrorist attacks, compared to 451 in 2002, a decline of more than 50 percent. The number of attacks also declined by almost 30 percent, from 5,301 in 2002 to 3,838 in 2003. A sharp decline was also registered in suicide bombings: 26 in 2003 compared to 60 in 2002 and 35 in 2001.[8]

However, this state of affairs did not weaken the CGS's belief in the need to maintain military pressure on Palestinian organizations: "We cannot stop; we cannot hesitate; we cannot show weakness. Yes, we can struggle over decisions, even agonize over them. We can feel contrite over wrongs we committed, and admit mistakes. But we should not divert our focus from the final objective, lest Arafat, who is alert to cracks in Israeli society—the political controversy over the future of the territories and public criticism of the lack of expectations from political activity —sees in them encouraging signs, which take the pressure off him to make concessions."[9]

By this time IDF strategists had also realized that a new stage had been reached in the intifada. While Operation Defensive Shield had transformed the arena, the hopes that the operation would put an end to the conflict were dashed. Control of the territories, the targeted killings of Hamas leaders, and the development of new battle techniques through unprecedented collaboration between the ISA, the land forces, and the air force had reduced the Palestinian use of force to a tolerable level. But the war looked as if it was going to go on for a long time.

Therefore, the IDF strategists began to speak of a new stage in the intifada, one of "regularization." This referred to the setting of new security arrangements, such as the security fence, that would enable the Israeli population to go on with their lives. As long as Arafat was alive, strategists believed, a peace agreement would not be reached. However, they did think it was possible to reach a *modus vivendi* with a tolerable level of controlled violence. So, even in this situation of unilateral management of the conflict, Ya'alon believed that if the stick must continue to be employed, the carrot must be offered to the Palestinians as well.

But division between the IDF and the government was not just based on differences over strategy; it was also based on personal friction between Ya'alon and Mofaz. Though Ya'alon had been loyal to Mofaz as his subordinate in the military, he grew unhappy with Mofaz's actions and decisions as defense minister, charging he favored his personal political interests over those of the military. For example, Ya'alon believed Mofaz had not fought within the cabinet against cuts in defense spending because Mofaz did not want to disrupt his relationship with the finance minister and prime minister. Another move by Mofaz that drew the military's ire was his decision to establish a political division within the Defense Ministry under Maj. Gen. (res.) Amos Gilead that would limit the role of the Planning and Policy Directorate. Ya'alon well understood that if the decision was implemented, the new civilian division would sharply curtail the General Staff's political activities, would leave the directorate involved only in force formation planning, and would reduce any influence the General Staff had over the conduct of battle with the Palestinians.

Though Mofaz's reform might indeed have been long needed, the fact that he proposed it only after he himself had moved from the military wing of the Defense Ministry compound, where the General Staff is located, to the civilian wing, led his recent colleagues to perceive it as hostile.[10] Adding to the conflict, Mofaz submitted to a ministerial committee a recommendation concerning reform of the IDF reserve system without prior military approval. Asked about the recommendation, Ya'alon commented with great understatement that the military does "not deem the moment appropriate for this reform." While the media emphasized the personal dispute between these two old friends, their differences of opinion also underscored two contentious political questions: how should the views of the military and its civilian supervisors be weighed in the formulation of defense and military policy and, indeed, what should Israel's policies toward the Palestinians be?

One reliable political commentator described the personal plight of the CGS in 2004 as follows: "Ya'alon believes that as head of Israel's military arm, he must sound the necessary alarm. If a volcano is about to erupt, the CGS must say [what must be said] and warn. If he issues his warning behind closed doors and does not get his message across, he must continue and say his piece directly to the public, as the public has a right to know." The analyst went on, observing, "Politics have already skewered him on more than a few occasions; his body is scarred and his soul is in turmoil. He must manage the military, fight the war, maintain the budgetary framework, defend the security fence, fight over public opinion, be wary of politics, watch over his back, and avoid Mofaz's shadow, all at the same time. It is not easy to be the CGS here."[11]

In early 2004, Ya'alon's doubts and misgivings were disclosed to few. But in mid-2005, in a revealing interview published in *Ha'aretz* on the day of his release from the IDF, he spoke of them openly:

> I remember myself coming to cabinet meetings and meetings of the Knesset's Foreign Affairs and Defense Committee during the war and asking myself where they are living and where I am living. The gaps are enormous. The feeling is that you are fighting over a hollow arena. . . . The most difficult moments of the war came during the meetings of the security cabinet. You try to exert influence about a certain matter and find yourself almost alone. You find yourself without agreement about who the enemy is and what the war is about. A commander is always alone, certainly a chief of staff, but in this case it was far beyond personal loneliness. It is the understanding that you perceive the situation in this way and everyone else perceives it differently. When what is at stake is the fate of your nation and your country, that is hard. Very hard.[12]

The IDF and the Disengagement Plan

Toward the end of 2003, Sharon also began to sense the impossibility of completely eliminating terrorism, the decline in public morale, and the ongoing political deadlock. The prime minister had always held the view that passiveness, on the battlefield as in politics, gives the adversary the opportunity to take the initiative and confront you with an established fact. Therefore, he believed you must always be the one to take the initiative and leave your adversary to respond. He also saw how the deadlock generated initiatives to which he was strongly opposed, such as the Geneva initiative of the Left, the strengthened U.S. demand to move forward with Bush's road map, and, above all, the continued promotion of conscientious objection. For this reason he decided to launch a new initiative that would restore his control of the field: a disengagement plan that involved completion of the security fence along the West Bank, and the withdrawal of the IDF and evacuation of the Israeli settlements from the Gaza Strip. The move was to be implemented unilaterally, without negotiations with the Palestinians. Not surprisingly, the plan and its rationale constituted yet another sore point between the military and the political echelon.

On December 18, Ya'alon and other members of the General Staff first heard, from the prime minister, of the dramatic change in government policy. Ya'alon objected to the evacuation of Gaza and the unilateral nature of the move. In his assessment, unilateral withdrawal, without any quid pro quo, would be viewed by the Palestinians as flight, as an admission of defeat in battle. Further, the manner of reaching the disengagement decision irked the General Staff: the prime minister made the decision in principle without first consulting the military. Ya'alon also took exception to the fact that representatives of the prime minister had already discussed a number of practical matters related to the disengagement plan with President Bush without first consulting the military. "Why rush without consulting the professional military echelon?" asked officers close to the CGS. "Why leave the military behind?"[13]

Additionally, the matter was reminiscent of Israel's unilateral withdrawal from southern Lebanon, a still sore wound on the military's psyche. More important, the military felt that unilateral withdrawal would turn Gaza into a terrorist haven, would threaten Israeli towns in the border areas, would validate Nasrallah's spiderweb theory, and would encourage

Palestinian terrorists to try to bring about withdrawal from Judea and Samaria as well.

In fact, Ya'alon supported the idea of announcing the evacuation as a tactical move to put pressure on the Palestinians to return to the negotiation table and proposed implementing the disengagement only within a framework of an agreed interim settlement with the Palestinian Authority. But the idea of actual unilateral disengagement troubled Ya'alon, and he continued to detail his objections to the plan in the many internal deliberations about it. In testimony to the Knesset Foreign Affairs and Defense Committee in December 2003, for example, he said, "The evacuation of [the settlement of] Netzarim will put a tailwind into the sails of terrorism."[14] Then, in mid-February 2004, Ya'alon issued the official IDF position on the disengagement plan. Its main point was simple: "[Israel] must withdraw from Gaza only by agreement and not unilaterally."[15]

However, Ya'alon constantly reiterated, as had every CGS before him, that the military would ultimately accept and implement any government decision, even though he was personally opposed to unilateral steps. He believed that there was still a chance to cooperate with the Palestinians and that the withdrawal should be implemented in consultation with them. "I recommend that no one here now become overly enamored of this move," he said at a cabinet meeting, directing his remark above all to Mofaz and Sharon. "We must exploit the element of threat in the move as a lever toward agreement with the Palestinians. We have to leave the door open to the Palestinians to return to negotiations." Those present did not need to be reminded of what Ya'alon had said at the conference of rabbis in August 2002, one month after assuming the post of CGS: "Unilateral withdrawal from the territories . . . would in effect be surrender to terrorism."

Nevertheless, Ya'alon was forced in the early months of 2004 to watch the plan continue to take shape. When he saw that he could not influence Sharon, he took a well-beaten path and appealed directly to the public through the media. On Sunday, March 7, during a tour of the Erez border crossing into the Gaza Strip, he responded to a journalist's question with the words, "a connection between a rise in acts of terrorism and talk of withdrawal should not be dismissed out of hand." The CGS's remarks had real impact, furnishing ammunition for opponents of Sharon's disengagement plan, including settlers and parties of the Right in the government coalition. What better reason could be given in the campaign against withdrawal than that the military opposed it? "IDF Asserts: Withdrawal Increases Terrorism" and "Withdrawal Equals Surrender to Terrorism" read posters. From the prime minister's office came a press leak that Sharon was furious and intended to summon Ya'alon to set matters straight and to reprimand him.

Once again the old ritual repeated itself: newspaper headlines announced a rift between the prime minister and his CGS; the media discussed the CGS's political views; debates focused on whether his actions were appropriate; and, finally, veteran commentators cynically concluded that the CGS had nothing to worry about. As one put it, "In Israel, you cannot argue with a serving CGS. The Israeli public loves its CGS, and does not like its prime minister so much. Therefore, Sharon will not have the nerve to hurt, or even rebuke, the CGS, come what may."[16] That, of course, is exactly what happened. In March 2004, the storm passed as had all those before it.

But Sharon and Mofaz did not forget and, unlike previous cases with former chiefs of staff and their political superiors, waited for the right opportunity to put the overly independent CGS in his place. It came in July 2005, when they decided not to extend Ya'alon's term of office. Since the 1950s, the term of almost every CGS had been extended by a year or more after its initial period had expired; in fact, this had become the norm and there were even some, such as Raphael Eitan, who had held the position for five years. Mofaz feigned ingenuousness, however, declaring that it was important to observe the letter of the law that set a three-year term of office. But it was clear to everybody that Boogy was being ousted. And while the media told a story of relations fraught with envy and hatred between Sharon and Ya'alon, they missed the deeper problems of their relationship—specifically, the political disagreement over how to treat the Palestinians and over the proper steps to take in the disengagement, and the structural tension between the military and the political echelon, which had reached new peaks during the years of the intifada.

Sharon was aware of this structural tension by 2004. Therefore, knowing he needed Ya'alon's support, he was ultimately compelled to moderate his original disengagement plan following the March crisis. With a cautious Ya'alon onboard, he was able to present his new modified plan as one fully supported by the military, the very outcome he had wanted from the beginning. After all, Sharon did not want to be seen as if he had devised his plan under pressure and wanted to market it as a proactive security measure, aimed at enhancing the security of the country and its citizens. Support from the military would enable him to do so.

As Ya'alon stopped expressing opposition to the withdrawal plan, and the IDF began cooperating in the preparations for its implementation, the IDF sought to prevent the withdrawal from being interpreted as a sign of weakness or capitulation. For that reason, the IDF intensified its operations in the Gaza Strip and submitted a proposal to eliminate Hamas's political leadership, which was endorsed by the government. This leadership-targeting strategy was meant to cause Hamas leaders to expend their energy on hiding rather than on organizing operations against Israel. The offensive against Hamas was also meant to weaken that organization in advance of the withdrawal to make it easier for moderates such as Muhammad Dahlan to take control of the Gaza Strip once the IDF left. What the officers referred to as preserving the IDF's deterrence capability was also interpreted by more critical observers as a flexing of muscles or even as revenge.

Then, on November 11, 2004, fate intervened, changing the nature of the Israeli-Palestinian relationship. After a long period of deteriorating health, Arafat died in a Paris hospital. Indeed, the assessment that was prevalent in every world capital, that the Israeli-Palestinian conflict would get back on the diplomatic track only after Arafat's departure, turned out to be correct. The "Rais's" place was taken without a struggle by the number two man in the Fatah leadership, Mahmud Abbas, who, over the previous four years had repeatedly expressed his opposition to the armed struggle. As a result, the United States, which had actually boycotted the Palestinian Authority, resumed contacts and even began to help it anew. The Israeli government, which had been sharply criticized in the past by the CGS for not helping Abbas when he was appointed prime minister by Arafat, also resumed contacts and a certain degree of cooperation with the Palestinian Authority.

This new chapter in the conflict commenced in the usual ritualistic style with an international conference. Representatives of Israel, headed by Sharon, and members of the Palestinian Authority, headed by Abbas, gathered at Sharm el-Sheikh on February 8, 2005. The king of Jordan also attended, as did President Mubarak of Egypt, who hosted the conference, stepping up his involvement in the diplomatic process in anticipation of the implementation of the disengagement plan.

Once again, Arab and Israeli adversaries spoke strongly about working toward peace, security, and economic development. Again they agreed to implement trust-building measures, and again they set timetables for the beginning of the political voyage, with Israel promising to ease its military pressure and the Palestinians promising to stop incitement and terror. In the internal Palestinian scene, too, there was a dramatic turnabout with the declaration of the *tahadiya* (meaning calm, as distinct from *hudna,* meaning truce) between the Islamic organizations and the Palestinian Authority, and the inclusion of the former in running the affairs of the Palestinian community in exchange for a temporary cessation of their violent activity against Israel. As a result, there was a decline in the number of victims on both sides in 2005.

However, as in each of the previous rounds of talks, the Palestinians and the Israelis ultimately did not live up to their promises. The Palestinian Authority did not disarm the organizations it said it would, and the attacks on Israel did continue; Israel, meanwhile, did not withdraw IDF units from the occupied cities, did not stop hunting down wanted men, did not facilitate movement in the territories, and did not release but very few prisoners. As in the past, each side justified its shortcomings with the excuse that the other side was not fulfilling its own commitments. Against this background, from April onward, gloomy predictions began to be heard that a new intifada, even more severe than the previous one, would break out immediately after the disengagement. As he had been doing since 2003, Ya'alon, still in uniform but feeling hurt, criticized his government for its stingy policy management toward the Palestinian Authority and its new head.

So Who Actually Won the Intifada?

Abbas's election to the presidency, the Sharm el-Sheikh conference, and the Islamic organizations' agreement to temporarily stop the terror attacks again raised the notion, albeit this time more qualified, that the intifada had come to an end. What could be more natural then, than to ask who won it? Indeed, this question gave rise to a major debate both among the public and within the IDF itself. The international media, too, contributed to the discussion, which began even before Arafat's death. For example, in an op-ed published in the *Washington Post* on June 18, 2004, after a significant drop in the number of terror attacks in Israel, Charles Krauthammer rushed to declare Israel the victor:

> While no one was looking, something historic happened in the Middle East. The Palestinian intifada is over and the Palestinians have lost. . . . The intent of the intifada was to demoralize Israel, destroy its economy, bring it to its knees, and thus force it to withdraw and surrender to Palestinian demands, just as Israel withdrew in defeat from Southern Lebanon in May 2000. . . . The end of the intifada does not mean the end of terrorism. There was terrorism before the intifada and there will be terrorism to come. What has happened, however, is an end to systematic, regular, debilitating, unstoppable terror—terror as a reliable weapon.

A few IDF officers who participated in the debate used equally unequivocal language. For example, in the summer of 2004, on the eve of his retirement as IDF commander of the Gaza Sector, Brig. Gen. Gadi Shamani stated, "We are winning in this conflict. In the military arena we are winning every day, several times a day." "But that is precisely the problem," reacted analyst Yossi Alper. "Is there any strategic meaning to the sort of victory that requires winning several times every day?" One of Shamani's senior officers also grasped the problem in his logic, noting that "the IDF had defeated all the terrorist gangs in Gaza save one: the population at large."[17]

Indeed, a thorough analysis of the costs and benefits of the intifada on both sides is necessary to truly evaluate its outcome. The IDF and the security forces certainly succeeded in achieving some of the goals they and the government had set for themselves. First and foremost, they prevented the Palestinian Authority from achieving its main objectives: escalating the insurgency into a violent regional confrontation; causing international intervention that would curtail Israel's control over the territories; diminishing Israel's motivation and perseverance in the conflict; undermining Israel's determination to maintain the status quo in all of the territories; and eventually forcing upon Israel the establishment of a Palestinian state.

Israel's security forces also succeeded in decreasing the level of violence and in reducing the number of terror attacks and their impact. Over the course of 2004, there was a significant decrease in the number of attacks, and the trend of preventing planned attacks continued, as only one out of every four such attacks was successfully carried out. The number of Israelis killed dropped from 214 in 2003 to 117 in 2004. Compared with 26 suicide bombings in 2003, killing 144, there were only 15 in 2004, killing 55.[18] Further, Nasrallah's spiderweb theory was proven to be baseless. While approximately one thousand Israelis were killed and six thousand were injured over the intifada's four years, with the overwhelming majority being civilians,[19] Israeli society did not disintegrate. The attempt to undermine Israel's resilience failed, as Israeli society developed mechanisms for coping with the conflict, enabling life's routines to continue despite the attacks.

But alongside the positive achievements, there were also significant setbacks. The war had a severe negative impact on Israel's economy. While there had been an annual growth rate of 4 percent in the years before the intifada, during it there were three years of 1 percent negative growth. In the four years of the intifada, the Israeli economy lost some 12 billion dollars (the relative damage to the Palestinian economy was three times more).[20] However, the impact of the intifada was not distributed evenly over the different classes of Israeli society. The terror hit the poorer classes much more, and for the first time in the history of the IDF most of the soldiers who were injured (75 percent of them) came from peripheral classes and groups.[21] This unequal distribution of the security burden, together with a deepening of the economic gap between the top 3 percent and the bottom ranks of Israeli society, diminished the sense of solidarity and cohesion within the country.

More detrimental to Israel was the pain connected to the dissipation of the peace dream and the loss of hope in a brighter future. The war also created a sense of a lack of personal security. Some scholars from Tel Aviv University who examined the subject found that one-third of the Israeli population reported that they had been personally exposed to terror attacks, 11 percent of them directly and 20 percent indirectly, such as through family members or friends who had been injured. According to the study, the intifada had caused approximately one out of every ten Israelis investigated to report feelings of dejection or depression, and stress or anxiety, and, in the authors' words, showed signs of post-traumatic stress syndrome as a result of the terror attacks.[22]

The decline in the number of casualties, due to the erection of the security fence, more extensive intelligence surveillance, and the elimination of Palestinian leaders, improved Israelis' daily lives but not their mood with respect to long-term prospects. After all, the intifada was a severe blow to Israeli society. For example, more Israelis were killed or injured by enemy hands during its four years than had been during the entire period since the establishment of the state in November 1947—11,356 compared with 4,319. This was also the first war in which more civilians were killed than soldiers: 8 out of 10 casualties were civilians.

The Palestinians were thus unsuccessful in achieving their strategic aims through violence, while Israelis, for their part, were not successful in bringing an end to the violence, as Sharon had demanded when he became prime minister, and as the military had promised it would do when it launched Operation Defensive Shield. Indeed, the conflict had not reached the stage that students of conflict resolution describe as "ripeness," allowing both parties to continue inflicting damage to each other even though they themselves suffered pain and agony as a result.[23]

Yet, in the summer of 2005, the Palestinians did score a major advantage. Though Sharon presented the withdrawal from the Gaza Strip as a military action that would shorten the lines of engagement with the enemy and improve Israel's security, the Palestinian interpretation sounded more persuasive: after almost five years of bloody struggle, Israel unilaterally withdrew from territories without getting anything in return. The armed struggle, for all its pain, had brought the Palestinians some gains.

Additionally, from a military point of view, the Palestinians presented unprecedented challenges for the formulators of Israel's national-security doctrine, and, for the first time since the state's establishment, succeeded in shaking some of the basic principles of that doctrine. For example, the intifada marked the first time that an adversary was able to compel Israel to conduct a war of attrition, a form of war traditional Israeli military doctrine had always viewed as unacceptable. The challenges Israel faced were so difficult precisely because of the asymmetry of postmodern war, whereby the probable winner is not necessarily the party possessing the greatest military power but rather is the party willing to pay the highest price.[24] And while Israeli society was already deep into the era of post-heroic wars, in which preserving the lives of soldiers is of supreme value, the Palestinians were willing to sacrifice life en masse, including the lives of women and children, in order to achieve their goals.

Therefore, when IDF officers began to point to the balance of casualties and to boast that the numbers were in Israel's favor, it seems that they had either failed to learn the first lesson of revolutionary wars or forgotten the famous words of Ho Chi Minh: "In the end they will kill ten of ours for every American who is killed, but they will tire first." The IDF officers only needed to look as far as Algeria to see the truth in such a statement. There, 25,000 French soldiers were killed, compared with 600,000 Algerians, yet the French were the ones who tired first.[25]

The Palestinian insurgents also succeeded in disturbing another basic principle in Israel's national-security doctrine: decision. This was the first of Israel's wars that was anything but decisive; indeed, a protracted war is exactly what the theory of fourth-generation warfare would predict. Col. (res.) Shmuel Nir, one of the main formulators of the LIC theory at the IDF, wrote about this in the military's journal, *Maarachot:* "The triangle [of basic principles in Israel's national-security doctrine], deterrence–advance warning–decision, which was like antibiotics that won over every disease, was confronted now with new germs that have developed resilience. The remedy we need in the present confrontation is the ability to adapt."[26]

But even the IDF's efforts at adaptation engendered antagonism among the more conservative officers who were not reconciled to jettisoning the traditional national-security doctrine for LIC doctrine. They accused the military command of a lack of determination. For example, the willingness of the IDF to get into a war of attrition with the Palestinians, wrote Col. (res.) Yehuda Wagman, meant that it accepts a lack of decision and accepts terrorism as a natural phenomenon that cannot be eliminated.[27] The policy of approaching the war as an LIC had failed, he stated, arguing that there was therefore a need to increase the intensity of engagement and revert to the traditional conduct of wars.

Finally, the intifada also elevated the IDF's involvement in political matters, leading to increased friction among the country's leadership. In particular, it illustrated the difficulties imposed on militaries in fourth-generation wars, in which the boundaries between the political and military spheres are blurred and in which the military becomes political. In Israel's case this was especially true given that most in the political echelon failed to recognize the constraints put on the military by the LIC.

In summary, while Israel succeeded in preventing the Palestinians from attaining most of their major strategic objectives, it did not succeed in achieving its own strategic objectives. That is, Israel brought about neither a Palestinian surrender nor a change in the adversary's perception, the main objective of counterinsurgency warfare. As the war continued, the IDF came to understand the major constraints placed on it not only by the United States and the international media but also by Israeli public opinion. Though these externally and internally imposed constraints limited the area in which the IDF could legitimately operate, the IDF learned to adapt, taking these constraints into consideration in setting strategy in the prime minister's office and in the course of planning tactical operations in IDF brigades and battalions. As a result, this "limited space of legitimacy" affected the IDF's operations throughout the intifada, as we have seen, both at the political level and at the tactical level.

14

Israel's Security Culture

Is There a Gap?

What attracted me to investigate the IDF's influence on Israel's policy toward the Palestinians was that it was the generals who, beginning in the late 1980s, advocated making a fresh start in relations with Israel's historic enemies. The military leadership supported the peace process with Syria and the Palestinians and urged the government to pursue both tracks, even if they led to costly territorial concessions. Further, they were so eager to see these negotiations succeed that when they later realized that Prime Minister Benjamin Netanyahu was hindering the process, they actively joined in the effort to topple him.

Yet with the same determination and vigor, when the Camp David peace talks failed in the summer of 2000 and the Palestinians embarked on an armed struggle, the military made a complete turnabout and pressed the government to implement an uncompromising policy toward the Palestinians. Indeed, the IDF also turned away from a military doctrine it had followed since its inception, one based on von Clausewitz's principles of war. Its newly developed political-military doctrine justified deeper penetration of uniformed men into the loci of national decision making and a relaxation of the strict moral code to which the IDF had previously held itself. Then, after about three years of mutual bloodshed, the IDF made another turnabout. Against the nationalist camp's vociferous demand for continuation of the battle, when victory seemed to them so certain and so close, the officers argued that without a "political horizon" no

213

amount of military pressure on the Palestinians would bring hostilities to an end.

Kohn rightly argues that the best way to gauge the extent and effectiveness of civilian oversight of the military is to weigh the relative impact of army officers against that of civilian officials in formulating government policy.[1] Both in extending an olive branch to the Palestinians in the early 1990s and in using the sword in the early twenty-first century—situations wherein the two elements of the IDF insignia were used—the military did play a major role in setting Israel's policy toward the Palestinians. But the key question to ask is whether the IDF officers have something in common that distinguishes them from nonuniformed policymakers—that is, are their actions and beliefs specific to a military culture or a military mind? This is a supremely important issue because if there is no difference between the two groups, then militarism—produced in the military—has no special influence over policy. Only if the officers have special characteristics that distinguish them from the civilians is there any meaning to the questions: in what direction are the IDF officers heading now, and where are they leading Israeli society?

In the United States in the 1990s, many worried that the U.S. military did not reflect civilian society, and therefore questions about military culture and the gap between the military and civilians occupied both scholars and practitioners a great deal.[2] But what is the situation in Israel? It is here, toward the end of the chronological descriptions of events that took place since the early 1990s, that we return to the questions with which I opened the first chapter: is Israeli society militaristic and do her generals have a military mind? To answer them, a retrospective examination of the period under discussion is first needed.

When studying the IDF's position toward the Palestinians and the peace process in the 1990s, one should distinguish between the attitudes of the officers as individuals and the official position of the IDF as an organization. As individuals, the officers who led the IDF first to the peace talks and then to war revealed the same patterns of attitudes and behaviors that have characterized IDF officers throughout the entire existence of the state of Israel. As in the past, today their perspectives spread across the entire political spectrum. The most extreme nationalist parties in the Knesset have been headed by former professional soldiers, but so have political parties on the Left. Some IDF officers have expressed racist views and supported the policy of "transferring" the Palestinians out of the country, while others began to establish contacts with the PLO in the early 1970s, when doing so was far beyond the national consensus and was perceived as treasonous.[3]

However, most senior officers who entered politics on retirement preferred one of the two major parties at the center of the political spectrum, the Labor Party and the Likud.[4] Within these two catchall parties, the officers fall along a continuum ranging from hawks to doves, with the majority being left of center. They are not disciples of the Greater Israel ideology, but neither are they post-Zionist peaceniks. Their approach to the conflict is practical and pragmatic. They see relations with the Arabs not from the perspective of rights based on God's promise to Israel or, alternatively, of moral injustice done to the Palestinians, but rather from a realpolitik approach. While a few top-ranking officers in the 1990s held a distinctly ideological view based on religious belief, such as Brig. Gen. Effy Eitam, and many more were strategic hawks, such as Maj. Gen. Amos Gilboa, or followers of the dovish tradition, such as Maj. Gen. Ami Ayalon, most were "dove-hawks."[5]

Clearly there is no commonality within the military on an ideological level, but might there be common character traits, personality structures, and natural inclinations among those in uniform? Military sociologists and psychologists are suspicious of what is called the military-mind theory, which postulates the existence of a psychological personality factor common to all officers, whatever their nationality or ethnicity. Rather, they suggest social organizations themselves develop their own cultures that come to be shared by members of the group.[6] This then leads to the question, could the IDF have developed its own culture like any other bureaucratic organization?

Defining organizational culture as "the set of basic assumptions, values, norms, beliefs, and formal knowledge that shapes collective understanding," Elizabeth Kier demonstrates how the culture of an organization "shapes its members' perceptions and affects what they notice and how they interpret it; it screens out some parts of 'reality' while magnifying others." She notes that "few institutions devote as many resources to the assimilation of their members as does the military."[7] However, the IDF is a much more open organization than most militaries, and its boundaries with civil society are permeable: the professional officers do not live in separate camps secluded from civil society; a substantial part of their lives is spent in civilian settings; and in the military they interact with civilians doing short periods of reserve duty. In such conditions it is not so easy to develop an organizational culture that distinguishes the officers from their civilian comrades. This absence of integral boundaries between the military and the civilian sectors has led some radical scholars to argue that the source of militarism in Israel is not the military at all but sectors within civilian society itself.

The question then of how to define Israeli culture could be solved by applying a term that suits a citizen's army or a nation in arms and calling it a "political-military culture," namely, a culture that includes those who wore a uniform in the past and those who wear a uniform in the present. More specifically, political-military culture refers to the "subset of the larger political culture that influences how members of a given society view national security, the military as an institution, and the use of force in international relations."[8] Peter Kazenstein has defined political-military culture as the "culture of national security," and both terms assert that social factors do shape different aspects of national-security policy.[9]

Scholars tend to frame this security culture opposite another one, known as the "civilian view" or the "diplomatic subculture." In analyzing Israel's foreign relations, Klieman rightly presents this dichotomous distinction as preferable to the ideological distinctions of dove-hawk, liberal-conservative, or left-right: "One principal dichotomy to look for in peace negotiations is one that pits a *diplomatic* subculture, with a distinctive worldview and particular set of cultural norms, premises, sensitivities, and preferences all pinned to the goal of normalized relations with the rest of the world, against a *security* subculture possessing a very different logic and orientation of its own."[10]

What, then, characterizes the security culture, whether maintained by uniform wearers or civilians? The ideal type in the Weberian sense would be those who think that mankind is inherently wicked, weak in character, and irrational. As a result, this thinking leads to the assumption that distributional and value conflicts can be resolved only by the use of force; that in international relations instability and uncertainty prevail and will always lead to wars between states; and that therefore the existential security threat is always immediate, and, hence, it is necessary to always be prepared for the worst possible scenario. By extension, military personnel and professional managers of violence come to occupy key roles in society, with the security sector expanding as more and more social resources are invested in countering the security threat. Therefore, although the political echelon is responsible for the military echelon, the political leaders should listen to the opinions of officers and heed their advice.[11]

The key point in this view is the attitude toward force. The basic belief is that the world does not function according to principles of justice and morality but serves as a battlefield for the disputes of the actors, namely the different states. Consequently, one cannot rely on settlements based on agreements, international law, contracts, and treaties; or international bodies, such as the United Nations and the International Court of Justice; or mediation and intervention by foreign states. Thus, the diplomatic method, negotiations, compromise, and reconciliation solutions are not really effective. What is effectual in the international arena is power, and, even if it has limits, the ability and readiness to use power is what counts. Reality is shaped by the use of force, and if diplomacy does not achieve national goals, war is not a choice to be decried.

Yehoshafat Harkabi, a theorist of strategy and international relations, aptly summarized the difference between these two approaches to international relations—the military and the diplomatic:

> The military recognize only one test of military actions—defeat of the adversary, victory, success; whereas diplomacy does not rest on one sole criterion. Diplomatic success has to be judged by many criteria, particularly because military action has immediate results, while diplomatic action is more gradual and finally depends on long-term results.
>
> Diplomatic thinking and military thinking differ in their mode and in their orientation. Military thinking deals with the event—the operation—and is more discontinuous, while diplomatic thinking deals with the process, with the flow of history and with historical results. In military thinking the enemy is an object to be overcome, and the orientation is manipulative. In diplomatic thinking the adversary is also a subject with whom it will be necessary to reach a peace agreement in the end, and therefore he should be seen as someone in his own right; it is necessary to talk to him, and thus the thinking is more communicative.
>
> In military thinking the adversary is a collection of targets to be hit; in diplomatic thinking the enemy is a human political entity who has to be persuaded and appeased. In military thinking we are indifferent to the pain of the adversary; furthermore, we attempt to increase his pain. In diplomatic thinking we have to be sensitive to his pain.

Military thinking tends to view confrontation as a zero-sum game—
one side's loss is the other's gain, and all this in a narrow framework of
us and our enemies—while diplomatic thinking starts with a zero-sum
game which finally ends in collaboration between the two sides, and has
to take into account not only the enemy but also the reaction of third
parties.

Military thinking is one-sided; diplomatic thinking is many-sided.
Military thinking tends to be means oriented, while political thinking
has to keep in mind object oriented aims, and to discuss long-term results
beyond the attainment of the immediate goal. Military thinking strives
to be rational with regard to the relationship between the means and
ends and the results, while diplomatic thinking has to aim for what is
reasonable in terms of the consequences of the results.[12]

The difference between the security culture and the diplomatic culture
may be institutional, as many researchers of the American situation believe.
They distinguish between the two according to their clothes. But in a
society where the boundaries between the military organization and the
civil sector are breached, where there is a two-way osmosis between the
civil and the military, one can find faithful representatives of the military
culture among people who are manifestly civilians, while some of those in
uniform might be better suited to the diplomatic culture.

In Israel, the existence of hard-line officers along with accommodationists indicates the pluralistic character of the IDF officer corps. Nevertheless, an examination of Israel's behavior toward the Palestinians during the 1990s—among civilians and officers alike—reveals another matter,
that the security culture is the dominant culture of Israel's political-military
elite. An abundance of such findings has been accumulated in the past
decade by anthropologists and culture scholars, who examined in Israel,
for example, the behavior of teachers in kindergartens and nurses in hos-
pitals.[13] This dominant security culture is also found in other spheres of
society,[14] particularly in the character and style of Israel's foreign relations.
"The primacy of national security impacts on every facet of Israeli life,
from literature and cinema to the quality of life and women's rights. . . . It
is also far and away the most influential culture subset shaping Israel's
negotiating stance."[15]

In general, however, Israel's political-military elite hold a different
view of the ideal type of security thinking. They distinguish between
such arguments in principle and the concrete Israeli reality. The typical

supporters of the security culture are not convinced that human nature is intrinsically bad, that there will always be wars, and that force is the only language that counts in international relations. Rather, their attitudes are specific to the situation with the Arabs in the Middle East at present.[16] They see their security culture as deriving from "objective," external structural factors: the nature of the threat; the behavior of the enemies; and the unstable, wild, and violent character of the arena. In the view of political scientists, this would be considered a realistic approach to international relations.

"However, though influenced by the real world, cultures, including political-military cultures, are not merely subjective reflections of objective reality."[17] More specifically, one's worldview is also influenced by social factors. And one cannot fail to see that Israel's security culture has resulted from cultural factors: for hundreds of years Jews lived as an oppressed national minority in conditions of constant danger and threat, and in the early stages of the national movement's development in pre-state Israel, Jews had to cope under British occupation while facing a rival Arab national movement. Israelis have also been influenced by incessant wars against hostile neighbors.

Although the IDF was ready to seek a political accommodation with the Palestinians, this was not because the diplomatic culture had gained strength. It was an accommodation in the spirit of the security culture. When negotiations broke down, Palestinian violence was perceived as proof that the security culture was right. As a result, the IDF's easy shift from the negotiating table to the battlefield was explained by the fact that the deceitful adversary had shown its true colors, that it had not wanted peace from the beginning, and that it had simply used the political process to make progress on its way to achieving its national aims. Even after Israel began negotiations again with the Palestinians, its dominant political-military culture did not change to a diplomatic one; its security-culture perspective persisted.

The Institutional Attitude

A thorough examination of the IDF's official positions throughout the various stages of the negotiations in the 1990s shows that although it supported the strategic move toward a settlement, the military—as an institution, not the individuals who were or had been officers—was reluctant to take steps that it saw as conceding too much, steps that were liable, in its view, to compromise Israel's security interests. In other words, it preferred steps that ensured broad margins of security over politically advantageous ones that carried military risks. The IDF also preferred concrete physical arrangements to principles, declarations, and statements of values.

This was especially evident at the end of the 1980s, when the IDF began to adopt the peace strategy. Despite its change in defense doctrine, the IDF did not undergo a paradigmatic revolution. The IDF's support for a peaceful accommodation did not stem from its adoption of the basic concepts of the ideological Left, which saw the conflict as a struggle between two equally just national movements and doubted the legitimacy of the occupation. And it certainly did not express acceptance of the analysis of revisionist historians, who claimed that even in the past some Arab leaders had wanted to arrive at peace agreements with Israel, but that it was Israel who had refused. Nor did officers who underwent a conceptual transformation at the end of the 1980s begin to think, like most of the supporters of Peace Now, that the settlements in the territories acquired in the 1967 war were a major obstacle to peace. Even when the IDF discussed the harmful effect of the counterinsurgency warfare that they had been conducting, they looked at the damage to the military primarily in professional and technical terms. The morality of their war actions was a lesser concern; actions were measured by their potential damage or benefit to the IDF and its reputation. Therefore, the conflict, and the ways to solve it, continued to be analyzed in terms of the realpolitik or *machtpolitik* paradigm, which does not see peace as a supreme goal in itself but primarily as a means of achieving security.

For this reason, the military showed little interest in the economic arrangements that were supposed to create the infrastructure and incentives to preserve the peace. For the same reason, they also paid little attention to the issues of preventing incitement and providing education about coexistence. In contrast, the minutest details of security arrangements on a hilltop or in a small neighborhood were given close scrutiny by IDF officers. Their answer when asked about this was, "It's our job to deal first of all with security arrangements." While one could argue that economic development and education about coexistence have a security value, the military's tendency as an organization was to attribute little importance to these matters.[18] In this respect, the change that occurred in the IDF's conception of security at the end of the 1980s matched the change that occurred in the overall security culture. In both there had been "conservative innovation," which, in the words of Cohen, "has fostered incremental change, but has resisted fundamental transformation."[19]

Though within the IDF an effort has always been made to prevent conservatism—an effort that gave the IDF tactical advantages in battles against the much more conservative Arab armies—it has not been immune to the conservatism that generally characterizes militaries. This has been particularly true in cases when the IDF has faced new situations marked by a lack of clarity. Whenever the security of the state is considered, military conservatism prefers known devils over uncertain courses of action. One expression of this type of conservatism was voiced at a meeting of the General Staff on September 11, 2001, to discuss the implications of that day's terrorist attacks on the United States. It was clear to all the participants that something of huge dimensions had happened that would change the world, yet it was hard to understand its meaning to Israel. What was the response of CGS Mofaz? He decided to raise Israel's level of preparedness for war against Syria. Ofer Shelah remarks sarcastically (and rightly) that the decision was taken not because the probability of war with Syria had increased, but because "that is what the Chief of Staff knows to do when something threatening and vague happens. And indeed, reserves were called up and trained, the state of alert was raised, precious time and money were wasted, and in the end Israel was well prepared for the scenario of October 1973, while what happened was the Intifada of 2001."[20]

Conservatism as an institutional military characteristic is liable to develop into a kind of rigidity that generally surfaces during conditions of fundamental change (for example, moving from peace to war or vice versa).[21] This is what happened when the long-held belief that Egypt would not start a war blinded IDF commanders in 1973, although there were abundant signs indicating that an Egyptian attack was imminent. Similarly, the belief that Egypt would never make peace with Israel blinded CGS Gur in 1978, even after President Sadat expressed his willingness to visit the Knesset to initiate peace negotiations with Israel.

The negative implications of such institutional conservatism intensify when it is accompanied by a worst-case-scenario approach. The head of the peace directorate, Col. Shaul Arieli, referred to such a circumstance when he described the difficulties he had with the commanders of the IDF in the course of preparing the ground for peace with the Palestinians: "Though we asked ourselves what shape peace would take, the military continued to think in terms of war. Officers were unable to understand that the whole idea was that we were moving into a state of peace, and that peace would bring security. They wanted to establish a framework, which would give us security as though there were no peace. This was unacceptable to our adversaries and rightly so."[22]

Foreign Minister Shlomo Ben-Ami, who also witnessed this phenomenon during the peace talks at Camp David, presented his thoughts at a cabinet meeting, stating, "We must define 'national security' in new terms: the depth of society, the quality of the education system, the character of our international relations, the upgrading of our strategic alliance with the United States, and above all by peaceful relations with the Arab and Muslim world."[23] He also spoke on other occasions of the importance of achieving international legitimization for the state of Israel in defined borders. But such views did not gain hegemonic status in Israel's political culture.

The fact that no paradigmatic revolution occurred was also apparent when considering the prevalence of security-based discourse. For example, the terminology used by peace advocates never changed. People spoke of "the struggle for peace" or "the war for peace," while victims of terrorist attacks were referred to as "victims of peace." Rabin even declared that he was "a soldier in the army of peace." Further, the language used in support of or against a given peace agreement was always packed with military terms; indeed, in discussing such issues, military experience, especially prestige acquired on the battlefield, gave the speaker an advantage. As we saw, this language also characterized the refuseniks of recent years.

The wish to reach a peace agreement with the states of the first circle, primarily Syria, was motivated and justified by the need to strengthen Israel's position against the states of the second circle, Iraq and Iran. In the same way, the willingness of Israel's political-military leadership to grant the Palestinian leadership territorial and political concessions was motivated by the expectation of receiving a reward for doing so—specifically, that the Palestinian Authority would stand firmly against militant Islamist organizations, such as Hamas, Islamic Jihad, and Hizbullah, and extreme left-wing Palestinian groups.

Indeed, throughout the entire peace process, the main criterion by which the Israeli negotiators judged the Palestinian leaders was the extent to which they succeeded in this task, that is, provided security to Israel against attacks by militants. The Palestinian Authority's failure to do so, particularly in 1996 and in the years since 2001, periods replete with terrorist suicide bombings, was seen by Israelis as proof that the Palestinians did not intend to establish real peace. The Palestinian Authority's argument that it could not totally control all the militant groups was dismissed as an excuse for avoiding responsibility. The fact that the Palestinian public received no visible return during the negotiations, such as economic development or the freezing of the settlements, which would have made it easier for the Palestinian Authority to conduct a civil war against the militant groups, was not perceived as relevant in Israeli security thinking.

We see here a vicious circle. Despite its readiness to make territorial concessions, the political-military leadership demanded very broad security margins, both in interim arrangements and in negotiations over a permanent settlement. Israelis saw this as vital to ensuring security in case a peace agreement was not implemented, but these very demands were perceived by the Palestinians as evidence of Israel's intention to continue the occupation by other means, a situation that could never bring about reconciliation between the Palestinian people and its powerful neighbor.

Palestinian negotiator Abdel Razek El-Yehye explained this in one of the meetings of the security committee in 1995: "You have a narrow view of the meaning of security. You need to understand that the answer lies in the change of psychological atmosphere. If you force us to do something, Arafat will not be able to survive it. If you appoint yourselves arbiters of what is right and wrong, you will destroy the good will that prevails between us and between our peoples. The way to bring about a radical change in the atmosphere, which in the end will serve the interests of both sides, is to create partnership in security."[24]

An alternative approach for the Israelis would have been to make more of an effort to put themselves in the place of the other side, to understand the causes that formed its perceptions, fears, motives, and personal and collective needs, while at the same time paying attention to real security considerations. The Israelis should have tried to defuse some of the security threats to their country by better understanding the other side.

Such an approach would not have ignored the vast importance of military power, but it would have been more balanced and preserved military capability while defusing some of the adversary's negative tendencies. An alternative approach would have been to settle for a lower level of prevention of the adversary's ability to threaten Israel in exchange for a weakening of its motivation to do so.

As Joseph S. Nye argues, a country that wishes to influence the behavior of others does not have to threaten the use of force to do so; it can use two other levers: economic power and soft power.[25] What traditionally characterized Israel's hegemonic conception was the unequivocal preference for the use of force rather than the use of soft power. However, this is not to say that the blame for the continued dispute rests solely on Israel's shoulders. After all, the Arab states did not recognize the Jewish people's right to have a country of their own in the Middle East, and it was the leaders of the Palestinian people who rejected various proposals for compromise—starting with the Partition Plan of 1947, which called for the establishment of two states. The PLO was established in 1965 with the aim of eliminating the Zionist entity; significantly, the organization was founded years before Israel conquered the territories in the Six Day War. But in the end Israel holds no small share of the responsibility for the continued conflict; in fact, largely because of its security culture, Israel holds a larger share than most Israelis are prepared to admit.

What particularly characterized Israel's dominant approach was its demand for absolute security, while it ignored the fact that this demand severely damaged other dimensions of the relations between the two sides. An alternative approach that focused on achieving security without military field glasses was advocated by Shimon Peres as prime minister in 1996 when he attempted to reach a political settlement with Syria. Itamar Rabinovich, former Israeli ambassador to the United States, who represented Israel in the negotiations with Syria, testified: "Peres' view of the Israeli-Syrian agreement was completely different from that of Rabin. . . . He did not regard security as the key issue. . . . In keeping with his overall view, the new prime minister believed that the way to establish a lasting peace was to create a network of joint economic interests and to enhance the prosperity of Syria itself. . . . For this reason Peres also did not believe in delegating senior military personnel to engage in the peace talks."[26]

In fact, the alternative approach adopted by Peres served to weaken somewhat the element of self-reliance in Israel's security culture. While this element had always been one of the basic characteristics of Israel's security doctrine, it was partially replaced in the alternative approach by broad regional security arrangements, international partnerships and alliances, the involvement of international forces, defense pacts, and even the establishment of a regional security regime.[27]

A striking expression of the difference between these two approaches can be seen in the speeches delivered by Yitzhak Rabin and Shimon Peres at a reception hosted by the Israeli delegation in Stockholm on December 9, 1994, on the eve of the Nobel Peace Prize ceremony. Peres spoke of peace as the continuation of a path taken in ancient times. Morality, namely a commitment and willingness to observe the moral imperatives of Judaism, is what determined more than anything the fate of the Jewish people, he said. This meant that the Jew has to oppose not only enslavement of his own people, but he also has to avoid conquering another people. In his mind, their trip to Oslo validated that the Israeli leadership had fulfilled its historical duty according to the Jewish tradition and thus served the interests of future generations. Rabin, in contrast, spoke of the agreement with the Palestinians in concrete, pragmatic, and tactical terms: "The art of negotiation requires understanding of when to yield and when not to yield."[28] The fact that these speeches were delivered in a small and closed forum and were not for publication made them particularly authentic.

If Peres and Rabin personify the two approaches of the second generation of Israeli leaders (with the founding fathers and mothers, Ben-Gurion, Meir, and Begin, composing the first generation), Barak and Beilin represent the differences in the third. As with Peres and Rabin, their attitudes toward peace and their reasons for wanting to achieve it reflect these differences. As Henry Kissinger describes, Barak saw the long-range danger to Israel as coming from guerilla war and weapons of mass destruction. According to Kissinger, Barak believed that "to resist both, Israel required American political support, guaranteed access to American intelligence, and advanced military technology" and that this "was achievable only so long as Israel was perceived as a reliable partner of America's quest for peace in the region."[29] Beilin, on the other hand, stated that he wished to achieve peace so that Israel might be able to live under normal conditions, where basic survival would not have to be at the top of the national agenda. Only then, he said, could Israel fulfill its destiny "of using the sense of mission that has existed for so many years in Israeli society to improve us and the world."[30]

The Military's Attitude toward Territory

An important element of Israel's security culture, which also is key in the IDF's institutional thinking, is the issue of territory. The IDF never supported the idea of Greater Israel. Nor did it subscribe to the political view that was once shared by the Herut Party on the Right and Ahdut Ha'avoda on the Left, both of which opposed the Partition Plan and saw the entire Land of Israel as the site for establishing a national home for the Jewish people. Indeed, after the United States and the Soviet Union pressured Israel in 1957 to withdraw from the Sinai peninsula, which it had conquered in the Sinai Campaign a year earlier, the IDF came to share the political-military consensus that the armistice lines of 1949 should be the future borders of the state of Israel.

The IDF's security doctrine accepted the territorial status quo as a given. Conquering and occupying an area for its own sake was not included in the IDF's war aims. Those who formulated Israel's national-security doctrine saw the occupied area as a by-product of war. They also viewed it as temporary, because world opinion would not condone it and because it would increase the Arab motivation to fight Israel. In Israel's security doctrine, the conquering of territory was designed to give Israel "a diplomatic and military advantage and a bargaining card for the stage of negotiations over the settlement after the war."[31]

Israel's view of itself as free of all territorial ambitions was also reinforced by an approach that was defined as offensive at the tactical level but defensive at the strategic level. Accordingly, the conquest of territory was intended primarily to solve Israel's problem of having a lack of strategic depth and to provide it with a space for exploiting the superiority of its striking force, where it could conduct mobile and armored warfare. But this, too, was a tactical goal. The trainees in IDF officer courses learned that Israel had no offensive strategic goals and no intention of initiating war.[32]

However, a careful examination of the IDF attitude toward territory reveals a more complex picture. First, in the military, as in civil society, there were some in the 1950s who hoped that one day the "fatal error" of the War of Independence, caused by Ben-Gurion's decision not to capture the entire area of the West Bank, would be corrected. Also, some IDF officers regarded settlement in the territories conquered in 1967 as a continuation of the fulfillment of the Zionist vision, as CGS Gur stated in the General Staff meeting described earlier. Second, an attempt at an objective assessment that does not read the doctrine and the written theory but simply examines the activity on the ground results in findings that might arouse skepticism about the professed territorial approach of the IDF. Every war that the IDF has fought since the War of Independence has ended with Israel controlling broader areas than it had before. And after each war, when Israel was called upon to withdraw from those territories, the IDF's General Staff strongly opposed doing so. Moreover, during the course of the wars it was often the military that dictated the final location lines of the forces, always pushing forward. In the Six Day War, for example, the officers decided to reach the shoreline of the Suez Canal, the banks of the Jordan, and the "Purple Line" (the cease-fire line) in the Golan Heights, while the political echelon only gave its approval post factum in a number of cases.

It may be that such operations were not planned in advance out of an ideological conviction, but were motivated by the IDF's professional goal and desire to win in battle. However, it is the result that counts. A victory in battle is measured by the destruction of the enemy's war machine and the conquering of its territories. Therefore, every time the IDF went to war it sought to maximize its military success in these two areas. The territory conquered was presented to the political leaders as a bargaining chip to be used in negotiating for a political accommodation. But, at the same time, the IDF made its own position very clear: it was of supreme importance to hold on to territories or part of them, as they granted security advantages by providing strategic depth, gave the IDF areas in which to deploy in case of a future attack, and brought the IDF closer to the enemy's highly populated areas.

Even Tal admitted, "Control of the territory conquered improves the IDF's strategic position. On the one hand, it gives Israel more defensive depth, and on the other hand, it enhances the IDF's deterrent power, since it is positioned closer to strategic targets of the enemy, increasing the threat to them."[33] During the period of euphoria between 1967 and 1973, there were even some who asserted that the territories were needed in order to provide the IDF, particularly the air force, with space for training and maneuvers. The military did not take into account that holding on to these territories would damage Israel and establish its image as an expansionist power. Those who saw themselves as security optimizers were invariably perceived by the other side as power optimizers, particularly as the number of settlements began to rise.

As is known to other settler societies, the establishment of settlements aids in territorial defense. For this reason, after 1948 the military helped to establish hundreds of agricultural settlements along the border through Nahal groups, "pioneering fighting youth," who wished to live in kibbutzim. For exactly the same reason, the IDF helped to set up Israeli settlements in the West Bank and the Gaza Strip after the Six Day War. This strategy began with what Rabin described as "security settlements," but it soon accelerated and continued with "political settlements" deep in the midst of populated Palestinian territories. Only later did the IDF's significant role in assisting these illegal outposts become clear.[34]

The IDF support of what was called in the early days of the Zionist lexicon "conquering the land" came up in one of the meetings of the General Staff immediately after the Six Day War. While some in the General Staff thought that Israel should return the occupied territories at once in order to allow for the establishment of a Palestinian state, others recommended strengthening Israel's hold on the territories. This is how Maj. Gen. Ariel Sharon expressed it: "These boundaries are not indeed peace borders . . . but they are borders that prevent war [and] destruction. . . . Today we are in an ideal position [because] there will be no normalization for decades. . . . The borders we must hold on to are the present borders, with no withdrawal, without any agreement that does not guarantee us total military control over the territory. That obviously means hold on to the present situation." Sharon also provided his opinion of the proper relationship between the military and civilian echelons: "We, the generals, have every right not only to express our opinions but also to influence opinion. What will largely dictate public opinion in Israel is the attitude of the IDF."[35] No wonder, when he finally took off his uniform and became a politician, he would become known as the father of Jewish settlement in Judea, Samaria, and the Gaza Strip.

The IDF's attitudes regarding the territorial issue go beyond the narrow sphere of security and extend to Zionist ideology. Ever since the beginning of the Zionist enterprise in Israel, the belief prevailed that, in the end, when the boundaries of the Jewish territory, and later the state, were set, they would follow the borders of the Jewish settlements. This view, which had become a national ethos in the 1920s in Tel Hay in Galilee, meant that territories were not seized just to serve as a bargaining tool for political negotiations but also to determine the shape of the future boundaries. The larger the territory occupied and the more stable the Jewish presence in it, it was believed, the greater the chance that it would remain within the borders of the state when the time came for a peace agreement. In fact, the formulas for peace presented by President Clinton and President Bush supported this perception.

Occupation Corrupts

Another matter that influenced the IDF's attitudes regarding the Palestinians was the ongoing occupation. For the IDF, an occupying force for well over a generation, it was hard to suddenly relate to the Palestinians as equal partners once the peace process began. The long occupation had created a sense of lordship, and the officers found it difficult to change its system of operating, to "change the diskette," as one of the participants in the Israeli-Palestinian talks described it.

Dennis Ross, an experienced U.S. diplomat who for years had been involved in Israeli-Palestinian negotiations, described the situation: "Even in the advanced stages of the negotiations, when the atmosphere was very positive, it was very difficult for the Israelis to relinquish the control mindset that had developed in them as a consequence of administering the territories for so long."[36] This is also what Uri Savir observed when, in the summer of 1995, the staff of the Civil Administration had difficulty removing restrictions they had imposed on the Palestinians and transferring administrative authority to the Palestinian Authority:

> Some of these restrictions stemmed from justified security needs, but most of them were products of the habits of a growing bureaucratic monster fed by an endless budget. In the course of the twenty-seven years of occupation almost every third Palestinian in the territories had at some time or another been imprisoned or detained, and the population as a whole had suffered great humiliation at our hands. Some of the wounds of that period may never heal. Now those who had ruled over

the Palestinians were asked to transfer their authority to their "subjects," and this caused them extreme distress, both conceptual and emotional. When we terminated the occupation . . . there were those among our people who found it very difficult to change.[37]

The behavior of the military was influenced not only by attitudes formed in the meetings of the General Staff or by the dynamics between Israeli and Palestinian negotiators but also to a very large extent by the experiences of soldiers and officers in the field. This influence was prevalent both in the IDF's deliberate actions, such as when executing policy decisions, and in the often troubling spontaneous behavior of its soldiers and officers. The sense of superiority that develops in an occupying army, the insensitivity of a bureaucratic machine that is not subject to public supervision, the soldiers' physical fear for their lives, and even the opportunities for release by people with questionable personalities all left their mark on the behavior of the military. Power corrupts, said Lord Acton, and absolute power—such as military rule over a foreign powerless people—corrupts absolutely.

Daily delays and humiliations in passing through roadblocks were not only the lot of Palestinians in the territories but also of their leaders with VIP cards, who were theoretically supposed to move without hindrance. The humiliation of these leaders on their way to political meetings often ruined the atmosphere around the bargaining table, as some members of the Palestinian team often complained.[38] "Perhaps because we were the first occupier in history who felt as if they were the occupied, our self-image as a humane society and as an eternal victim of history, coupled with the Arab antagonism, blinded us to what was happening in the territories," wrote Savir, adding, "It is always possible to explain evil behavior toward the Palestinians as a function of the fear of terrorism—and not without reason. But part of this behavior comes from deeper erosion of norms in human relations. Very few understood that if we did not treat the Palestinians with respect, as equals, across the whole range of interactions, we would pay for it in areas where there was mutual dependence of the two sides, particularly in security."[39]

However, among the Israelis who took part in the talks, as among IDF officers in general, there were many who could not be included in Lord Acton's category of "corrupt." Their behavior was in fact the reverse.

For instance, Maj. Gen. Ya'akov Orr was described in the IDF as someone "who was ready to lie on the IDF roadblocks in order to allow the gas
tankers to enter the Gaza Strip in the middle of the intifada and ease the
suffering of the civilian population."[40] No wonder his fellow officers called
him the "ambassador of Palestine on the General Staff." He explained his
position by stating, "I don't agree with the thesis of 'Let's squeeze a bit
more and they'll give in.'"[41]

In fact, over the course of the negotiations, IDF officers showed
sensitivity toward Palestinian attitudes in many instances, revealing an
openness in their thinking and a needed flexibility to further the negotiations. For example, Gilead Sher testified that Brig. Gen. Gadi Eisencott,
Prime Minister Barak's military secretary, "tirelessly urged Barak to make
more use of the mediating endeavors of Shahak and Ginnosar."[42] Ami
Ayalon's efforts since the summer of 2001 should be seen in the same
way, as should the work and activities of many others.

So what conclusions should be derived from this analysis? The common perception of there being a distinction between the military mind and
the civilian mind is an oversimplification that does not correspond to
Israel's reality. The political-military partnership that exists in Israel has
strengthened the ability of the security culture and diplomatic culture to
coexist, whereby each exerts a hold on civilians and those in uniform.
However, despite the emergence of the peace era, the security-culture
school remained dominant, and when institutional military conservatism—
combined with the desire of military officers to safeguard the military's
institutional interests—was added to that culture, the resultant foreign
policy did not include appropriate conditions for historic reconciliation
and compromise. Indeed, the characteristics of the Israeli security culture
and their negative implications were evident both at the dramatic Camp
David summit in 2000 and throughout the intifada.

This statement, however, does not imply that the Israeli side was
primarily responsible for the failure of the peace talks and the outbreak of
the intifada. The Palestinians' share of the blame for these two events is
far greater than that of the Israelis. Though reasons for the failure of
Camp David and the outbreak of the intifada necessitate further study,
this book does not offer a detailed description or analysis of the Palestinian dynamic. Rather, my focus is on only the Israeli dimension.

15

Camp David and the Intifada— What Went Wrong?

The Security Culture at Camp David

The security-culture perspective that is characteristic of the Israeli political-military elite surfaced throughout the peace negotiations of the 1990s. This mindset—though not the prime cause—contributed to the unhappy end of the Camp David summit in July 2000, an event that brought to a halt a decade of negotiations and ushered in an era of dreadful violence with the second intifada. While the records of the Camp David negotiations constitute one of the more compelling *Rashomon*-like narratives in contemporary international relations literature, what adds to the riddle of why they collapsed is that the detailed personal memoirs, reflections, and assessments of the negotiations subsequently offered by many of the participants failed to offer any clarity on events there,[1] as one account conflicted with the next. In the words of U.S. diplomat Aaron David Miller, "there were 12 people at Camp David 2, and so far there have been at least 10 different versions of what happened there; a perfect case study in post-modernism."[2]

Debate about the causes of the Camp David negotiations' failure started shortly after the end of the summit and became more intense following the outbreak of the intifada. The question on everyone's mind was, "What went wrong?" Members of the Israeli, Palestinian, and U.S. negotiating teams, as well as statesmen and scholars, took part in these debates. While the Israeli delegation included both military personnel and civilians, representing both the security culture and diplomatic culture, about two-thirds of the delegation were officers, former officers, and former ISA personnel. The delegation's tone was set by Prime Minister Barak, an erudite and brave man with a broad political worldview and sharp intellect who is himself a typical product of Israel's security culture. Itamar Rabinovich, former Israeli ambassador to the United States and a participant-observer of the peace process, divided the various narratives of what went wrong at Camp David into four versions.

The first version, called by Rabinovich the "orthodox version," was best presented by Barak, Clinton, and others, who totally blamed Arafat for the failure of the negotiations, emphasizing his refusal to respond to Barak's "generous offer," the most far-reaching proposal ever extended to the Palestinians by any Israeli prime minister. Meanwhile, the "revisionist version," according to Rabinovich, was initially presented by Robert Malley, a member of the U.S. delegation, and by Hussein Agha, a Palestinian. This version, which cast the Palestinian position in a more positive light, held that Israel and its policies were mainly responsible for the failure of Camp David and criticized the U.S. management of the negotiations. Rabinovich defined the third version as "determinist," which was presented in Israel by Maj. Gen. Amos Gilead and in the United States by people such as Norman Podhoretz. According to this hard-line version, there was no chance from the start of reaching an accord, and there would be no chance in the future due to the Palestinian stand that denied and would continue to deny Israel's right to exist. The determist and the orthodox versions encouraged the widespread belief in Israel that the state had no partner for negotiations. The fourth and final interpretation offered by some participants and observers is known as the "eclectic version," reflected, among other places, in the books of Gilead Sher, Yossi Beilin, and Menachem Klein; this perspective avoids the deterministic interpretations of the other three versions. Rabinovich himself also offered an integrative explanation in answer to the question, "What went wrong?"

While the causes of the failure of the negotiations merit a profound analysis, for the present study, the relevant questions from Camp David relate to the tension between Israel's security and diplomatic worlds. How was the military presence in the Israeli delegation manifested? Were there behavioral differences between the military personnel and the civilian members of the delegation? And, if so, in what way were these differences expressed? A critical reading of the voluminous publications on the summit and the numerous interviews I conducted with most of the Israeli participants and many non-Israeli delegates led me to the following conclusions.

First, the members of the Israeli delegation varied in their attitudes regarding the Palestinian positions and in their willingness to recognize those positions. Therefore, one may place the Israeli negotiators on a scale, ranging from hard-liner to accommodationist, according to their positions on different issues and their negotiation styles. In the former group were those who emphasized strict elements of security (such as secure borders and the presence of Israeli military bases in Palestine) and those who also underlined other matters (such as sovereignty over the holy sites in Jerusalem and other symbolic issues). In the latter group were those who, to varying degrees, were willing to listen to the Palestinian point of view, modify their own original positions during the negotiations, and consider the different compromises suggested by the U.S. brokers. Though in reality all these approaches should be seen as part of a continuum, for now it is simpler to deal with them as two opposing stands—that of the hard-liner and that of the accommodationist.

Second, the school to which a member belonged was completely independent of his profession; each of the two positions was represented by the full range of attendees: acting officers, former military personnel, and civilians. The stands articulated by the various participants during the negotiations, their arguments, their openness toward the positions of the other side, and their willingness to change their original points of view were not specific to any one profile. Former minister Meridor, for example, was a civilian representing the hard-liners, while former CGS Shahak clearly belonged to the accommodationists.

Third, the centrality of Barak to the Israeli delegation (whose position was analogous to Arafat on the Palestinian side) and the tone he set throughout the negotiations deeply impacted its outcome. The orthodox version of "what went wrong" was widely accepted in Israel, as well as outside the state, largely because of the successful media spin carried out by Barak, with Clinton's assistance. According to this narrative, Barak reached out toward the Palestinians more than any other prime minister before him; he was willing to renounce more than 90 percent of the territories and to accept the partition of Jerusalem. Arafat, meanwhile, rejected every

Israeli suggestion and did not extend any concrete counteroffers. In other words, Barak was seen as the follower of Rabin, the general who became a soldier in the army of peace, and perhaps even surpassed Rabin when he bravely dared to challenge fundamental positions held by Israel since 1967. On the surface, his actions represented the exact opposite of what one might expect from a member of Israel's security culture.

Although this description is not groundless, a deeper examination of Barak's stands, of his rationalizations, and even more so of his performance, behavior, and management of the negotiations, reveals a number of characteristics that do not fully align with the accommodationist school. True, Barak's positions were based on compromise, particularly when compared to Arafat's intransigence, but he behaved in the typical fashion of an adherent of the security culture. This was obvious from the first day of the summit meeting, as was reflected in the initial images broadcast from Camp David.

In the first media clip from the negotiations, Clinton, Barak, and Arafat are seen walking toward one of the cabins on the ranch. Clinton enters first, and then Arafat and Barak extend their hands forward, politely inviting each other to step in next. It should not be forgotten that this polite gesture was carried out by the prime minister of an occupying state and the leader of the occupied people. However, those sensitive to symbolic politics and familiar with the analysis of cultural texts could not avoid noticing the events that followed. Each of the two leaders insisted, out of politeness, that the other enter first; neither of them stepped forward. At a certain point, Barak grabbed Arafat's arm with one hand, placed his other hand on Arafat's back, and pushed him in, while the two of them laughed and appeared playful. On first glance, one might be inclined to believe Barak gave Arafat the honor of entering first. But, in effect, he forced him to enter, even using physical force to do so. The subtext of this incident underscored the nature of their relationship. As Arafat would later complain to Madeleine Albright, "Barak treated me like a slave."[3]

To be sure, for a process to be successful, chemistry and friendship among leaders are not sine qua nons. A readiness to take risks, to stretch things to the limit, and to sell the agreement to the respective constituencies are more important. However, the allegedly playful event on the first day of the negotiations reflected the state of affairs throughout the entire summit. One must keep in mind that Arafat had initially rejected this meeting and was only there because he had been forced to participate. He was sure that the United States and Israel would trick him, and he had therefore preferred a postponement of the summit, stating that conditions were not ripe. Indeed, hindsight showed that not enough preparations had been made for the meeting, either by the United States or by Israel. The gap between the Israelis and the Palestinians was still too wide and too many issues were still unresolved when Arafat was compelled to take part at Camp David. Under these circumstances, Barak's demand to conclude the summit with an agreement that would put an end to one hundred years of conflict was not realistic. Furthermore, no follow-up mechanisms or contingency plans had been prepared in case the talks collapsed, even though many knew there was a real probability that failure would lead to a resumption of hostilities and violence.

It is true that Barak showed a willingness to compromise and was courageous in presenting positions that deviated from long-standing Israeli principles. On the subject of Jerusalem, for instance, the Israeli delegation presented no less than twenty-six proposals. Arafat's historic mistake was that he rejected Israeli offers and did not propose alternative ones instead. But Barak's approach to the negotiations also contributed to the failure of the talks. He saw the summit as decisive, and his message to Arafat was that if both sides did not come to an agreement then they never would. Therefore Barak pressured Arafat to make a final decision on the termination of the dispute, without making any effort to understand Arafat himself or the constraints under which he acted. If Barak had done so, he would have understood that Arafat might be able to accept another interim solution, even a solution to the problem of 1967, but not to the problem of 1948–49, something to which the PLO bodies had never acceded and had never authorized. But Barak, confident of his own boundless abilities, thought he could convince or coerce his interlocutor to accept the deal. So when Arafat rejected his "termination of the dispute" formula, Barak interpreted this as an unwillingness on Arafat's part to make a historic decision and declared that this proved Gilead's suspicions correct.[4] Barak could have made progress at Camp David if he had been willing to accept something short of a final peace treaty. But without meeting face to face with Arafat and without a profound and genuine readiness on his part for a joint move based on mutual agreement, it was impossible to do so.

After the failure of the talks, many were disappointed with Barak, but some had foreseen what would transpire. Shlomo Ben-Ami relates in his diary how in June he asked Barak "to develop a more personal and empathetic approach toward Arafat."[5] Barak, as usual, listened attentively but did nothing about it. After the talks, Ben-Ami concluded, "Barak really did have severe personality defects, which led to his downfall in the end. He expected his interlocutors to fall in with his wishes, according to the scenario that he had prepared for himself and for them, and when this did not happen he tended to lose his composure, to entrench himself deeply in his positions, thus, in effect, helping to block the dynamics of negotiation."[6] Barak's unwillingness to conduct open and intimate talks with Arafat, his failure to establish mutual trust, and above all his ignoring of Arafat's needs, typified the working style of the security-culture school, or, as Klieman would define it, the national-security approach. Consider Klieman's analysis of Israeli negotiating culture:

> Applying many of the principles of IDF warfare to bargaining, soldiers in mufti are prone to treating diplomatic talks as analogous to wars of attrition and conducting them according to one of two models: either as a game of waiting out the opponent, or as a lightning offensive aimed at breaking the back of resistance. If the former, then the objective is to wear down one's adversary in a battle of wills through such stratagems as looking for the tactical high ground, refusing to budge, and fighting for every inch and centimeter by wrangling over even seemingly trivial technical details. If the latter, then the enemy's bargaining position is best taken by storm by using intimidation and bluff. Apply mounting pressure, if warranted, by constantly devising and tabling fresh counter-proposals. Insist on *quid pro quo*. Outsmart the opponent by probing for openings, soft spots, and weakness. Bring constant pressure to bear. Present maximum demands in the knowledge that one can always back down and offer concessions; especially symbolic ones, further along the negotiation. . . . The basic inclination is to assume neither goodwill nor magnanimity on the part of the Arab opponents.[7]

Theoretical concepts articulated by researchers of the conflict resolution school can further clarify the problem with Barak's negotiating style at Camp David. According to Louis Kriesberg, reconciliation as a means of resolving conflicts requires building mutual trust based on a common set of values and dealing with each side's sense of justice.[8] According to this conception, it is possible to promote a peace process only if the two adversaries erase feelings of contempt and disrespect, develop an understanding of the other side's suffering and demands for justice, build mutual trust, believe in each other, and agree on a set of common values.[9] Those in Israel who subscribed to the diplomatic approach expressed these elements of reconciliation, but they were a minority; the majority adhered to the ideas of the security culture.

In a nation facing continuous conflict, and in a military that is constantly fighting, sometimes against suicidal terrorists, it is hard for the above-mentioned elements of reconciliation to develop. It may be that Israeli society deserves praise for the fact that, despite the dominance of the security culture, a relatively large group of decision makers were ready for reconciliation with the Palestinians. However, it is clear that those with this inclination faced heavy pressure from different cultural agents. Consider, for example, Rabin's body language during the ceremony marking the mutual recognition of Israel and the PLO on the lawn of the White House in Washington, D.C., in 1993, when he and Arafat famously shook hands. Many Israeli viewers who watched the event concluded that Rabin's gestures reflected the doubt and suspicion accompanying the process of allying oneself with an individual who not long before had been considered a duplicitous enemy. Indeed, footage from the event shows Rabin standing far from Arafat, not moving any closer to him for the handshake. Then, Rabin hastily reaches out his hand, almost hesitating midway; the handshake itself looks loose. Rabin was clearly disconcerted by the physical contact with Arafat, which comes across in his facial expression as well.[10]

Just as Rabin's manner in this instance provided some insight into his internal state, so too did Barak's behavior toward Arafat at Camp David reflect his own personal distrust, suspicion, and disapproval of the Palestinian leader. So while it is worth conducting a detailed analysis of the Israeli and Palestinian positions in the Camp David negotiations to determine what went wrong, these positions are only one element of the entire interaction. The security culture that was demonstrated so clearly in Barak's conduct also contributed to the failure of Camp David. Barak reflected the patronizing ways of the strong, who try to dictate a whole process, presenting his offers in a take-it-or-leave-it manner (though, in fact, he did withdraw from original positions throughout the negotiations). Further, he used a go-for-broke strategy, not understanding that

Arafat could not conclude a final deal. His domineering and patronizing behavior and his inability to understand the other side's needs and limitations are characteristic of those in the security culture, and such traits were an obstacle to Barak's solving the long-lasting conflict and reaching an agreement. In his memoirs published in 2004, Clinton alluded to this when he described Barak's "brusque bullheadedness":

> [Barak] was brilliant and brave and he was willing to go a long way on Jerusalem and on territory. But he had a hard time listening to people who did not see things the way he did, and his way of doing things was diametrically opposed to honored customs among the Arabs with whom he'd dealt. Barak wanted others to wait until he decided the time was right, then, when he made his best offer, he expected it to be accepted as self-evidently a good deal. His negotiating partners wanted trust-building courtesies and conversations and lots of bargaining. The culture clash made my team's job harder.[11]

While Clinton reflected on the cultural clash between the Palestinians and the Israelis, he could have just as easily commented on the culture clash that also persisted among Israelis throughout the 1990s. Members of the Israeli delegations to the negotiations who tried to show desire for reconciliation, to express empathy for the Palestinian feeling of historic injustice, and to establish mutual respect and trust, were perceived as weak, naive, and unsophisticated negotiators. Although taking even a few measures to build trust inspires the adversary to try to do the same, adherents of the security culture decried such measures, arguing that they strengthened the importunity, obstinacy, and self-confidence of the other side and would cause them to raise their demands.

Aaron David Miller addressed this very issue, arguing that "Israel's peace accords with Egypt as well as with Jordan succeeded due to the fact that they were based on a parity of interests and not on a balance of power. This was the mistake the Israelis made in regard to the Palestinians. The Israelis thought about power instead of thinking about interests. The Palestinians, however, were also stricken by the same line of thought."[12] Indeed, in the final analysis, the basic Palestinian attitude, which is at the heart of the difficulty of bringing the Israeli-Palestinian conflict to an end, also found expression at Camp David. Even Rob Malley, who wrote the most sympathetic version of the Palestinian position regarding Camp David, said that the collapse was a question of "the Palestinians' inability to accept

Israel's moral legitimacy."[13] In particular, this attitude was manifested in Arafat's total inflexibility during the summit. But, ultimately, the security culture that was reflected at the negotiation table in Camp David came to be even more intensely expressed in the battle zone of the second intifada, which broke out three months later.

The IDF's Behavior during the Intifada

Just as there are different opinions regarding who is to blame for the failure of Camp David, there are also disagreements over several questions regarding the intifada. One of them relates to the specific role of Arafat. Was the intifada a popular uprising carried out by an occupied and suppressed people or a violent process orchestrated from above by the Palestinian leadership?

Immediately after the intifada's outbreak in September 2002, a clear, sharp, and unequivocal conception took root among the Israeli public: Arafat had planned the intifada, gave the directive that launched it, and was the one who orchestrated it. This idea was eagerly embraced by the majority of Israelis, since it aligned completely with the dominant belief about the reason for the failure of the Camp David talks. Indeed, Gilead had predicted the outbreak of violence even before the Camp David summit collapsed.

Although Barak had dismissed Gilead's vision in June, he adopted it eagerly in September. On numerous occasions after his return from Camp David, Barak explained that he had gone there with the idea that he would either reach an agreement or expose Arafat's true self—that is, expose him as someone who had no intention of ever making peace with Israel. Barak believed that at the summit he did, in fact, reveal Arafat's true intentions. But might it not also be argued that by imputing to Arafat the planning and management of violence, Barak had a plausible explanation for the failure of the talks, thereby clearing himself of any trace of shared responsibility for their undoing?

Barak's explanation of Arafat's behavior was, naturally, acceptable to the nationalist camp and to its leader, Sharon. This was what they had been asserting throughout the Oslo process. And thus it happened that the political leadership—both the government and the opposition—and the military leadership shared the same view. They sold it to the media, and the public bought it completely. This is significant not only for understanding the past but also for understanding the future. In the minds of these Israelis, if what they were seeing was the true Arafat, and this was his policy, they must not negotiate with him at all. As a saying that took root in Israel made plain, "There is no one to talk to." This idea was further legitimized by the professional opinions of the experts, in other words, the military leadership—the CGS, the deputy CGS, and other senior staff officers; they based their explanations on Gilead's assessments. In the end, the confidence crisis in relations with the Palestinians became deeper than ever.

During the first two years of the intifada, no dissenting voice to the above narrative was heard. But after the intifada had taken a heavy toll and many hundreds were dead, and after an alternative to the hegemonic version of what went wrong at Camp David came to light, a second explanation about what caused the intifada to break out also began to circulate among the members of the political class. Since the violent outbreak, there had actually been a few people, mainly researchers of Palestinian society, who believed that the intifada was not planned by the Palestinian leadership at all but, in fact, was a popular uprising: "It broke out spontaneously without preparation, without planning, and without organization."[14] It erupted from below, they believed, and was generated by events occurring within Palestinian society—Islamic radicalization, an economic crisis, widespread unemployment, and daily suffering under closures, curfews, and other expressions of the yoke of Israeli occupation. These scholars further argued that the early stages of the intifada were, to some degree, a protest against both the corrupt Palestinian Authority and Arafat himself. This implied that Arafat's response to the intifada was reactive. He supported the movement precisely because he did not want to lose any more public support. He also knew that by riding this public wave, he could possibly induce Israel to be more flexible in its position toward the Palestinians.

According to this interpretation, Arafat had not abandoned the path of a political resolution to the conflict and did not use the peace process to camouflage his intentions to destroy the state of Israel. He remained faithful to the idea of two states for two peoples. The violence simply served as another method for furthering his strategic aim of reaching a settlement. This meant that there really was someone to talk to.

What became clear in 2002, though few paid attention to it, was that this explanation had supporters within the military itself, particularly within the top echelons of the MID.[15] It was supported not only by Col. Ephraim Lavie, head of the Palestinian desk, but also by the head of the MID, Maj. Gen. Amos Malka. In fact, prior to the Camp David summit, Malka had warned the prime minister that Arafat was not ready for the move Barak was planning. But Malka's explanation differed from that of Gilead. According to Malka, it was not that Arafat did not want a settlement and preferred violence. Rather, he believed Arafat could not accept Barak's ultimatum that the settlement would put an end to Palestinian demands on Israel. Malka did maintain, however, that by applying pressure Barak could make diplomatic gains.[16]

Thus, the operative conclusion of this alternative conception is that notwithstanding the conflagration and violence, there was someone to talk to and there was something to talk about. The intifada was not an overt expression of the Palestinians' original plan to destroy Israel, nor was it a change of direction and a retreat from the peace process back to the violent struggle. It was the continuation of negotiations by other means. Hence, Israel too should have and could have proceeded on a dual course, reacting to violence but at the same time continuing diplomatic negotiations in search of an agreed solution.

Why did the military adopt the position of Gilead rather than that of Malka and Lavie? Why were the members of the political class ignorant for such a long time of the fact that there was another viewpoint in the military apart from the one presented by Gilead? And why did the Israeli public know nothing of this internal division until the summer of 2004, when it was exposed in a series of articles in *Ha'aretz*?[17] The answers to these questions are related to the nature and workings of the political-military partnership and particularly to the military's mode of influence on civilian decision makers.

From the beginning of the peace process, successive heads of the MID research division were principal proponents of the hard-line. Within military ranks, Amidror, Gilead, and Joseph Kopervasser were among the most skeptical about the peace process and the most suspicious of Arafat. Gilead, a knowledgeable and articulate officer who is also highly opinionated, assertive, and determined, gained a status in Israel's political community that Malka had not managed to achieve.[18] This partly stemmed from the fact that Malka, though head of the MID, lacked the experience of Gilead. But Gilead's victory over Malka within the military, and therefore also in the political corridors, was not just a matter of personality or experience. Gilead was also able to influence the top brass of the military because of the previously mentioned structural characteristics of the military, namely, its conservatism, its tendency to plan according to worst-case scenarios, and its reluctance to take risks. Since 1996, MID research division assessments had been persuading the IDF to prepare for a violent clash with the Palestinians. Just prior to Camp David, the belief in an imminent violent clash intensified because of the growing currency of another assessment. This assessment ascertained that the Palestinian Authority would unilaterally declare a Palestinian state if no agreement was reached, which would lead to a violent confrontation between Palestinian security forces and the IDF. In fact, the very preparations for such a possible confrontation predisposed the top military brass to share this position, thereby marginalizing every other view of the situation.

While the IDF was responsible for military operations, keeping a close watch on the Palestinian leadership, it remained oblivious to other processes—social, economic, and even political. For example, the IDF was not sufficiently attentive or sensitive to the prevalent mood among the younger generation of PLO leaders who were discouraged by the corruption in the Palestinian Authority and at odds with its veteran leadership, particularly Arafat, and his conciliatory policy toward Israel. Further, most military leaders failed to hear complaints among Palestinians that the Oslo Accords had not brought about any improvement in their situation and criticisms that Israel had not honored its agreements. As Brig. Gen. Mike Herzog, military secretary to the defense minister, stated, "If you want to make an in-depth assessment, you also have to know the society, its state of mind, the poetry, the literature, not just what happens in the leadership and the security mechanisms. I think that all the intelligence systems in Israel have the same problem and none of them goes deeply into the question of what is truly happening in the Palestinian mind. In this we are definitely lacking."[19]

And thus it happened that the IDF continued, and even stepped up, its preparations for a violent encounter with the Palestinian Authority. It was at this stage that the top military brass determined that in this confrontation the IDF would have to mold the Palestinian consciousness, so the Palestinians would recognize that they would get nothing from Israel through violence. The military's view dominated, but it suffered from collective stereotyping and groupthink, leaving no room for doubt and completely overshadowing any dissenting view. For example, in April 2003 Maj. Yaron Nir, a young deputy commander in the IDF School for Leadership Development, published an article in *Maarchot,* in which, like the child in the well-known fable "The Emperor's New Clothes," he asked the questions that no one had had the courage to ask: Is it correct to present the Palestinian stand as monolithic? Doesn't the extensive research literature on international relations warn of the tendency to see the adversary as acting in greater unison than it does in reality? Why do we ignore the abundant evidence for the existence of a variety of opinions among the Palestinians and instead focus just on those that call for Israel's annihilation? Does not the fact that in Israel itself there is a new interpretation of events on which there was no debate in the past—here he referred to the new historians' iconoclastic approach to the Zionist narrative—justify a more hesitant, skeptical, and diversified approach to Palestinian society? But voices such as Nir's were quickly marginalized.[20]

The hegemonic viewpoint remained the same, despite the fact that even Avi Dichter, as head of the ISA, disagreed with it. Dichter, who as ISA head knew more about the ins and outs of the Palestinian population than anyone else, dismissed the MID research division's view and presented a different interpretation of events. He argued that Arafat had no overall plan at all but acted according to the constraints of the moment: "Arafat is a survivor type who reacts to events, not a leader who advances according to a preconceived plan."[21] But, as time passed, due to the ongoing escalation of the violence and the strong influence of the IDF, the ISA "surrendered to the power of the IDF and to the extreme stress caused by its preventative role, leaving the military to be the sole factor determining the Israeli narrative in regard to the true state of events."[22]

Meanwhile, the manner in which the IDF influenced political perceptions of the Palestinians is illustrated by the following case. During Operation Defensive Shield, many PA documents were confiscated by the IDF. A few select ones, found in Arafat's headquarters in Ramallah, were handed to a *Yedioth Ahronoth* journalist, Ronen Bergman, an IDF confidant who later published a book titled *Authority Given.*[23] In that book, he explained how Arafat had conceived a well-organized scheme to use the peace process in order to continue the violent confrontation with Israel under easier circumstances, and how he used his control over the Palestinian Authority to build underground militias to engage in the fighting. This led Danny Rubinstein, an expert on Palestinian affairs, to comment: "This is a kind of distorted presentation of things, based mainly on the partial and tendentious information provided by the Israeli MID, thus turning Bergman into a propaganda channel. An examination of the events leading to the outbreak of the Intifada from a Palestinian point of view reveals a completely different story."[24] Clearly, even if the Palestinians had started the cycle of violence, the IDF's security culture contributed to its continuation. The policy of the IDF fueled the flames, contributing to a vicious cycle of violence right from the first stage of the intifada.

This argument by no means diminishes the Palestinians' responsibility for the outbreak of the intifada, but a more restrained response on the part of the IDF, one that did not emanate from the security culture, might have lowered the flames and made it easier to contain the intifada at a lower price.[25] If another approach had been adopted, Israeli leaders, by recognizing the mood of the Palestinian population and the limitations on the Palestinian leadership, may have been better positioned to help mobilize Palestinian support for the path to peace.

The narrative of events described here serves to illustrate the character of the military-political partnership. The political echelon was ultimately responsible for the policy pursued by the IDF in the intifada, but the power of the dominant camp and its control of the production and dissemination of the military's security information led the media to completely accept the hegemonic view. Therefore, the Israeli public only heard one position without even knowing any other point of view existed. So powerful was the influence of this hegemony that even when the extent of the division within the MID came to light, it did not lead to any real public debate, except in *Ha'aretz*, which was suspected a priori of having a critical attitude toward Sharon's government and of being "too soft and understanding" of the Palestinian position. In the second half of 2004, the number of articles, interviews, and books criticizing the hegemonic narrative of the intifada proliferated, but because the impact of the hegemonic narrative had been so strong, their influence in changing attitudes was marginal.

The Stages of the Intifada

The second intifada went through four distinct stages. It broke out as a popular uprising, and eventually Palestinian security forces started to deliberately shoot at Israelis. The IDF retaliated with excessive force and succeeded in inflicting much harm on the Palestinian side and reducing the number of Israeli casualties. Its actions also resulted in four negative implications for Israel. The Palestinians' status in international public opinion improved, the idea that the Palestinians were responsible for the failure of the Camp David negotiations was forgotten, and once again the Palestinians were presented as the weak party in the conflict, a victim of Israel's military strength. For example, the image of a Palestinian child throwing a stone at an Israeli tank became an iconic picture of the war. Finally, the numerous Palestinian casualties also increased the Palestinians' motivation and determination to continue the battle.

After about two months, the popular uprising faded and the confrontation became more organized and institutionalized. The radical Islamic organizations fought to prevent the possibility of an agreement, initiating attacks in the territories and also within Israel, including those by suicide bombers. Meanwhile, other Palestinian organizations, such as Fatah and the Tanzim, focused on carrying out violent hits against the IDF and settlers in the occupied territories to force Israel to make concessions.[26] By the second half of 2001, the escalation of violence led Arafat to change his approach to the conflict. Although in the first stage he had tried to continue negotiations with Israel, in the second stage he adopted a more radical stance familiar to militant Palestinian Islamic organizations, one which called for the violent expulsion of all Israelis from the territories. At this time, the IDF was pushing for expansion of military action against all Palestinian organizations, including the Palestinian Authority, without carefully considering that different tactics might be needed for different groups. The guiding principle at this second stage was no longer one of containment but one of leverage. To achieve this goal, the IDF eventually penetrated areas controlled by the Palestinian Authority, though only for specific operations and for short periods of time.

This stage lasted until September 11, 2001, which marked the beginning of a new period in the Israeli-Palestinian confrontation. The

U.S. decision to fight international terror led Arafat to conclude that he must create a clear distinction between the Palestinian struggle and that of groups perceived by the United States as terror organizations, such as al-Qaeda and Hizbullah. Accordingly, Arafat tried for a while to reduce the level of violence but failed to do so because he could no longer control the Islamic Palestinian organizations.[27] Sharon and the military, on the other hand, felt that the war against international terrorism improved Israel's position in the international arena, especially in the United States. They also sensed that Arafat was weakening and therefore extended further operational freedom to the IDF. It was at this stage that Palestinian political leaders also became targets of the IDF. For example, among other actions, the IDF carried out the killing of Ra'ad Carmi, the head of the Tanzim in Tul Karem. In turn, radical Palestinian organizations pressured the Palestinian Authority to react.

As Palestinian violence escalated, the IDF began taking measures directly against the Palestinian Authority with the hopes of crushing the intifada altogether. Palestinian suicide attacks reached their climax on the evening of Passover in March 2002 at the Park Hotel in Netanya; the next day the Israeli military commenced Operation Defensive Shield, entering all the West Bank territories until then under the control of the Palestinian Authority. However, it soon became clear that the operation was a tactical victory but not a strategic one, and the conflict continued.

By December 2002, Palestinian society had grown increasingly dissatisfied with its leadership. Criticism of Arafat and the Palestinian Authority had become more vociferous, particularly with regard to corruption and the high human and material costs of the intifada. There was also a growing willingness to undertake the course set out by the United States for implementing internal reforms in the Palestinian Authority. These pressures led to the establishment of the Abbas government, which declared that it was willing to resume a political exchange with Israel. But Abbas remained in the minority and lacked support, especially from Arafat. This ultimately brought down Abbas's government and put an end to any further attempt among Palestinians to travel down a new path. In fact, at this stage, Ya'alon hoped that Abbas would succeed with his reconciliatory steps, but this hope was not shared by Sharon or Mofaz.

Toward its fourth year, the intifada entered yet another new stage. Sharon realized that although there had been a decrease in the number of violent attacks on Israelis, the IDF had failed to squash the insurgency. However, he was unwilling to give up his demand that negotiations would be resumed only after the Palestinian Authority renounced violence and, in his words, acted against the terror organizations. This led Sharon to a new strategy of underlateralism and disengagement. Construction of the wall and withdrawal from the Gaza Strip and part of the West Bank would, in Sharon's estimation, serve to stabilize the conflict for several years and strengthen Israel's hold on the remaining territories that, in the course of time, would become part of Israel.

This idea contradicted the basic principle that the IDF had been upholding since September 2000: vigorous rejection of a unilateral withdrawal. It argued that evacuating settlements before signing an agreement would mean surrendering to terror, even if it gave Israel certain benefits. Thus, the IDF found itself adopting a new approach; after attempts at containment, leverage, and forcing an end by military victory, it turned to what it termed "regularization."[28] But the military wanted regularization based on a bilateral approach. Not surprisingly, the government rejected such an approach out of hand. Just as Mofaz had been forced by Barak to implement the unilateral withdrawal from Lebanon, so too was Ya'alon forced to accept Sharon's decision, one that also had the support of Sharon's protégé, Mofaz.

On the face of it, Arafat's death could have removed the major cause of the stagnation that had overcome the diplomatic process. Indeed, talks between the sides did resume following his death, but after four years of bitter warfare, the Israelis' basic mistrust of the Palestinians' intentions was stronger than ever. And, although Ya'alon argued that in order to maintain a low level of conflict it was also important to offer the Palestinians a political horizon, he was far from optimistic about the chances of reaching a political settlement with them in the foreseeable future. One day after his release as CGS on June 1, 2005, Ya'alon publicly revealed this view, offering the bleak and pessimistic assessment that the Palestinians were not ready to recognize Israel's right to exist as a Jewish state. He argued that the Palestinians had not given up the principle of the right of return—and that their ultimate aim remained the destruction of Israel. He also stated that Israel is in continuous retreat and that the Palestinians will keep up the violence in order to continue the process of Israel's retreat. The solution of two states living in coexistence is not realistic or stable, he concluded, stating,

> A Palestinian state will be an irredentist one and will undermine Israel's existence. . . . I do not see an end to the Israeli-Palestinian dispute in my lifetime. . . . We need to think of a long process, not something that stops here and now and brings us an end to the dispute. There is no such solution now. . . . we must recognize that we are destined to remain a warring society. . . . The achievement of the war after 2000 was to make the Palestinians understand that terror does not pay, but Israel is fated to live by the sword for a long time.[29]

Only the liberal newspaper *Ha'aretz* reacted sharply to his statements, publishing a critical editorial on June 2:

> One can treat the former chief of staff's statements as the opinion of security expert No. 1: lose hope, and sit hidden away in bomb shelters in anticipation of the next wave of terror that he predicts. Regrettably, one can also say that it is, in fact, the State of Israel—and first and foremost the former chief of staff—that has proved that it understands only force. Israel has yet to try the only solution acceptable to the Palestinians, most Israelis, and the entire world—the solution of a withdrawal from the occupied territories and the dismantling of the settlements. The Palestinians are not alone in mistakenly dreaming about a return. While they continue to dream of Jaffa, the Israelis not only dreamed of returning to Hebron, but actually settled there. These two untenable dreams have dragged the conflict down to its low point . . . [and now] Ya'alon is doing his bit for the renewal of the violence.[30]

16

Conclusion
The IDF—Sword or Olive Branch?

How Would Other Armed Forces Act?

Throughout the history of the state of Israel, two cultural systems have coexisted: a security culture and a diplomatic culture. Despite fluctuations in their relative influence and despite the fact that the diplomatic culture began gaining currency within Israel in the late 1980s, the security culture has always been dominant. The long tradition of deep Arab hostility toward Israel has made it particularly difficult for supporters of the diplomatic culture to increase their influence on Israeli society. In fact, when the intifada erupted, many of them lost confidence in their own belief in diplomacy and voted for Sharon, who personified the security culture.

Fear of terrorism, the barbaric nature of suicide bombings, and a wave of patriotism all enabled advocates of an ironfisted approach toward the Palestinians to blur the two dimensions of the conflict: it is both a struggle for national liberation and a war of attrition that includes the use of terror against Israel and Israelis. While the Palestinian national liberation movement is directed against Jewish settlements, with the purpose of putting an end to the occupation, the terror campaign is carried out within Israel's 1967 borders and expresses a denial of Israel's right to exist as the Jewish homeland. In the first, the targets are soldiers and settlers; in the second, they are also civilians, including children and the elderly.

After suicide bombers took virtual control of Israel's main streets, the security approach overwhelmingly came to dominate the Israeli psyche and made no distinction between these two separate dimensions of the war. As Ya'alon believed, the violent conflict that began in 2000 represented a "continuation of Israel's 1948 war of independence" and the ultimate goal of the Palestinians was the destruction of the state of Israel. Thus, in the Israeli mindset the LIC acquired one single meaning, and the Palestinian struggle for independence was blanketed under the label of "terror."

Incidentally, this Janus face of the Israeli-Palestinian conflict largely explains why Israel's positions are supported by the United States but criticized by Europe, with the media there being even more critical than the officials. Since the United States commenced its campaign against international terrorism and, more precisely, against Islamist terrorism, Washington and the U.S. media have related to Israel as a partner in this campaign. In Europe, however, postcolonialism is the hegemonic paradigm, and Israel is regarded as trying to hold on to its colony, denying an occupied, indigenous people from realizing its right to self-determination.[1]

On an operational level, Israel's stance led the IDF to respond harshly to the Palestinian armed struggle, indirectly contributing to its escalation, increasing Palestinian hatred of Israel and its intentions, and intensifying Palestinian motivation for war, even to the point where a greater number of Palestinians enlisted to become suicide bombers. Thus, the IDF acted contrary to the most elementary principle of counterrevolutionary warfare, which calls for differentiation between those who support the insurrection and those who do not, or, as Mao Tse-tung put it, "distinguish[ing] between the fish and the sea." The long curfews in the territories and the closures, arrests, sieges, roadblocks, and collective means of punishment harmed the entire population and, instead of eroding public support for militant organizations, heightened their popularity and weakened the moderate elements.

Israel could have implemented another approach that distinguished between the Palestinian terror aimed at Israel and the Palestinian demand for self-determination and national independence. This perspective would have required recognizing the armed struggle as a strategy often undertaken by the weak to gain advantage in negotiations with the mighty and not as a manifestation of a desire to annihilate the state of Israel. Had the reconciliatory approach rather than the security-culture approach been the inspiration of Israel's strategy, Israel would have followed a double path: it would have used tough measures against terrorism and fought the Palestinian attempt to dictate conditions of negotiation through violent confrontation, and also expressed its understanding of an occupied people's wish for freedom and national liberation. Subsequently, it would have offered the Palestinians a positive political future, while not compromising its own quest for security.

By empathizing with the Palestinians' suffering and sense of being unjustly treated, Israel, as the stronger side, would have made clear to the Palestinians that it was not interested in pursuing territorial expansion and that it was willing to accept a historic compromise, one that would both take into consideration symbolic Palestinian needs and answer the basic needs of Israel as a Jewish state. This would have meant a genuine and generous acceptance of the basic idea of two states for two peoples— the Palestinians and the Jews.

Adopting this approach would not necessarily have made Israel the beloved friend of the Palestinian people. Indeed, many Middle Easterners do not accept, and might never accept, the existence of a Jewish state on sacred Muslim land. Nevertheless, such a reconciliatory approach is not folly; it is both rational and realistic in the sense that it would have helped strengthen those within Palestinian society who want to live in peace and tranquility. Furthermore, even if such a strategy did not bring full peace, at least it would have reduced the number of critics of Israel worldwide—and, more important, the number of those volunteering to become suicide bombers.

This encapsulates the main difference between the two cultures that exist in Israel: the security culture views the main goal as decreasing Arab capabilities to threaten Israel, whereas the diplomatic culture sees the main objective as decreasing Arab motivation to continue the conflict. The former sees military superiority as a precondition for coexistence; the latter —while not ignoring the need for military superiority—seeks international legitimacy for the state's existence. The former believes that in the Middle East only hard power talks, while the latter also advocates the use of soft power.[2] Ultimately, the difference is between those who believe that security will bring peace and those who believe that, at the end of the day, only real peace will bring lasting security.

According to the reconciliatory approach, negotiations should be handled between two equal partners, in a generous and kind way; there should be an understanding that this is not a zero-sum game but that Israel has a true interest in Palestinian acceptance of an agreement. Such an approach might help engender a similar perspective on the Palestinian side. Of course it is difficult to expect officers in the midst of bloody battle, particularly when disguised civilians act as human bombs, to adopt a reconciliatory perspective. But even if they were inclined to reconciliation, most IDF officers could not have effectively voiced such opinions during the four years of fighting given how the security culture resonated in the cabinet room more than ever.

Indeed, an analysis of the two recent eras in Israeli-Palestinian relations —during the search for peace in the 1990s and the regression to war in the new millennium—demonstrates that ultimately the political echelon does have the power and ability to force its decisions on the IDF and direct its course of action if it so desires. Whenever political leaders express a clear stand, the military echelon follows the decisions they make. From this point of view, Eliot Cohen is right when he talks about an "unequal dialogue." It is when politicians are indecisive, fail to use the means available to them, and dodge responsibility, that the military is compelled to fill the vacuum.

Is it then justified to criticize military officers for overemphasizing security concerns above other, loftier, considerations? Are they not acting like any other bureaucratic organization that sees the world through its own subjective lens and self-interests? Should not IDF generals be praised, then, rather than criticized, for the fact that despite the prolonged war—and despite their having been bred in the security culture— most of them wanted to engage in the peace process at the beginning of the 1990s? And should they not be commended, since even after four years of counterinsurgency combat, many nevertheless advocated the adoption of a policy that was more conciliatory than the one pursued by their government? Indeed, one wonders how militaries in other democracies would behave in similar circumstances.

A broader historical view of the relations between the IDF and its political masters reveals an interesting phenomenon. At four critical landmarks in Israel's history, when there were historic breakthroughs in the Israeli-Arab dispute that involved withdrawal from territories, final decisions regarding military affairs were made by determined statesmen, despite the reservations of the military. In 1957, Ben-Gurion decided to withdraw from the Sinai after the Suez campaign despite the opposition of CGS Dayan. Begin responded to Sadat's peace initiative at the end of the 1970s and was ready to give up the whole of the Sinai, despite the opinion of CGS Gur. Rabin, Peres, and other leaders negotiated the Oslo Accords without the involvement of the military and CGS Barak. In 2000, meanwhile, Prime Minister Barak decided to withdraw from southern Lebanon in direct opposition to the opinion of CGS Mofaz. On the other hand, those who made such dramatic decisions—including Rabin, Barak, Dayan, and Weizman—had only recently doffed their military uniforms for civilian dress. The same pattern occurred in the summer of 2005, when the IDF, under CGS Halutz, evacuated the Gaza Strip according to Sharon's disengagement plan—despite former CGS Ya'alon's reservatons.

However, these statesmen were also invariably helped by the presence of certain senior officers whose opinions differed from that of their chiefs of staff. Collectively, the above examples illustrate how wrong it is to characterize civil-military relations in Israel with simplistic definitions. Further, according to the most important indicator of the strength of civil control of the military—that is, whether the military submits to civil authority even when it disagrees with the course of action—Israel has managed to maintain its democratic traditions despite the ongoing conflict.[3] But how can we explain the rigid position of the IDF in those cases where fateful decisions about the future of the state had to be taken? One explanation is that the CGS and the entire senior command as an organization held negative attitudes toward proposed agreements because their professional duty was to act as the prosecution, not as the defense or the judge. As those responsible for security, they believed that they needed to examine the given problem from a narrow military point of view and place military considerations above all others; looking at the entire picture was not their concern. After all, blame for any failure in military assessment would fall on them.

Such an explanation, however, is only partially valid. There appears to be another explanation for the IDF perspective, which is related to its conservative organizational approach. In each of the cases cited above, the military was asked to adapt to a radical change in the political environment. And, in general, when armed forces come to a crossroads where they have to choose between following an old, familiar path and taking a new, unfamiliar path with a higher level of uncertainty, they tend to choose the former. This is not because of the attitudes of individual officers —some standing officers and even more retired officers will generally support such a move—but because the collective body, the organization, and those who are formally responsible for it, are risk averse and will resist such change.

The Future of Political-Military Relations

Political-military relations in Israel during the past decade have been quite problematic. The tensions between the two echelons are caused by four factors. The first is the ongoing political crisis, reflected in the weakness of the political echelon, the government's inability to formulate clear directives, and its tendency to dodge responsibility, casting it on the military. The second is the weakness in the structural mechanisms of civilian control over the military.[4] The third is the nature of the citizen's army, which blurs the boundaries between the civilian population and the military. And the fourth is the nature of the conflict with the Palestinians. The combination of these factors deepened the IDF's involvement in the political process and in policymaking, both in matters related to the conduct of the war and in diplomatic negotiations.

As a result, resentment of the military's involvement in political affairs has increased in many circles, as has criticism of the country's security culture, which some have referred to more bluntly as militarism. Books such as *Wars Don't Just Happen, The Israeli Army: A Radical Proposal, A Different Army for Israel, The Seventh War,* and *Boomerang,* all express such resentment and criticism[5] as have other publications, such as a special 2003 issue of the journal *Seder Yom,* which is published by the Rabin Center for Israel Studies, an institution that reflects the views of the political-military establishment.[6]

"The ongoing war against terror brought about a situation in which the military commanders became those who outline the state's policy," Brig. Gen. (ret.) Zeev Drori, former commander of the IDF's radio station, wrote in the journal.[7] "The political leadership saw in the IDF commanders a political asset with which it could achieve different factional-governmental goals, and that caused the blurring of the needed clear line between politics and military," added Maj. Gen. (ret.) Yossi Peled, former head of the Northern Command.[8] Maj. Gen (res.) Uzi Dayan went even further, stating,

> The vast majority of the civilians believe that in the conflict against the Palestinians Israel does not have the upper hand because the political echelon did not define clear goals for the war, and did not determine the strategy required in order to achieve them. In other words, it is unclear what the definition of victory is in this war. One who does not have a vision and a way is bound to fail in giving clear guidance and direction to the military echelon. The result is that the two echelons are occupied in managing the crisis and not in solving it.[9]

But the formulas used in the past for ensuring civilian control of the military do not provide a comfortable prescription for present problems. Kenneth Kemp and Charles Hudin wrote in the 1990s that the key to good civil-military relations is the military's respect for the principle of civilian supremacy. They maintained that this principle in fact has two parts: (1) that civilians in the end decide on policy, while the military is responsible for the means; and (2) that civilians decide where the line between the end and means is drawn. "In other words, the military are to be policy implementers, not policymakers."[10]

However, the history recounted in this book shows how simplistic this distinction is. The hybrid situation that has prevailed since the eruption of counterinsurgency warfare renders obsolete such distinctions between the roles of the military and of the politicians. While LICs make friction between the civil and military echelons almost inevitable,[11] the problem becomes more acute in the case of a nation in arms, such as Israel. A higher degree of civilian involvement in the military can, in certain circumstances, strengthen the "civilianization" of the military, and thus also increase its subordination to the political echelon. But, in other circumstances, particularly when the political sector is weak, the high degree of civilian involvement in the military can be a recipe for discord and can lead to the strengthening of the military. More specifically, in peacetime, a pattern of political-military partnership—or, using Douglas Bland's term, a "civilian direction" of the military[12]—rather than civilian control can generate positive and harmonious relations between society and the military. But weak political statesmanship in times of a fourth-generation war may cause the military to cross the threshold of legitimate activity in a democracy.

In contrast to Mofaz, who as CGS explained away any discordant relations between the military and the political echelons as isolated incidents, Ya'alon was more open and straightforward, explaining to anyone who was ready to listen that there was a structural problem in these relations. Moreover, he did not refrain from voicing criticism of the political echelon—specifically, of the prime minister and of the defense minister— for exacerbating this situation. Following his lead, other senior officers began to criticize the absence of a clear directive from their civilian superiors.[13]

What retired officers said openly, those still in uniform expressed more discreetly but no less emphatically. They debated the issue not only in informal talks among themselves but also in formal meetings of the General Staff and discussions with civilians.[14] The officers' frustration was palpable in these debates, and two trends among the IDF generals could be distinguished. One position held that the IDF should take a few steps back and disentangle itself from the intricate political snarl as much as it could. The other, more radical, position argued that the nature of the conflict and the political conditions were such that the IDF needed to participate more directly and aggressively in the political game. The supporters of this stand recommended that the IDF become more proactive by taking on extra responsibility, by pursuing additional political initiatives, and especially by providing more often its own viewpoints directly to the public. This position gained increasing support among senior officers in early 2005 as the date for withdrawal from the Gaza Strip approached. Opponents of disengagement, meanwhile, directed their vociferous criticism not only at the government but also at the IDF.

As early as 2004, the IDF began to implement conceptual and organizational reforms. As part of these reforms, which included adding a level to the IDF structure between the strategic and tactical levels, the IDF began debating some issues that had never before been raised, including discussion of war aims and the meaning of victory in future wars. After examining the outcome of past wars, the military analysts reached the conclusion that there existed "an imbalance between the large amount of effort put into planning and using power during wartime, and the small amount of consideration put into the preplanning and aftermath stages."[15] This was a gentle way of saying that in the past the IDF had gone to war without being told directly by its civilian authority what the war aims were, other than to repel a threat to Israel's existence. If this is the case, they concluded in the summer of 2004, should not the IDF determine war goals by itself?

Criticism of the political echelon for not having provided the IDF with political directives regarding the goals of war is not uncommon in the history of the IDF. What was new in 2004 was that, following the intifada, the military decided not to wait any longer for such directives but to determine them on its own. Such an approach would institutionalize and legitimize the growing influence of the military in the political-military partnership. But to avoid further steps toward greater military sway in politics, one must first confront the factors that provoke such steps.

The easiest problem to repair is the lack of formal structural and institutional supervision of the military by civilians. One change that could help empower civilian authority would be the breaking of the IDF's monopoly in the fields of designing and shaping defense policy; this could be accomplished by strengthening the National Security Council and its civilian branches. By providing a National Net Estimate, a strong council could break the monopoly of the MID's intelligence estimate and provide decision makers with an analysis that integrates civilian and military viewpoints. Detailed recommendations for empowering civilian institutions have been outlined in numerous reports and white papers published since the Yom Kippur War but have never been implemented.[16] Indeed, in August 2005, Maj. Gen. (res.) Giora Eiland resigned as head of the council, a position he assumed less than two years earlier. This was the fourth resignation of a National Security Council head in less than seven years. All of them resigned for the same reason: they all ultimately realized they had no real power.

One of the latest recommendations for change in the intelligence field was presented by Uzi Arad, who formerly held a senior position in the Mossad and was a political adviser to Prime Minister Netanyahu. In a document presented at the Herzliya Conference of the Institute for Policy and Strategy in December 2004, he argued that it was time to effect a radical reform in the structure of the security services in the spirit of the recent reforms instituted in Britain, the United States, and Australia. Arad described the pluralistic structure of the Israeli intelligence community as "fossilized" and was particularly critical of the fact that the MID defined itself as the national evaluator even though it did not integrate and incorporate in its assessment processes the resources and inputs of the Mossad, the ISA, or the foreign ministry. This left a pluralistic structure with no real civilian inspection, no national adviser on intelligence, and no civilian superstructure for the evaluation of intelligence.[17]

Furthermore, the weakness of the political echelon compared to the military is manifested in Israel's relations with the Arab states. In Israel's relations with the Palestinians, the situation is especially severe because the intelligence organizations, the ISA and the MID, are not only bodies that evaluate what is done within the Palestinian Authority and society but are also active players in the relationship. Wrote Ephraim Halevy, a former head of the Mossad who became chief of the National Security Council under Sharon in 2003 and resigned soon after, "The Military Intelligence Directorate has become an actor that carries great weight in the daily political dialogue and its voice has become the dominant one in the bilateral discourse."

Halevy defined this situation as "unique and unprecedented in the history of the intelligence community" and observed that "instead of occupying itself with gathering and analyzing information, [the MID] runs the battle in the field, conducts the talks with the Palestinians, and is also the one whose intelligence assessments are most highly valued by the administration and considered the most authoritative and accurate." The result is a vicious circle in which "the force that operates in the field is also the one that evaluates the political meaning of its actions, and is also the one that conducts the dialogue with its adversaries and also influences more than anyone else the cabinet's understanding of the situation."[18] While this structure may have led to certain successful results in Israel's war against the Palestinian armed struggle, one cannot fail to see the negative implications of this manner of decision making and the weak civilian control of the military.

Another possible reform is to strengthen the power of the cabinet and the Ministry of Defense to implement changes that would reinforce their civilian nature and thus alleviate military influence on them. Detailed recommendations for implementing such changes, as well as the rationale for doing so, were formulated among others by Maj. Gen. (ret.) Israel Tal in the mid-1990s; yet, despite his prestige, and despite the fact that similar recommendations have been presented several times since then, they have remained words on paper only. Maj. Gen. (res.) Yaari added to this recommendation, pointing to two facts: on the one hand, the prime minister and defense minister lack the tools that would enable them to exert their authority; but, on the other hand, they have at their disposal tools that are not used properly.[19]

The need for reform applies to parliamentary control as well. In 2004, an unprecedented situation occurred when the chairman of the Knesset's Foreign Affairs and Defense Committee, Yuval Steinitz, decided to strengthen the supervision of his parliamentary committee over the military. The CGS was deeply resentful of this and did not allow officers to testify before the committee. Only after long deliberations involving the CGS, the defense minister, the Knesset speaker, and the committee chair was the crisis resolved. It became clear that the Knesset was willing to change its passive and unassertive role with respect to control of the military. For that purpose, a second committee was established, led by former justice minister Amnon Rubinstein, to develop recommendations for reform in this area. In December 2004, the committee presented its recommendations, which included steps for tightening parliamentary control by enhancing the status of the Knesset Foreign Affairs and Defense Committee vis-à-vis both the military and the executive branch. One concrete step, for example, would require civil servants and security personnel to testify before the committee (Israel's constitutional law does not have such an obligation, except for the State Audit Committee), and another would require the CGS to report to the committee on his activities once a month. The recommendations also called for a radical change in the procedures for approving the defense budget, thereby giving more power to the Foreign Affairs and Defense Committee.[20]

A set of relatively minor recommendations might also have a valuable overall effect on the political-military relationship. One such recommendation relates to the status of the military secretary of the prime minister. Currently, the military secretary is a senior officer whose military career is determined by the CGS. Thus, while the secretary should serve as the eyes and ears of the highest civilian authority inside the military, he is in fact a representative of the IDF within the prime minister's chamber. A similar situation exists with regard to the defense minister and his military secretary. Only if the defense minister has a powerful, developed, and sophisticated staff unit can he be an effective supervisor of the military. Without such a staff, he is totally dependent on the military and becomes either a "super chief of staff" or a weak minister.

Another move that might heal the ailing civil-military relations is to stop the parachuting of officers directly into cabinet benches. A more robust "cooling system," by which officers are legally forbidden to enter politics for a set time, might also contribute to increased civilian supervision of the military. The current waiting period in Israel is only one hundred days for participating in Knesset elections and six months for accepting a ministerial position in the cabinet. Ideally, newly retired officers should have to wait two or three years before being able to enter the Knesset, and perhaps four or five years before being able to hold a cabinet position, such as defense minister or prime minister. The absence of a substantial cooling period facilitates the politicization of the military and the militarization of politics.

But such a law has not yet been seriously considered. Those who need to act are the politicians, the party bosses in particular, and they are the very ones who profit from the present situation. For example, in April 2005, with the announcement that the commander of the air force, Dan Halutz, would become the next CGS, the press already began to speculate that there would be two contestants for leadership of the Likud in 2009: Halutz and Mofaz, the man who had just appointed Halutz as CGS. As for Ya'alon, he always expressed a dislike for politics and regularly confessed that he would never enter this arena. Yet his anger at his dismissal and the warmth he received from the public—as the honest guy who fell victim to cynical politicians—was mentioned by commentators as a driving force that might push him into a major public position in the near future.

The growing public concern over the weakness of civilian control of the military and the security services and the increasing number of recommendations put forward for reform are evidence of a rise in consciousness regarding the problematic relations between the military and Israel's political leaders. It is especially interesting that many of those who demand reform are former military personnel who know the situation from the inside and acquired a civilian perspective after their release. However, while many recommendations have been made, most of them deal only with administrative and procedural dimensions and do not address the fundamental problems that led to the current situation: the ongoing conflict with the Palestinians, the weakness of the political system in general, and the nature of Israel's security culture in particular.

Beyond the obvious institutional changes, some of which I have just described, Israeli society must do something more difficult: it has to undertake a radical transformation and develop its own civil culture. The prolonged conflict—whether it has been forced on Israel from the outside, as the conservative researchers of civil-military relations claim, or has been a governing practice directed by the state power-elite, as the radical researchers suggest—has nurtured the culture of national security to such an extent that it harms Israel's democratic being. As a result, the security ethos and the culture of power dominate the public and private spheres. Machismo exceeds civility.

Perhaps it is too much to expect such a profound change without there first being a change in the state's present existential condition, namely, a resolution to its conflict with the Palestinians and broader Arab world. But finding a solution to this ongoing problem is the most difficult challenge the country faces. In fact, Israel's recent political crises derive from the inability of its political leadership to make the bold decisions necessary to end the conflict with the Palestinians. This lack of courage has meant that the fundamental question on most Israeli minds has not been properly tested: are the Palestinians truly ready to realize the vision of two independent states coexisting peacefully?

Maybe the pessimistic perspective of the MID's research division and of former CGS Ya'alon is more realistic and the answer to this question is no, but it is equally possible that the land-for-peace formula—a formula that has not been fully tested—could yet bring an end to the conflict. In either case, the intifada has certainly not made finding a solution to the conflict any easier. But was the insurgency a manifestation of a Palestinian strategy aimed at the eventual destruction of Israel, or was it just one means among many designed to bring about a negotiated settlement between two sides on a more equal footing? Regardless, one thing is sure: as long as Israelis and Palestinians choose to shed each other's blood rather than pursue a serious dialogue, there will be no peace in the Holy Land. A compromise reached through negotiation will inevitably entail concessions on both sides, such as Israel giving up its dream of annexing territories and the Palestinians waiving their right of return. In the meantime, more generals, whether in uniform or in mufti, will continue to occupy cabinet seats, and the security culture will continue to dominate, engendering more friction between the military and the political echelon, between the military and civilian society, and between segments of the civilian population itself.

Appendix 1
Glossary

CGS   Chief of General Staff, a Lieutenant General

DMI   Director of Military Intelligence, a Major General

GSS   General Security Service

IDF   Israel Defense Forces

ISA   Israel Security Agency, formerly known as the Israel Security Service (ISS) and the General Security Service (GSS), or Shaback (in Hebrew)

LIC   Low-Intensity Conflict

MID   Military Intelligence Directorate, formerly known as the Military Intelligence Division

MK   Knesset Member

NIE   National Intelligence Estimate, a yearly assessment of Israel's strategic posture prepared by the MID

PA   Palestinian Authority

PLO   Palestine Liberation Organization

Appendix 2
Chronological List of Key Events

September 17, 1978 — Israel and Egypt sign the Camp David Peace Accords.

March 26, 1979 — The Israeli-Egyptian peace treaty is signed.

February 6, 1982 — The Lebanon War begins.

December 7, 1987 — The first intifada begins.

January–February 1991 — Israel is attacked by Iraq during the Gulf War.

October 30, 1991 — The Middle East Peace Conference convened in Madrid.

August 23, 1992 — Yitzhak Rabin is elected prime minister of Israel.

January 1993 — The PLO and Israeli representatives begin secret negotiations in Norway.

August 19, 1993 — The declaration of principles (DOP) is secretly signed in Oslo.

September 13, 1993 — The PLO and the Israeli government sign the DOP in Washington; Yasser Arafat and Rabin shake hands.

April 1994 — The Palestinian Authority and the Israeli government sign the agreement for economic cooperation in Paris.

May 4, 1994 — In Cairo, Rabin and Arafat sign the agreement for Palestinian "self-rule" in Gaza and Jericho.

August 29, 1994 — The PLO and the Israeli government sign the preparatory transfer of powers and responsibilities in the West Bank.

October 26, 1994 — The Israeli-Jordanian peace treaty is signed.

January 1995 — Amnon Lipkin-Shahak is appointed IDF chief of general staff.

Summer 1995 — The Israeli and Syrian chiefs of staff conduct negotiations in the United States.

September 28, 1995 — The PLO and the Israeli government sign Oslo B, an interim agreement to transfer control of major Palestinian populated areas in the occupied territories.

October 4, 1995 — Rabin is assassinated.

May 29, 1996 — Benjamin Netanyahu is elected prime minister of Israel.

September 24, 1996 — The Hasmonean tunnel in Jerusalem is opened.

January 15, 1997 — The PLO and the Israeli government sign the protocol concerning redeployment in Hebron.

October 23, 1998 — Netanyahu and Arafat sign the Wye River Memorandum.

January 1999 — Shaul Mofaz is appointed IDF chief of general staff.

May 17, 1999 — Ehud Barak is elected prime minister of Israel.

September 4, 1999 — The PLO and the Israeli government sign the Sharm El-Sheikh Memorandum.

April–June 2000 — "Swedish Channel" negotiations between Israeli and Palestinian representatives take place.

May 15, 2000 — Nakba Day

May 22–23, 2000 — The IDF pulls out of southern Lebanon.

July 11–25, 2000 — President Bill Clinton mediates the Camp David Summit between Israeli and Palestinian delegations.

September 28, 2000 — Ariel Sharon visits the Temple Mount/al-Haram al-Sharif. The next day the Al-Aqsa Intifada begins.

December 23, 2000 — Clinton presents his ideas for a peace agreement between Israel and the Palestinians.

January 21–27, 2001 — The Taba round of negotiations between Israeli and Palestinian delegations occurs.

February 6, 2001 — Sharon is elected prime minister of Israel.

March 29, 2002 — Operation Defensive Shield begins.

June 24, 2002 — President George W. Bush presents his vision for peace in the Middle East, which includes the establishment of a Palestinian state.

November 4, 2002 — Mofaz joins the cabinet as defense minister.

January 28, 2003 — Sharon is elected prime minister of Israel for the second time.

March 14, 2003 — Bush presents his road map for an Israeli-Palestinian peace agreement.

March 19, 2003 — The Iraq War begins.

June 4, 2003 — The Aqaba Summit is held between Israeli and Palestinian delegations.

December 1, 2003 — The Geneva Accord is signed.

April 2004 — Sharon initiates his disengagement plan.

November 11, 2004 — Arafat dies.

June 1, 2005 — Dan Halutz is appointed IDF chief of general staff.

August 2005 — Sharon's Gaza disengagement plan is implemented.

Appendix 3
Interviews

Below is a partial list of the individuals I interviewed for this study, along with their affiliation(s) at the time of the interview.

Doron Almog, Maj. Gen. (res.), commander of Southern Command

Ya'akov Amidror, Maj. Gen. (res.), commander of the National Defense College and former head of research in the MID

Shaul Arieli, Colonel (res.), former head of the peace directorate

Ehud Barak, Lieut. Gen. (res.), former prime minister and CGS

Nahum Barnea, senior political analyst for *Yediot Ahronoth*

Yossi Beilin, MK, former minister of justice

Shlomo Ben-Ami, former foreign minister

Eitan Ben-Zur, former Foreign Ministry director-general

Gadi Blatianski, former media adviser to Prime Minister Barak

Uzi Dayan, Maj. Gen. (res.), head of the National Security Council and former deputy CGS

Reuven Erlich, Col. (ret.), director of the Intelligence and Terrorism Information Center

Yossi Genosar, former liaison between Israeli prime ministers Rabin and Peres and PA president Arafat

Eiten Haber, director of the Prime Minister's Bureau for Prime Minister Rabin

Michael Herzog, Brig. Gen., military secretary to the minister of defense

Martin Indyk, former U.S. ambassador to Israel

Ron Kitrey, Brig. Gen., former IDF spokesperson

Menachem Klein, former adviser to Foreign Minister Ben-Ami

Amnon Lipkin-Shahak, Lieut. Gen. (res.), former minister of transport and IDF CGS

Zeev Livne, Maj. Gen. (res.), former military secretary to the prime minster

Robert Malley, former special assistant for Arab-Israeli affairs to President Clinton

Dan Meridor, MK, member of the Foreign Affairs & Defense Committee, former minister of justice and finance

Aaron David Miller, senior adviser for Arab-Israeli negotiations, U.S. Department of State

Amram Mitzna, Maj. Gen. (res.), mayor of Haifa, former commander of the Central Command and head of the IDF planning branch

Amir Oren, military analyst for *Ha'aretz*

Yitzhak Rabin, prime minister

Itamar Rabinovich, president of Tel Aviv University, former Israeli ambassador to the United States

Elyakim Rubinstein, attorney general, later Supreme Court justice

Yossi Sarid, MK, former chairman of the opposition and minister of education

Ze'ev Schiff, military analyst for *Ha'aretz*

Yoel Singer, Col. (res.), legal consultant, former IDF Judge Advocate

Ephraim Sneh, Brig. Gen. (res.), minister of transportation and former deputy minister of defense

Moshe Ya'alon, Lieut. Gen., IDF CGS

Shlomo Yanai, Maj. Gen (res.), former head of the IDF Planning and Policy Directorate

Amos Yaron, Brig. Gen. (res.), Defense Ministry director-general

Ruth Yaron, Brig. Gen., IDF spokesperson

Dani Yatom, Maj. Gen. (res.), secretary to the prime minister, former head of the Mossad, and later MK

Notes

Introduction

1. *Sipri Year Book* (New York: Oxford University Press, 2002*)*, 63.

2. Israel Tal, *National Security* [in Hebrew] (Tel Aviv: Dvir, 1996), 31.

3. Samuel P. Huntington, *The Soldier and the State: The Theory and Politics of Civil-Military Relations* (New York: Vintage Books, 1964).

4. S. E. Finer, *The Man on Horseback: Military Intervention into Politics* (Harmondsworth, UK: Penguin, 1975).

5. Richard H. Kohn, "Out of Control: The Crisis in Civil-Military Relations," *National Interest,* Spring 1994, 5–17.

6. Charles J. Dunlap Jr., "The Origins of the American Military Coup of 2012," *Parameters* (Winter 1992–93): 2–20.

7. Ibid.

8. Emanuel Wald, *The Curse of the Broken Tools* [in Hebrew] (Jerusalem: Schocken, 1987), 208.

9. Tal, *National Security,* 115.

10. Eliot A. Cohen, *Supreme Command* (New York: Free Press, 2002). Rebecca L. Schiff, "Civil-Military Relations Reconsidered: A Theory of Concordance," *Armed Forces and Society* 22, no. 7 (1995): 18.

11. Dana Priest, *The Mission* (New York: W. W. Norton, 2003).

12. See Defense and the National Interest, http://www.d-n-i.net/second _ level/fourth_generation_warfare.html.

13. See Avi Kover, "Low Intensity Conflicts: Why There Is a Gap between Theory and Practice," in *Low Intensity Conflict,* ed. Haggai Golan and Shaul Shai (Tel Aviv: Maarachot, 2004), 69–101.

14. Yoram Peri, *The Israeli Military and Israel's Palestinian Policy: From Oslo to the Al Aqsa Intifada,* United States Institute of Peace Peaceworks 47 (November 2002).

15. See, for example, Golan and Shai, eds., *Low Intensity Conflict;* Amos Harel and Avi Isacharoff, *The Seventh War* (Tel Aviv: Miskal-Yedioth Ahronoth Books,

2004); Yaacov Bar-Siman-Tov, Ephraim Lavie, Kobi Michael, and Daniel Bar-Tal, *The Israeli-Palestinian Violent Conflict 2000–2004: The Transition from Conflict Resolution to Conflict Management* (Jerusalem: Jerusalem Institute for Israel Studies, 2005). All of these books have also been published in Hebrew.

16. Yoram Peri, *Between Battles and Ballots: Israeli Military in Politics* (Cambridge: Cambridge University Press, 1983).

1. Civil-Military Relations in Israel

1. This idea was elaborated and updated in recent years. See Jay Stanley, "Harold Lasswell and the Idea of the Garrison State," *Society* 33, no. 6 (September–October 1996) and Harold D. Lasswell, "The Garrison State," *American Journal of Sociology* 46 (1941).

2. The most prominent representatives of this school are Horowitz, Lissak, and Perlmutter. See also Gabi Ben-Dor, "Civil-Military Relations in the Mid-1990s," in *Independence: The First 50 Years* [in Hebrew], ed. Anita Shapira (Jerusalem: Shazar Center, 1998), 471–486.

3. Shulamit Carmi and Henri Rosenfeld, "The Emergence of Militaristic Nationalism in Israel," *International Journal of Politics, Culture and Society* 3, no. 1 (1989).

4. Moshe Lissak, "The Ethos of Security and the Myth of the Militarized Society" [in Hebrew], *Democratic Culture* 4-5 (2001): 187–212.

5. Zeev Rosenhak, Daniel Maman, and Eyal Ben-Ari, "The Study of War and the Military in Israel: The Social Construction of Knowledge," in *In The Name of Security,* ed. Majid Al-Haj and Uri Ben-Eliezer (Haifa: Haifa University Press, 2003), 185–214.

6. Orna Sasson-Levy, "Masculinity as a Protest Identity Construction Among Blue-Collar Soldiers" [in Hebrew], *Israeli Sociology* 5, no. 1 (2003): 15–48.

7. Yagil Levy, *The Other Army of Israel* [in Hebrew] (Tel Aviv: Miskal, 2003), 20.

8. Baruch Kimmerling, "Political Subcultures and Civilian Militarism in a Settler-Immigrant Society," in *Concerned with Security: Learning from Israel's Experience,* ed., Daniel Bar-Tal, Dan Jacobson, and Arahon Kliemann (Greenwich, Conn.: JAI Press, 1998), 395–416.

9. Uri Ben-Eliezer, "From a Nation-in-Arms to a Postmodern Army: Military Politics in 'New Times' Israel" [in Hebrew], *Democratic Culture* 4-5 (2001): 56–57.

10. Ibid.

11. Ibid.

12. Yagil Levy, "How Militarization Drives Political Control of the Military: The Case of Israel," *Political Power and Social Theory* 11 (1997): 105.

13. Motti Golani, *Wars Don't Just Happen* [in Hebrew] (Ben-Shemen: Modan, 2003). Ofer Shelah, *The Israeli Military: A Radical Proposal* [in Hebrew] (Tel Aviv: Kineret Zmoroa Bitan Dvir, 2003). Levy, *The Other Army of Israel*. Al-Haj and Ben-Eliezer, eds., *In The Name of Security*.

14. See, for example, Dan Horowitz and Moshe Lissak, *Troubles in Utopia* (Albany: SUNY Press, 1989).

15. See Finer, *The Man on Horseback*, 17–19. For further analysis of objective and subjective control, see Peri, *Betwen Battles and Ballots*.

16. Ze'ev Maoz, *Ha'aretz*, October 16, 1996.

17. David Ben-Gurion, *Singularity and Mission* (Tel Aviv: Maarachot, 1971), 141–142.

18. The short and charismatic Uzi Dayan is a nephew of Moshe Dayan, Israel's former defense minister and CGS.

19. Uzi Dayan, "What Is Needed and What Prevails in the Relations between the Political and the Military Echelons" [in Hebrew], in *Civil-Military Relations in Israel: Influence and Restraints*, ed. Ram Erez (Tel Aviv: Jaffee Center for Strategic Studies at Tel Aviv University, 2003), 23–27.

20. Yehuda Ben-Meir, *Civil-Military Relations in Israel* (New York: Columbia University Press, 1995), 179.

21. Ibid.

22. Aviezer Yaari, *Civil Control of the Military*, Memorandum 72 [in Hebrew] (Tel Aviv: Jaffee Center for Strategic Studies at Tel Aviv University, October 2004).

23. Peter J. Roman and David W. Tarr, "Military Professionalism and Policy Making: Is There a Civil-Military Gap at the Top? If So, Does It Matter?" in *Soldiers and Civilians: The Civil-Military Gap and American National Security*, ed. Peter D. Feaver and Richard H. Kohn (Cambridge, Mass.: MIT Press, 2001).

24. Gregory D. Foster, "The Culture of Military Bureaucracy: Civil-Military Relations in Democracies Today," *Public Manager* 29 (2000): 41–42.

25. For Cohen's analysis of Churchill, see Cohen, *Supreme Command*.

26. Amos Perlmutter, *The Military and Politics in Modern Times* (New Haven, Conn.: Yale University Press, 1977), 251–280.

27. Shlomo Gazit, *Fools in a Trap* (Tel Aviv: Zmora Bitan, 1999).

28. See the analysis of the IDF's actions in the territories in Shelah, *The Israeli Military*, 99–107.

29. Levy, *The Other Army of Israel*, 22–23.

30. Emanuel Sivan, "The Assassination in Paris, The Assassination in Tel Aviv," in *Political Assassination* [in Hebrew], ed. Charles S. Liebman (Tel Aviv: Am Oved, 2000), 22–32.

2. The Geostrategic Transformation of the 1990s

1. Eliot A. Cohen, Michael J. Eisenstadt, and Andrew J. Bacevich, *Knives, Tanks, and Missiles: Israel's Security Revolution* (Washington, D.C.: Washington Institute for Near East Policy, 1998).

2. Eytan Bentsur, *The Road to Peace Crosses Madrid* [in Hebrew] (Tel Aviv: Yedioth Ahronoth Books, 1997), 81.

3. Ibid., 114.

4. Ephraim Sneh, *Responsibility: Israel after Year 2000* [in Hebrew] (Tel Aviv: Yedioth Ahronoth Books, 1996), 68.

5. I had many discussions with Rabin about this. See also Yoram Peri, "Rabin: From 'Mr. Security' to Nobel Prize Winner," afterword in *The Rabin Memoirs,* by Yitzhak Rabin (Berkeley and Los Angeles: University of California Press, 1996), 380–399.

6. Yair P. Hirschfeld, *Oslo: A Formula for Peace* [in Hebrew] (Tel Aviv: Am-Oved, 2000), 148.

7. Carmi Gilon, *Shin-Beth between Schisms* [in Hebrew] (Tel Aviv: Yedioth Ahronoth Books, 2000).

8. Cohen, Eisenstadt, and Bacevich, *Knives, Tanks, and Missiles,* 20.

9. Maj. Gen. Doron Almog, interview by author.

10. Tel Aviv Security Workshop, Tel Aviv University, December 30, 2003, at which Maj. Gens. Yitzhak Ben-Israel and Eval Giladi lectured on Israel's new security perception following the war in Iraq.

11. Shimon Peres, interview on Israeli Television, April 14, 1994. See also Shimon Peres, *The New Middle East* (New York: Henry Holt, 1993). Since the 1990s, the IDF has been developing war scenarios in which enemy formations will be destroyed from a distance, without the need to conquer territories. See Amir Oren, *Ha'aretz,* April 25, 2004.

12. Yoram Peri, "Media, War, and Citizenship," *Communication Review* 3, no. 4 (2000): 1–29.

13. Stuart Cohen, *The IDF and Israeli Society* [in Hebrew] (Ramat-Gan, Israel: BESA Center for Strategic Studies, Bar Ilan University, 2001). See also Avner Ben-Amos and Daniel Bar-Tal, *Patriotism* (Tel Aviv: Dyonon, 2004).

14. See "Public Trust in the Media," Research Project at the Herzog Institute for Media Politics and Society, Tel Aviv University, http://www.tau.ac.il/institutes/herzog/.

15. Shahak's speech received dramatic coverage in the media. See *Ha'aretz,* October 31, 1996.

16. Yitzhak Rabin, in discussion with the author. See also Peri, afterword to *The Rabin Memoirs,* 339–380.

17. Uri Sagi, *Lights within the Fog* [in Hebrew] (Tel Aviv: Miskal-Yedioth Ahronoth Books, 1998), 27.

18. Ibid., 105.

19. Ibid., 147–155.

3. The Political Arm of the Military

1. See Ben-Gurion's perception in Peri, *Between Battles and Ballots*.

2. The Planning and Policy Directorate was previously called the Strategic Planning Division in English. Though the name has not changed in Hebrew, the preferred English translation changed to eliminate the confusion in using the term "division" for both its headquarters and field units.

3. Aviezer Yaari, "Intelligence Assessment in Israel's Conditions of Uncertainty," [in Hebrew] in *Intelligence and National Security*, ed. Zvi Offer and Avi Kover (Tel Aviv: Maarachot, 1987), 213.

4. Asher Arian, *Security Threatened* [in Hebrew] (Tel Aviv: Papirus, 1999), 57.

5. For many of these recommendations, from those of the Yadin-Sherf commission in 1963 to the Vardi recommendation in 1975, see Shlomo Gazit, *Between Warning and Surprise: On Shaping National Intelligence Assessment in Israel*, Memorandum 66 [in Hebrew] (Tel Aviv: Jaffee Center for Strategic Studies, Tel Aviv University, 2003).

6. These questions were at the center of one of Israel's most complicated political crises, "The Lavon Affair." See Peri, *Between Battles and Ballots*.

7. The security service in Israel—the Shin Bet or Sherut Habitahon Haklali—had previously been called the ISS and was later called the Israel Security Agency, or ISA.

8. Shlomo Brom, "The War in Iraq: An Intelligence Failure?" *Strategic Assessment* 6, no. 3 (November 2003).

9. Yaari, "Intelligence Assessment in Israel's Conditions of Uncertainty," 213. For additional evidence, see also Yehoshafat Harkabi, *War and Strategy* [in Hebrew] (Tel Aviv: Maarachot, 1990).

10. Gazit, *Between Warning and Surprise*, 55–56.

11. Dan Meridor, interview by author.

12. Ehud Barak, interview by author.

13. Shelah, *The Israeli Military*, 70.

14. Maj. Gen. Ya'akov Amidror, interview by author.

15. Sagi, *Lights within the Fog*, 106.

16. David Halberstam, *War in a Time of Peace* (New York: Scribner, 2001).

17. See also Gazit, *Between Warning and Surprise*.

18. Ephraim Halevy, "The Role of the Intelligence Community in Planning Israel's Strategic Alternatives" [in Hebrew], *Maarachot,* July 2003, 40.

19. Yossi Beilin, *Manual for a Wounded Dove* [in Hebrew] (Tel Aviv: Miskal-Yedioth Ahronoth Books, 2001), 256–257.

20. M.K. Sarid, interview by author.

21. Uzi Benziman, *Ha'aretz,* August 10, 2001.

22. See interviews with the DMI in *Yedioth Ahronoth,* April 11, 2004, and with the CGS in *Yedioth Ahronoth,* March 26, 2004.

23. All quotes are taken from Ben-Meir, *Civil-Military Relations,* 143–158.

24. Ibid., 146.

25. Avraham Tamir, *A Soldier in Search of Peace* (London: Weindenfeld and Nicolson, 1988), 232.

26. Ibid., 147.

27. Maj. Gen. Shlomo Yanai, interview by author.

4. The Modus Operandi of the Military

1. Among these professional officers are the head of the research division in the Planning and Policy Directorate, high-ranking officers in the Planning and Policy Directorate and the MID, the coordinator of activities in the territories, the prime minister's and defense minister's military secretaries, professionals in areas such as law and finance, and those in charge of media relations.

2. Eitan Haber (Rabin's bureau chief), interview by author.

3. David Makovsky, *Making Peace with the PLO* (Boulder, Colo.: Westview Press, 1996), 101.

4. Barak, interview by author.

5. As a result of this thinking, Barak, after becoming prime minister, did not fulfill Israel's obligations toward the two additional stages of retreat, believing too many territorial assets had already been lost. Arafat was forced to agree to Barak's position, but since Barak did not carry out his promises, the Palestinians lost trust in him.

6. Gilon, *Shin-Beth between Schisms,* 209.

7. Col. (res.) Shaul Arieli, interview by author.

8. Ibid.

9. See Comptroller's Report for 2000, September 2001.

10. Yair P. Hirschfeld, *Oslo: A Formula for Peace* [in Hebrew] (Tel Aviv: Am-Oved, 2000), 156.

11. Gilon, *Shin-Beth between Schisms,* 208.

12. Martin Indyk, interview by author.

13. Arieli, interview by author.

14. Meridor, interview by author.

15. Daniel Dor, *The Suppression of Guilt: The Israeli Media and the Reoccupation of the West Bank* (London: Pluto Press, 2005)

16. IDF spokesperson Brig. Gen. Ruth Yaron, interview by author.

17. Editorial, *Ha'aretz,* October 8, 2001.

18. Gilon took over from Peri as ISA head; after retiring from that position, he served as the head of the Peres Institute for Peace. Ginossar became a confidant of Arafat. Gilon's successor at the GSS was a former navy commander, Maj. Gen. Ami Ayalon, who later established a joint Israeli-Palestinian NGO to promote peace between the two nations. See chapter 10.

19. Uri Savir, *The Process* [in Hebrew] (Tel Aviv: Miskal-Yedioth Ahronoth Books, 1998), 125.

5. The "Democratic Putsch" of 1999

1. Benjamin Netanyahu, lecture, Israel's National Security College, August 14, 1997.

2. Shelah, *The Israeli Military,* 78.

3. Maj. Gen. Oren Shachor, interview in *Yedioth Ahronoth,* August 15, 1997.

4. Amir Oren, *Ha'aretz,* January 22, 1999.

5. Amir Oren, *Ha'aretz,* February 4, 1998.

6. Ze'ev Schiff, *Ha'aretz,* May 9, 1997.

7. Yoram Peri, *Telepopulism: Media and Politics in Israel* (Stanford, Calif.: Stanford University Press, 2004).

8. *Seven Days* (supplement), *Yedioth Ahronoth,* January 22, 1999.

9. I am referring here only to career officers who ended their military service with the rank of colonel or higher. Many Israeli citizens whose careers are not in the military serve as officers in the reserve forces.

10. For a detailed analysis, see Peri, *Between Battles and Ballots.*

11. Horowitz and Lissak, *Troubles in Utopia.*

12. Baruch Kimmerling, "Militarism in Israeli Society" [in Hebrew], *Theory and Criticism* 4 (1993). Uri Ben-Eliezer, "Do the Generals Rule Israel?" in *Society in the Mirror* [in Hebrew], ed. Hanna Herzog (Tel Aviv: Ramot, 1999), 235–267.

13. Another case involved a group of major generals, headed by former CGS Yigal Yadin, who created the Dash Party in 1976. Also, when CGS Rafael Eitan left the IDF in 1983, he founded a new party, Tzomet, which ran in the 1985 elections, and was even a minister in rightist governments. Other officers founded political parties as well. For example, Maj. Gen. (res.) Rechavam Ze'evi and Brig. Gen. (res.) Avigdor Kahalani founded the Moledet Party and the Center Party, respectively. In

November 2005, Sharon split from the Likid and established a new party called Kadima, while Maj.-Gen. (res.) Uzi Dayan formed a new party called Tafnit.

14. *Ma'ariv,* October 1, 1997.

15. Yossi Verter and Yerach Tal, *Ha'aretz,* January 25, 1999.

16. *Seven Days* (supplement), *Yedioth Ahronoth,* February 5, 1999.

17. Dalya Shahori, *Ha'aretz,* December 24, 1997.

18. *Ha'aretz,* November 7, 1996.

19. *Yedioth Ahronoth,* August 15, 1997.

20. Maj. Gen. Shahor, interview by Amira Hass, *Seven Days* (supplement), *Yedioth Ahronoth,* January 22, 1999.

21. David Agmon, *Channel One News,* February 8, 1998.

22. *Yedioth Ahronoth,* January 15, 1998.

23. Ibid.

24. Amnon Shahak, interview by author.

25. Ehud Barak, *Channel One News,* June 7, 1999.

26. Barak, interview by author.

27. Among the major generals, in addition to the prime minister himself, were Ministers Vilnay, Shahak, and Mordecai.

6. The IDF Confronts a New Intifada

1. Barak, interview by author.

2. Dan Naveh, *Executive Secrets* [in Hebrew] (Tel Aviv: Yedioth Ahronoth Books, 1999), 50.

3. Maj. Gen. Doron Almog, interview by author.

4. For a detailed analysis of these negotiations by a participant observer, see Itamar Rabinovich, *Waging Peace* [in Hebrew] (Tel Aviv: Dvir, 2004).

5. The deteriorating relations with the Palestinians attracted Israelis' attention to such a degree that very few paid any attention to the failed negotiations with Syria. Though an account of the negotiations was first published by Raviv Drucker in *Harakiri, Ehud Barak: The Failure* [in Hebrew] (Tel Aviv: Yedioth Ahronoth Books, 2002), only in 2004 was Barak's role in this affair criticized, when President Clinton and Dennis Ross also blamed him for failing to achieve peace with Assad. The author's interview with Martin Indyk also brings this to light.

6. Shelah, *The Israeli Military,* 67.

7. This quote is taken from the author's interview with Arieli, but many other officers also affirmed that this was characteristic of Mofaz's mode of work.

8. Uzi Dayan, interview by author. See also Dayan, "What Is Needed and What Prevails in the Relations between the Political and the Military Echelons."

9. Ibid.

10. Amos Gilead, lecture, Jaffee Center for Strategic Studies, Tel Aviv University, May 23, 2002. See also Gilead's testimony in Yaacov Bar-Siman-Tov, ed., *Views of the Generals: On the Collapse of the Oslo Process and the Violent Israeli-Palestinian Conflict* [in Hebrew] (Jerusalem: Leonard Davis Institute for International Relations, Hebrew University of Jerusalem, 2003).

11. Amos Malka, "The Regional System in the Stability Test," in Bar-Siman-Tov, ed., *Views of the Generals*.

12. The Palestinians demand an arrangement based on justice. Hence, they are prepared to reach a settlement with Israel, but not one that legitimizes a war that Israel—as they see it—waged against them in 1948–1949. Ephraim Lavie, lecture, Peres Center for Peace, May 18, 2003.

13. Barak, interview by author. The term "hubris" was used by his media adviser, Gadi Blatiansky, in an interview by author.

14. The best description published to date on the first period of the war appears in a book by Amos Harel and Avi Isacharoff, *The Seventh War* [in Hebrew] (Tel Aviv: Miskal–Yedioth Ahronoth Books, 2004).

15. Harel and Isacharoff, *The Seventh War*, 74–75. Fogel went further saying that the military's modus operandi also had profound political significance. "Our actions destroyed the PA's administrative apparatus. We didn't create the Hamas, but we helped it to grow."

16. Ben Caspit, *Ma'ariv*, September, 6, 2002.

17. Ibid.

18. Shlomo Ben-Ami, *A Front with No Rear* [in Hebrew] (Tel Aviv: Miskal–Yedioth Ahronoth Books, 2004), 321.

19. Gadi Blatiansky, interview by author.

20. Kobi Michael, *The Violent Israeli-Palestinian Conflict: From Conflict Resolution to Conflict Management* (Jerusalem: Jerusalem Institute for Israel Studies, forthcoming). This found expression in a March 2004 Foreign Affairs and Security Committee report that was very critical of the assessments of the intelligence community before and during the Iraq war.

21. Quoted in Harel and Isacharoff, *The Seventh War*, 87.

22. Harel and Isacharoff, *The Seventh War*, 39.

23. Yossi Beilin, interview by author.

24. Ephraim Sneh, interview by author.

25. Gilead Sher, *Just beyond Reach: The Israeli-Palestinian Negotiation, 1999–2001* [in Hebrew] (Tel Aviv: Yedioth Ahronoth Books, 2001).

26. Col. Gal Hirsch, "From 'Cast Lead' to 'Another Way': The Development of the Military Campaign in the Central Command [in Hebrew] *Maarachot* (February 2004): 26–31.

27. Drucker, *Harakiri*, 325.

28. Mazal Mualem, *Ha'aretz,* October 14, 2001.

29. Hirsch, "From 'Cast Lead' to 'Another Way,'" 28.

30. Amos Harel, *Ha'aretz,* December 12, 2000.

31. Sher, *Just Beyond Reach,* 367.

32. Amos Harel, *Ha'aretz,* December 29, 2000.

33. Ze'ev Schiff, *Ha'aretz,* December 31, 2000.

34. For further details, see Drucker, *Harakiri,* 326.

35. Ofer Shelah, *Yedioth Ahronoth*, December 22, 2000.

36. Ibid.

37. For a broad expression of Ya'alon's conception regarding the war against the Palestinians, see Ari Shavit, interview in *Seven Days* (supplement), *Ha'aretz,* August 29, 2002.

38. Amnon Shahak, interview by author.

39. Sher, *Just beyond Reach,* 368.

40. Ben Caspit, *Ma'ariv,* September 6, 2002.

41. Drucker, *Harakiri*, 331–333.

42. Ben-Ami, *A Front with No Rear,* 397.

43. Arieli, interview by author.

7. Sharon's Double-Headed Government

1. For the "fuzziness" of low-intensity conflict, see Stuart A. Cohen, "Why Do They Quarrel? Civil-Military Relations in LIC Situations," in *Democracies and Small Wars,* ed. Efraim Inbar, (London: Frank Cass, 2003) 21–40.

2. Harel and Isacharoff, *The Seventh War,* 108.

3. Yoel Markus, *Ha'aretz,* June 22, 2002.

4. Harel and Isacharoff, *The Seventh War,* 114–115.

5. Amir Oren, *Ha'aretz,* February 15, 2002.

6. Harel and Isacharoff, *The Seventh War.*

7. Harel and Isacharoff, *The Seventh War,* 223–225.

8. CGS Moshe Ya'alon related that "We restricted the use of tanks because of the harsh effect of the photograph of a tank confronting a child. Later we used helicopters for a few minutes only, or at night so that it would not be possible to photograph them." Moshe Ya'alon, lecture, Israeli Communication Association Conference, April 20, 2005.

9. Gilead Sher, *Just beyond Reach,* 368.

10. Kenneth W. Kemp and Charles Hudin, "Civil Supremacy over the Military: Its Nature and Limits," *Armed Forces and Society* 19, no. 1 (1992): 7–26.

11. Ze'ev Schiff, *Ha'aretz*, March 4, 2001.

12. Moshe Arens in *Ha'aretz*, January 7, 2002.

13. Amos Harel, *Ha'aretz*, October 30, 2002.

14. Arik Bender, *Ma'ariv*, January 23, 2002.

15. Ben Caspit, *Ma'ariv*, May 30, 2002.

16. Amos Harel, *Ha'aretz*, April 5, 2002.

17. Amir Oren, *Ha'aretz*, September 28, 2001.

18. *Yedioth Ahronoth*, September 28, 2001.

19. Amir Oren, *Ha'aretz*, September 5, 2001.

20. Uzi Benziman, *Ha'aretz*, September 30, 2001.

21. Nahum Barnea, *Yedioth Ahronoth*, November 24, 2000.

22. Gal Hirsch, *Maarachot*, 2004.

23. Ofer Shelah, *Yedioth Ahronoth*, December 22, 2000.

24. These dramatic accusations were published on December 28, 2001, in an interview with Brig. Gen. Dov Zadka by none other than the IDF journal *Bamahane*.

25. Explicit cases will be described in the following chapters.

26. Institute for Anti-Terrorist Policy Survey, April 15, 2001. Also at http://new.walla.co.il.

27. "The Peace Index," Tami Steinmetz Center for Peace Research, Tel Aviv University, April 2001. See also Zeev Schiff, *Ha'aretz*, February 17, 2002.

28. Editorial, *Ha'aretz*, October 28, 2001.

29. Eli Kamir, *Ma'ariv*, October 19, 2001.

30. For details of this incident, see Eli Kamir, *Ma'ariv*, September 19, 2001.

31. Nitzan Horovitz, *Ha'aretz*, September 9, 2001.

32. Eli Kamir, *Ma'ariv*, October 19, 2001.

33. B. Michael, *Yedioth Ahronoth*, May 31, 2000.

8. Political-Military Relations in Low-Intensity Conflict

1. Although Harel and Isacharoff call this the seventh war, as they do not count the first intifada as one of Israel's wars, it is really the eighth.

2. Although Israel was involved in this sort of conflict for many years, it was only at the beginning of this decade that material on LIC began to be published in Israel, first in articles in the military journal *Maarachot* and later in books. See Efraim Inbar, ed., *Democracies and Small Wars* (London: Frank Cass, 2003); Haggai Golan and Shaul Shay, eds., *Low Intensity Conflict* [in Hebrew] (Tel Aviv: Maarachot, 2004).

3. Shmuel Nir, *The Limited Confrontation* (IDF, 2001). Nir laid down the written foundation for the new concept within the IDF.

4. Shmuel Nir, "The Nature of the Limited Conflict," in *Low Intensity Conflict,* ed. Golan and Shay, 19–45.

5. *Tatzpit* (IDF Training Division, December 2000). The text quotation is taken from a British army handbook: *Operations Short of War/Counter Insurgency Handbook* (Camberly, UK: Staff College, 1993).

6. Nir, *The Limited Confrontation.*

7. Amir Oren, *Ha'aretz.*

8. Shmuel Nir, "Attrition and the Test of Adaptation," in *Studies in National Security* 4 [in Hebrew] (March 2003): 164–174.

9. Uzi Benziman, *Ha'aretz,* July 13, 2001.

10. Nir, *The Limited Confrontation.*

11. Giora Eiland, lecture, Tel Aviv Workshop for Science, Technology and Security, Tel Aviv University, December 30, 2004.

12. Shmuel Zakai, interview in *Ma'ariv,* June 3, 2005.

13. See Eitan and Ya'alon pronouncements in *Ma'ariv,* March 29, 2002. Ya'alon is quoted in Kobi Michael, "The End to the Deterministic Distinction," in *Low Intensity Conflict,* ed. Golan and Shay, 201–238.

14. Alex Fishman, *Yedioth Ahronoth,* May 18, 2001.

15. Ze'ev Schiff, *Ha'aretz,* May 18, 2001.

16. "Peace Index," April 2002.

17. Gideon Alon, *Ha'aretz,* May 26, 2002. Uzi Benziman, *Ha'aretz,* March 7, 2002.

18. Amos Harel, *Ha'aretz,* April 24, 2003.

19. At one point, in summer 2004, 60 percent of Israelis supported the dismantling of most settlements on the West Bank and all Israeli settlements in the Gaza Strip (*Ma'ariv,* July 12, 2004).

20. Col. (ret.) Reuven Erlich, director of the Intelligence and Terrorism Information Center, in an interview by author, argued that this was done by retired officers and therefore did not involve serving MID officers.

21. Aharon Yariv, interview by author, 1980.

9. The Tragedy of CGS Ya'alon

1. To be precise, Ya'alon was not exactly fired; he was allowed to complete his three-year term of office, but he did not receive a year's extension, a long-held custom with chiefs of general staff.

2. In March 2004, Mofaz, as defense minister, suddenly changed his mind and began to support Sharon's proposal for unilateral withdrawal from the Gaza Strip. Commentators cynical about this strange volte-face noted that Mofaz's political partnership with, even dependence on, Sharon made it necessary.

3. Harel and Isacharoff, *The Seventh War,* 91.

4. Yo'av Limor, *Ma'ariv,* July 25, 2002.

5. Uzi Benziman, *Ha'aretz,* August 30, 2002. Ben Caspit, *Ha'aretz,* August 20, 2002.

6. Uzi Benziman, *Ha'aretz,* August 30, 2002.

7. Yo'av Limor, *Ma'ariv,* July 25, 2002.

8. Eliot A. Cohen writes, "But perhaps the most important cost of elite units is the damage they can cause to sound civil-military relations. By subverting the chain of command, courting favor with politicians, and distorting perceptions, they disturb the professional basis of healthy civil-military relations." See Cohen, *Commandos and Politicians,* 40.

9. Ben Caspit, *Ha'aretz,* August 26, 2002.

10. Moshe Ya'alon, interview by Ari Shavit, *Seven Days* (supplement), *Ha'aretz,* August 29, 2002.

11. Uzi Benziman, *Ha'aretz,* August 30, 2002.

12. B. Michael, *Yedioth Ahronoth,* August 30, 2002.

13. Doron Rosenblum, *Ha'aretz,* August 30, 2002.

14. Aluf Ben, *Ha'aretz,* August 30, 2002.

15. Moshe Ya'alon, "Preparing the Forces for the Limited Confrontation," *Maarachot,* December 2001, 380–381.

16. Shmuel Nir, *The Limited Confrontation.*

17. Ya'alon, interview by Shavit.

18. Doron Rosenblum, *Ha'aretz,* August 30, 2002.

19. Nahum Barnea, *Yedioth Ahronoth,* July 11, 2003.

20. Uzi Benziman, *Ha'aretz,* July 10, 2003. See also Ari Shavit, *Ha'aretz,* July 10, 2003.

21. Nahum Barnea, *Yedioth Ahronoth,* July 11, 2003.

22. Amos Harel, *Ha'aretz,* January 22, 2004.

23. Uzi Benziman, *Ha'aretz,* October 29, 2003.

24. Yitzhak Harel, interview by author, April 2004. Up to 2004, suicide bombings accounted for only .5 percent of terrorist attacks, yet inflicted 50 percent of all casualties.

25. Ben Caspit, *Ma'ariv,* October 31, 2003.

26. Nahum Barnea, *Yedioth Ahronoth,* October 29, 2003.

27. Amos Harel, *Ha'aretz,* December 5, 2003.

28. This was the headline over Barnea's lead article in *Yedioth Ahronoth.* The headlines in the other two papers that day were similar.

29. Armam Mitzna, *Ha'aretz,* November 2, 2003.

30. See interviews with Ya'alon and assessments, inter alia, in Nahum Barnea, *Yedioth Ahronoth,* October 29, 2003, and Alex Fishman, *Yedioth Ahronoth,* December 26, 2003.

31. Ya'alon in a briefing to the Herzog Institute for Media, Politics and Society, Tel Aviv University, February 18, 2005. See also Kobi Michael, "The End of the Deterministic Distinction," 201–238.

32. Aharon Zeevi-Farkash, in conversation with the author. Zeevi-Farkash also spoke in a similar manner in a lecture he gave to veterans of the IDF intelligence community, Tel Aviv, January 18, 2004.

33. Ben Caspit, *Ma'ariv,* January 9, 2004.

34. See Drucker, *Harakiri.*

35. Ya'alon in *Ha'aretz,* June 1, 2005.

10. The Chief of Staff as a Political Actor

1. Ben-Meir, *Civil-Military Relations,* 85.

2. The Israeli CGS takes on a role similar to the ones held by Eisenhower and Marshall in World War II. Or, drawing a comparison from the 2003 war in Iraq, the Israeli CGS wears four hats: that of General John Abizaid, CINC Central Command (CENTCOM); that of General Richard B. Myers (the CJCS); that of the CGS of the United States Army, General Peter Schoomaker; and that of the commander of the United States Army service component of CENTCOM, General Abizaid (COMDR ARCENT).

3. Ben-Meir, *Civil-Military Relations,* 92.

4. Yaari, *Civil Control of the Military.*

5. *Duyikat et al. v. the Israeli Government et al.,* Supreme Court verdict 390/679, P.D.(Piskey Dinn) LD (1) 1.

6. Rafael Eitan, *A Story of a Soldier* [in Hebrew] (Tel Aviv: Ma'ariv, 1985), 182. Another case was that of the deputy CGS, Maj. Gen. Tal, who refused to carry out a command by Defense Minister Moshe Dayan. In March 1974, Dayan ordered Tal to renew the fighting of the Yom Kippur War, despite the corroboration of a cease-fire. Tal argued that Dayan's request was illegal and asked Dayan to present it to him in writing. Dayan drew back, and the fighting did not take place. See interview with Maj. Gen. Israel Tal in Peri, *Between Battles and Ballots,* 257–259.

7. Dan Naveh, *Executive Secrets* [in Hebrew] (Tel Aviv: Yedioth Ahronoth Books, 1999), 17.

8. Amos Perlmutter, *The Military and Politics in Modern Times* (New Haven, Conn.: Yale University Press, 1977).

9. Motti Golani, "The 1956 Sinai War: Political and Military Aspects" [in Hebrew] (PhD diss., Haifa University, 1992).

10. Ibid., 394.

11. Mordechai Gur, *Chief of Staff* [in Hebrew] (Tel Aviv: Ma'arachot, 1998), 56.

12. Ibid., 57.

13. Ibid., 94.

14. Ibid., 94.

15. *Yedioth Ahronoth,* November 15, 1977.

16. Gur, *Chief of Staff,* 312.

17. Ibid., 343.

18. Ibid., 320.

19. Ibid., 337.

20. Eitan, *A Story of a Soldier,* 20.

21. Moshe Arens, *Peace and War in the Middle East, 1988–1992* [in Hebrew] (Tel Aviv: Yedioth Ahronoth Books, 1995), 229.

22. Gur, *Chief of Staff,* 349.

23. Ibid., 352.

11. Is It a Just War?

1. Cohen, "Why Do They Quarrel? Civil-Military Tensions in LIC Situations," 21–40.

2. For an elaboration of this issue and references from court rulings, see Judge Amnon Straschnov, in *Civil-Military Relations in Israel: Influence and Restraint,* Memorandum 68, ed. Ram Erez (Tel Aviv: Jaffee Center for Strategic Studies, Tel Aviv University, 2003), 39–44.

3. *Ha'aretz,* April 4, 2002.

4. See Dalia Lev-Sade, "Communal Strength—the Social Challenge in National Resilience Building" (paper, Fourth Herzliya Conference, Institute for Policy and Strategy, Lauder School of Government, Diplomacy and Strategy, Interdisciplinary Center, Herzliya, December 2003).

5. *Betzelem Report on Human Rights in the Occupied Territories* (Jerusalem: Betzelem, May 2002).

6. The IDF declared that it would not publicize the new directives, as they were "operational regulations which if made known will make it difficult for the soldiers to perform their duty." See appendix to ibid.

7. Ze'ev Schiff, *Ha'aretz,* August 16, 2002.

8. Alex Fishman, *Yedioth Ahronoth,* January 19, 2001.

9. Ze'ev Schiff, *Ha'aretz,* February 18, 2002.

10. These phenomena were widely documented. The most detailed documentation appears in a series of reports published on a nearly monthly basis by the Israeli

Information Center for Human Rights in the Territories, known as "Betzelem." These reports refer to specific events or deal extensively with a fundamental issue (e.g., maltreatment at roadblocks, use of live fire to enforce curfews, and firing at ambulances).

11. Alex Fishman, *Yedioth Ahronoth,* January 19, 2001.

12. Hearings of the Knesset Constitutional Committee, June 22, 2003. In January 2004, the military chief advocate published a document revealing that in the first three years of the intifada, during which approximately 2,500 Palestinians were killed and about 14,000 injured, the military police conducted seventy-two investigations of death cases, from which only thirteen resulted in legal charges. See Akiva Eldar, *Ha'aretz,* January 6, 2004.

13. See Dor, *The Suppression of Guilt.*

14. See Sara Leibovich-Dar, *Ha'aretz,* January 23, 2002. This situation kept on deteriorating, as the Ministry of Foreign Affairs spokesperson and the military spokesperson admitted in interviews with the author.

15. *Seven Days* (supplement), *Ha'aretz,* August 30, 2002.

16. Bo'az Ha'etzni, *Besheva,* May 5, 2005

17. *Seven Days* (supplement), *Ha'aretz,* August 23, 2002.

18. *Yedioth Ahronoth,* April 15, 2004.

19. The story was extensively covered by the media. See, for example, Ariela Ringel-Hoffman, *Yedioth Ahronot,* February 23, 2005.

20. Asa Kasher and Amos Yadlin, "Military Ethics of Fighting Terror: An Israeli Perspective," *Journal of Military Ethics* 4, no. 1 (2005): 3–32.

21. Ibid.

22. Ibid. There were some, among them the vice minister of security, Ze'ev Boim, who extended this definition even further, to also include those who supported terrorism ideologically.

23. Ibid.

24. *Geneva Convention Relative to the Protection of Civilian Persons in Time of War* (Geneva, August 1949), part 3, section 1, articles 28 and 29.

25. Arik Diamant, *Ha'aretz,* March 2, 2004.

12. Conscientious Objection

1. See also Alek D. Epstein "On the Collapse of the Normative Framework of Citizens' Commitment to the Army in the 1990s," [in Hebrew] in *In the Name of Security,* ed. Majid Al-Haj and Uri Ben-Eliezer (Haifa: Haifa University Press, 2003).

2. Courage to Refuse, http://seruv.org.il.

3. Yoram Peri, "Israel: Conscientious Objection in a Democracy under Siege," in *The New Conscientious Objection,* ed. Charles C. Moskos and John Whiteclay Chambers II (New York: Oxford University Press, 1993).

4. See Courage to Refuse, http://www.seruv.org.il.

5. John Rawls, *A Theory of Justice* (Oxford: Oxford University Press, 1973).

6. Interview, *Ha'aretz,* February 2002.

7. Ami Ayalon, *Channel One News,* February 1, 2002.

8. Michael Ben-Yair, *Ha'aretz,* March 3, 2002.

9. Ibid. In May 2004, the Attorney General Mazuz also expressed an "understanding" of the moral drive of the conscientious objectors, although he agreed that they should be punished.

10. *Ma'ariv,* December 17, 2003.

11. *Shein vs. the Minister of Defense,* Supreme Court ruling 734/83, PDI, LH (3)303. Incidentally, this ruling constituted, in a dialectic manner, an achievement for the Israeli Association of War Objectors. It was the first time after thirty-five years of public strife that the court ruled in favor of the right to conscientious objection. There have been very few applicants though: in the years prior to the intifada, there were only a few dozen applications, and less than 10 percent were accepted. See Arieh Dayan, *Ha'aretz,* March 3, 2002.

12. Alek D. Epstein, "On the Collapse of the Normative Framework."

13. Ibid.

14. Michael Keren, "Justifications of Conscientious Objection: An Israeli Case Study," *International Journal of the Sociology of Law* 26 (1998).

15. Lilli Galili, *Ha'aretz,* May 3, 2002. History professor Aviad Kleinberg also claimed that using the military identity in acts of protest damages civil society in Israel and imposes militant characteristics on the public struggle. See *Ha'aretz,* December 28, 2003.

16. The pilots' ad was published in *Ha'aretz* on September 26, 2003.

17. See, for example, MK Michael Ratzon, *Ha'aretz,* September 26, 2003.

18. Editorial, *Ha'aretz,* September 29, 2003. See references to the media's handling of the pilots' case in *Ha'yn Hashvi'yt* 47 (November 2003).

19. *Yedioth Ahronoth*, September 29, 2003.

20. *Ha'aretz,* May 15, 2002, which also reports that pressure from the reserve units succeeded in stopping the operation in Gaza.

21. *Seven Days* (supplement), *Ha'aretz,* December 5, 2003.

13. Who Won the Intifada?

1. Dichter made these remarks at the Herzliya Conference on December 16. See the relevant news item in *Ha'aretz,* December 17, 2003.

2. *Yedioth Ahronoth,* July 13, 2001.

3. *Ma'ariv,* January 21, 2001.

4. *Yedioth Ahronoth,* November 14, 2003.

5. People's Voice, http://www.mifkad.org.il/FAQ.asp.

6. The Knesset, http://www.knesset.gov.il/process/docs/geneva_eng.html.

7. Ben Caspit, *Ma'ariv,* January 9, 2004.

8. ISA report, published in the press on January 9, 2004.

9. Ben Caspit, *Ma'ariv,* January 9, 2004.

10. Ze'ev Schiff, *Ha'aretz,* July 16, 2003.

11. Ben Caspit, *Ma'ariv,* January 9, 2004.

12. Ya'alon, interview by Ari Sahvit, *Seven Days* (supplement), *Ha'aretz,* July 3, 2005.

13. Brig. Gen. Ruth Yaron, interview by author.

14. Ze'ev Schiff, *Ha'aretz,* March 9, 2004. During that same testimony, Ya'alon took a shot at the government, stating, with his usual frankness and honesty, that "some of the encampments [preliminary settlements] were established by permission of the political echelon, and not necessarily in accordance with the law."

15. Amir Rapoport, *Ha'aretz,* February 19, 2004.

16. Ben Caspit, *Ma'ariv,* March 9, 2004.

17. Bitterlemons.org, http://www.bitterlemons.org.

18. Annual report of the ISA, *Ha'aretz,* January 7, 2005.

19. Only 260 of those killed, and 1,700 of those injured, were security forces personnel.

20. *Ma'ariv,* December, 16, 2004. In 2005, the IDF confronted a serious problem of conscientious objection from the Right. This occurred when nationalist-clerical rabbis ordered soldiers and officers to disobey commanders and to not take part in the evacuation of Jewish settlers from the Gaza Strip. Though the IDF feared thousands of soldiers might disobey orders, only five professional soldiers and sixty-three reservists refused to obey their commanders during the disengagement process. They were punished by their military commanders or tried by courts and imprisoned. These events have dramatically deepened the gap between the military and the national-religious sector of Israeli society. This topic calls for serious research and analysis.

21. Gil Levy examined the personal data of 229 soldiers who were killed in direct confrontations with Palestinians over the course of the intifada and found that most of them came from lower social classes, a departure from the past, when IDF combat units reflected the traditional elites—middle-class Ashkenazis; members of old, established rural communities; and graduates of prestigious high schools in the big cities. Yagil Levy, *Ha'aretz,* February 4, 2005.

22. Lecture, Trauma Center for Victims of Terror and War, Tel Aviv, December 3, 2004.

23. Bar-Siman-Tov, ed., *Views of the Generals,* 46.

24. Edward N. Luttwak, "A Post-Heroic Military," *Foreign Affairs* 75, no. 4 (1996): 33–44.

25. Harel and Isacharoff, *The Seventh War,* 98.

26. Col. (res.) Shmuel Nir, "There Is No Catch Here," *Maarachot,* January 2003, 68–70. Lt. Col. (res.) Dani Reshef revealed the same thought process when he wrote, "The IDF has to adopt a completely new war doctrine, which is totally different from, and in fact the opposite of, the doctrine it had developed for war against the regular armies of the Arab states." Dani Reshef, "A New Approach to Low Intensity Conflict," *Maarachot,* April 2003, 9–11.

27. Col. (res.) Yehuda Wagman, "The Limited Conflict Catch," *Maarachot,* September 2002, 68–77.

14. Israel's Security Culture

1. Richard H. Kohn, "How Democracies Control the Military," *Journal of Democracy* 8, no. 4 (1997): 140–153.

2. See, for example, Peter D. Feaver and Richard H. Kohn, eds., *Soldiers and Civilians: The Civil-Military Gap and American National Security* (Cambridge, Mass.: MIT Press, 2001); the extensive CIS Project on the American Military Culture in the Twenty-First Century, February 2000; and the Working Paper Series of the U.S. Post-War Civil-Military Relations of the Olim Institute for Strategic Studies at Harvard University.

3. At the end of December 1989, Prime Minister Shamir demanded the resignation of Minister Weizman, accusing him of endangering the security of the state when he met a representative of the PLO, Nebil Ramlawi, in Geneva. Shamir later settled for Weizman's exclusion from the defense cabinet. See Yossi Beilin, *Touching Peace* [in Hebrew] (Tel Aviv: Miskal-Yedioth Ahronoth Books, 1997), 44.

4. In 1982, a demonstration was held in Tel Aviv's city square, Kikar Malkei Yisrael, against Israel's involvement in the Lebanon War. The demonstrators called for the resignation of Defense Minister Ariel Sharon because of the Christian massacre of Muslims in the Sabra and Shatila refugee camps. Dan Halutz, then a civilian, held a counterdemonstration expressing support for Sharon. Twenty-three years later Halutz was nominated CGS by Sharon's government.

5. The tradition of newly retired officers entering the Knesset along the entire political spectrum continued in the beginning of the twenty-first century. Brig. Gen. Eitam became the leader of the National Religious Party and Brig. Gen. Eldad joined the National Unity Party on the right, while Maj. Gen. Danny Yatom joined the Labor Party.

6. Benget Abrahamsson, *Military Professionalism and Political Power* (Beverly Hills, Calif.: Sage, 1972).

7. Elizabeth Kier, "Culture and French Military Doctrine before World War II," in *The Culture of National Security: Norms and Identity in World Politics,* ed. Peter J. Katzenstein, (New York: Columbia University Press, 1996) 202–203.

8. Thomas U. Berger, "Norms, Identity, and National Security in Germany and Japan," in *The Culture of National Security, Norms and Identity in World Politics,* 326–327.

9. Peter J. Katzenstein, ed., *The Culture of National Security, Norms and Identity in World Politics* (New York: Columbia University Press, 1996).

10. Aharon Klieman, "Israeli Negotiating Culture," in *How Israelis and Palestinians Negotiate: A Cross-Cultural Analysis of the Oslo Peace Process,* ed. Tamara Cofman Wittes (Washington, D.C.: United States Institute of Peace Press, 2005), 87.

11. On this matter, see Baruch Kimmerling, "Militarism in Israeli Society," [in Hebrew] *Theory and Criticism* 4 (1993): 123–140. See also Abrahamsson, *Military Professionalism and Political Power.* Abrahamsson enumerated five characteristics of military thinking, which include a pessimistic view of human nature, a belief that there will always be war, alarmism regarding the dangers constantly awaiting the state, and a high level of nationalism.

12. Yehoshafat Harkabi, *War and Strategy* [in Hebrew] (Tel Aviv: Ministry of Defense, 1990), 512.

13. Edna Lomsky-Feder and Eyal Ben-Ari, eds., *The Military and Militarism in Israeli Society* (Albany: State University of New York Press, 1999).

14. Daniel Bar-Tal, Dan Jacobson, and Aharon Klieman, eds., *Security Concerns: Insight from the Israeli Experience* (Stanford, Conn.: JAI Press, 1998).

15. Klieman, "Israeli Negotiating Culture."

16. These findings emerged clearly from a study I conducted of one hundred senior IDF officers (unpublished).

17. Berger, "Norms, Identity, and National Security in Germany and Japan," 326–327.

18. This point has been raised repeatedly by some, including Eitan Bentsur, past director-general of the Foreign Ministry, in interview by author, July 2001.

19. Cohen, Eisenstadt, and Bacevich, *Knives, Tanks, and Missiles,* 79.

20. Shelah, *The Israeli Military,* 53–54.

21. Emanuel Wald, *The Curse of the Broken Tools* [in Hebrew] (Jerusalem: Schocken, 1987). See also Kobi Michael, "The Army's Influence on the Transition Process from War to Peace: The Israeli Case" (PhD diss., Hebrew University, Jerusalem, 2004).

22. Arieli, interview by author.

23. Shlomo Ben-Ami, *A Front with No Rear* [in Hebrew] (Tel Aviv: Miskal-Yedioth Ahronoth Books, 2004), 107.

24. Uri Savir, *The Process* (Tel Aviv: Miskal, 1988).

25. Joseph S. Nye, *Soft Power* (New York: Foreign Affairs, 2004).

26. Itamar Rabinovich, *Waging Peace* [in Hebrew] (Tel Aviv: Dvir, 2004), 71.

27. Yagil Levy, "How Militarization Drives Political Control of the Military: The Case of Israel," in *Political Power and Social Theory* 11 (1997).

28. Hirschfeld, *Oslo,* 160.

29. Henry Kissinger, *Does America Need a Foreign Policy?* (New York: Simon & Schuster, 2001), 176.

30. Yossi Beilin, *Touching Peace* [in Hebrew] (Tel Aviv: Miskal-Yedioth Ahronoth Books, 1997), 223.

31. Tal, *National Security,* 58.

32. The first open deviation from this since the Sinai campaign was in the Lebanon War in the summer of 1982, when Prime Minister Begin spoke in praise of an initiated offensive war as a "just war."

33. Tal, *National Security,* 58.

34. Ofer Shelah, *Yedioth Ahronoth,* March 11, 2005.

35. From a study by Maj. Gen. (res.) Haim Nadel, quoted by Amir Oren in *Ha'aretz,* April 13, 2004.

36. Dennis Ross, interview by author.

37. Savir, *The Process,* 237.

38. See Saib Arikat, interview by Amira Lam, *Yedioth Ahronoth,* January 26, 2001.

39. Savir, *The Process,* 246.

40. Akiva Eldar, *Ha'aretz,* December 20, 2000.

41. *Ha'aretz* supplement, September 14, 2001.

42. Sher, *Just Beyond Reach,* 322.

15. Camp David and the Intifada—What Went Wrong?

1. For a very good summary of this literature, see Rabinovich, *Waging Peace,* 116–163.

2. Aaron David Miller, lecture, Annual Jimmy Carter Lecture at Tel Aviv University, Tel Aviv, May 2, 2004.

3. Ben-Ami, *A Front with No Rear,* 473.

4. Ephraim Lavie, head of the Palestinian desk of the MID, lecture, Peres Peace Center, Tel Aviv, May 18, 2003.

5. Ben-Ami, *A Front with No Rear,* 473.

6. Ibid., 144.

7. Klieman, "Israeli Negotiating Culture."

8. Louis Kriesberg, "Paths to Varieties of Inter-Communal Reconciliation," in *From Conflict Resolution to Peacebuilding*, ed. Ho-Wong Jeong, (Fitchburg, Mass.: Dartmouth, 1999).

9. Louis Kriesberg, "Negotiating the Partition of Palestine and Evolving Israeli-Palestinian Relations," *Brown Journal of World Affairs* 7 (2000): 63–80.

10. In fact, Rabin even discussed with President Clinton when they rehearsed the ceremony his concerns about physical contact with Arafat.

11. Bill Clinton, *My Life* (New York: Knopf, 2004), 913.

12. Aaron David Miller, interview by author.

13. As quoted in Ben-Ami, *A Front with No Rear*, 230.

14. Danny Rubinstein, Robert Malley, Hussein Agha, Ehud Barak, and Benny Morris, *Rashomon Camp David* (Tel Aviv: Yedioth Ahronoth, 2003), 51. Maj. Gen. Amos Gilead, lecture, Jaffee Center for Strategic Research, Tel Aviv University, May 23, 2002. See also his testimony in Bar-Siman-Tov, *Views of the Generals*, 13–25.

15. Saar Raveh and Maaya Pecker-Rinat, "To Win and Stay Humane," *Maarachot*, September 2002, 20–25.

16. Maj. Gen. Amos Gilead, lecture, Jaffee Center for Strategic Research, Tel Aviv University. See also his testimony in Bar-Siman-Tov, *Views of the Generals*, 13–25.

17. See http://www.haaretz.co.il/hasite/pages/LiArtSR.jhtml?objNo=56433/.

18. Gilead became such a central figure that on the eve of the Iraqi war in 2003 he was given the role of "national explainer," that is, the government's chief public analyst, despite the fact that he was an officer in uniform. In retrospect, it turned out that he was wrong in his assessment concerning the existence of weapons of mass destruction in Iraq, and in the summer of 2004 his public status declined considerably.

19. Herzog, interview by Ben Caspit, *Ma'ariv* (weekend edition), August 27, 2004.

20. Yaron Nir, "Recognition of the Need for a Diversified Approach to the Palestinian Standpoint," *Maarachot*, April 2003, 18–23.

21. Briefing by Dichter, June 18, 2004.

22. Shelah, *The Israeli Military*, 70–71.

23. Ronen Bergman, *Authority Given* [in Hebrew] (Tel Aviv: Yedioth Ahronoth Books, 2002).

24. Rubinstein, Malley, Agha, Barak, and Morris, *Rashomon Camp David*.

25. It is worth mentioning that this position also has many supporters within the IDF itself. Bar-Siman-Tov, Lavie, Michael, and Bar-Tal, *The Israeli-Palestinian Violent Conflict 2000–2004*, 48–52.

26. Gal Hirsch, "From 'Cast Lead' to 'Another Way': The Development of the Military Campaign in the Central Command [in Hebrew] *Maarachot,* February 2004, 26–31.

27. Harel and Isacharoff, *The Seventh War.*

28. Hirsch, "From 'Cast Lead' to 'Another Way.'"

29. Ya'alon, interview by Ari Shavit, *Seven Days* (supplement), *Ha'aretz,* June 3, 2005.

30. Editorial, *Ha'aretz,* June 2, 2005.

16. Conclusion: The IDF—Sword or Olive Branch?

1. See Robert Kagan, *Of Paradise and Power* (New York: Knopf, 2003).

2. On the concept of hard versus soft power, see Joesph S. Nye, *Soft Power* (New York: Foreign Affairs, 2004).

3. Michael C. Desch, "Soldiers, States, and Structure: The End of the Cold War and Weakening U.S. Civilian Control," *Armed Forces and Society* 24, (1998): 389–346.

4. See Aviezer Yaari, *Civil Control of the IDF,* Memorandum 72 [in Hebrew] (Tel Aviv: Jaffee Center for Strategic Studies, Tel Aviv University, 2004).

5. The Hebrew title of the book *Boomerang* is translated as *The Failure of the Leadership in the Second Intifada.* It was published by two Israeli journalists when *Generals in the Cabinet Room* went to press and illustrates many of its arguments.

6. *Seder Yom (Agenda)* (Special Issue on military and politics in Israel), October 3, 2003.

7. Brig. Gen. Zeev Drori, *Seder Yom,* 22.

8. Maj. Gen. (res.) Yossi Peled, *Seder Yom,* 25.

9. Maj. Gen (res.) Uzi Dayan, *Seder Yom,* 17.

10. Kemp and Hudin, "Civil Supremacy," 8.

11. Charles J. Dunlap, Jr., "The Origins of the American Military Coup of 2012," *Parameters* (Winter 1992–93): 2–20.

12. Douglas L. Bland, "A Unified Theory of Civil-Military Relations," *Armed Forces and Society* 26, no. 1 (1999).

13. This complaint against the political echelon was reiterated by almost all of the senior officers who were interviewed for this study.

14. Some of these discussions were held at the Israeli Institute for Democracy in Jerusalem and the Jaffee Center for Strategic Studies at Tel Aviv University.

15. Amnon Barzilai, *Ha'aretz,* April 16, 2004.

16. One of the best and most well-argued documents on this matter is one by a former DMI, Maj. Gen. (ret.) Shlomo Gazit. See Gazit, *Between Warning and Surprise: On Shaping National Intelligence Assessment in Israel,* Memorandum 66 [in Hebrew] (Tel Aviv: Jaffee Center for Strategic Studies, Tel Aviv University, 2003).

17. Uzi Arad, "National Intelligence at the Highest Level" (working paper, Herzliya Conference, Herzliya, December 13–16, 2004).

18. Ephraim Halevy, "The Role of the Intelligence Community in Planning Israel's Strategic Alternatives," [in Hebrew] *Maarachot,* July 2003, 41.

19. Yaari, *Civil Control of the IDF.*

20. "Report of the Public Commission on Parliamentary Supervision of the Defense System and Ways to Improve It," Knesset, December 2004.

Works Cited

Abrahamsson, Benget. *Military Professionalism and Political Power*. Beverly Hills, Calif.: Sage, 1972.

Arens, Moshe. *Peace and War in the Middle East, 1988–1992* [in Hebrew]. Tel Aviv: Yedioth Ahronoth Books, 1995.

Arian, Asher. *Security Threatened* [in Hebrew]. Tel Aviv: Papirus, 1999.

Aron, Raymond. "War and Industrial Society: A Reappraisal." *Millennium* 7, no. 3 (1979): 195–200.

Avant, Deborah. "Conflicting Indicators of 'Crisis' in American Civil-Military Relations." *Armed Forces and Society* (Spring 1998): 375–385.

Barak, Ehud. "The Pull-out from Lebanon: A Case Study in Political-Military Relations." In *Civil-Military Relations in Israel: Influence and Restraints,* edited by Ram Erez, 29–38. Tel Aviv: Jaffee Center for Strategic Studies, Tel Aviv University, 2003.

Bar-Siman-Tov, Yaacov, ed. *Views of the Generals: On the Collapse of the Oslo Process and the Violent Israeli-Palestinian Conflict* [in Hebrew]. Jerusalem: Leonard Davis Institute for International Relations, Hebrew University of Jerusalem, 2003.

Bar-Siman-Tov, Yaacov, Ephraim Lavie, Kobi Michael, and Daniel Bar-Tal. *The Israeli-Palestinian Violent Conflict 2000–2004: The Transition from Conflict Resolution to Conflict Management*. Jerusalem: Jerusalem Institute for Israel Studies, 2005.

Bar-Tal, Daniel, Dan Jacobson, and Aharon Klieman, eds. *Security Concerns: Insight from the Israeli Experience*. Stanford, Conn.: JAI Press, 1998.

Beilin, Yossi. *Manual for a Wounded Dove* [in Hebrew]. Tel Aviv: Miskal-Yedioth Ahronoth Books, 2001.

———. *Touching Peace* [in Hebrew]. Tel Aviv: Miskal-Yedioth Ahronoth Books, 1997.

Ben-Ami, Shlomo. *A Front with No Rear* [in Hebrew]. Tel Aviv: Miskal–Yedioth Ahronoth Books, 2004.

Ben-Amos, Avner, and Ilana Bet-El. "Militaristic Education & Commemoration: National Memorial Ceremonies in Israeli Schools." In *In the Name of*

Security, edited by Majid Al-Haj and Uri Ben-Eliezer. Haifa: Haifa University Press, 2003.

Ben-Dor, Gabi. "Civil-Military Relations in the mid-1990s" [in Hebrew]. In *Independence: The First 50 Years,* edited by Anita Shapira. Jerusalem: Shazar Center, 1998.

Ben-Eliezer, Uri. "Do the Generals Rule Israel?" In *Society in the Mirror* [in Hebrew], edited by Hanna Herzog, 235–267. Tel Aviv: Ramot, 1999.

———. "From a Nation-in-Arms to a Postmodern Army: Military Politics in 'New Times' Israel" [in Hebrew]. *Democratic Culture* 4-5 (2001): 55–98.

———. *The Making of Israeli Militarism.* Bloomington: Indiana University Press, 1998.

Ben-Gurion, David. *Singularity and Mission.* Tel Aviv: Maarachot, 1971.

Ben-Meir, Yehuda. *Civil-Military Relations in Israel.* New York: Columbia University Press, 1995.

Bennett, Lance W., and Robert M. Entman. *Mediated Politics: Communication in the Future of Democracy.* New York: Cambridge University Press, 2000.

Bentsur, Eytan. *The Road to Peace Crosses Madrid* [in Hebrew]. Tel Aviv: Yedioth Ahronoth Books, 1997.

Berger, Thomas U. "Norms, Identity, and National Security in Germany and Japan." In *The Culture of National Security: Norms and Identity in World Politics,* edited by Peter J. Katzenstein, 317–375. New York: Columbia University Press, 1996.

Bergman, Ronen. *Authority Given* [in Hebrew]. Tel Aviv: Yedioth Ahronoth Books, 2002.

Betzelem Report on Human Rights in the Occupied Territories. Jerusalem: Betzelem, May 2002.

Bland, Douglas L. "A Unified Theory of Civil-Military Relations." *Armed Forces and Society* 26, no. 1 (1999): 7–25.

Brom, Shlomo. "The War in Iraq: An Intelligence Failure?" *Strategic Assessment* 6, no. 3 (November 2003): 3–6.

Carmi, Shulamit, and Henri Rosenfeld. "The Emergence of Militaristic Nationalism in Israel." *International Journal of Politics, Culture and Society* 3, no. 1 (1989): 387–393.

Clinton, Bill. *My Life.* New York: Knopf, 2004.

Cohen, Eliot A. *Commandos and Politicians,* Harvard Studies in International Affairs 40. Cambridge, Mass.: Harvard University Press, 1978.

———. *Supreme Command*. New York: Free Press, 2002.

Cohen, Eliot A., Michael J. Eisenstadt, and Andrew J. Bacevich. *Knives, Tanks, and Missiles: Israel's Security Revolution*. Washington, D.C.: Washington Institute for Near East Policy, 1998.

Cohen, Stuart. *The IDF and Israeli Society* [in Hebrew]. Ramat-Gan, Israel: BESA Center for Strategic Studies, Bar Ilan University, 2001.

———. "The Peace Process and Its Impact on the Development of a 'Slimmer and Smarter' Israel Defense Force." *Israel Affairs* (Summer 1995): 1–21.

———. "Why Do They Quarrel? Civil-Military Relations in LIC Situations." In *Democracies and Small Wars,* edited by Efraim Inbar, 21–40. London: Frank Cass, 2003.

Dayan, Uzi. "What Is Needed and What Prevails in the Relations between the Political and the Military Echelons" [in Hebrew]. In *Civil–Military Relations in Israel: Influence and Restraints,* edited by Ram Erez, 23–27. Tel Aviv: Jaffee Center for Strategic Studies, Tel Aviv University, 2003.

Desch, Michael C. "Soldiers, States, and Structure: The End of the Cold War and Weakening U.S. Civilian Control." *Armed Forces and Society* 24, (1998): 385–406.

Dor, Daniel. *The Suppression of Guilt: The Israeli Media and the Reoccupation of the West Bank*. London: Pluto Press, 2005.

Drucker, Raviv. *Harakiri, Ehud Barak: The Failure* [in Hebrew]. Tel Aviv: Yedioth Ahronoth Books, 2002.

Drucker, Raviv, and Ofer Shelah. *Boomerang* [in Hebrew]. Jerusalem: Keter, 2005.

Dunlap, Charles J. Jr. "The Origins of the American Military Coup of 2012." *Parameters* (Winter 1992–93): 2–20.

Eitan, Rafael. *A Story of a Soldier* [in Hebrew]. Tel Aviv: Ma'ariv, 1985.

Epstein, Alek D. "On the Collapse of the Normative Framework of Citizens' Commitment to the Army in the 1990s" [in Hebrew]. In *In the Name of Security,* edited by Majid Al-Haj and Uri Ben-Eliezer. Haifa: Haifa University Press, 2003.

———. "The Struggle for Legitimization: The Development of Conscientious Objection in Israel since the Founding of the State to the War in Lebanon." *Israeli Sociology* A, no. 2 (1999): 319–354.

Erez, Ram, ed. *Civil-Military Relations in Israel: Influence and Restraints,* Memorandum 68. Tel Aviv: Jaffee Center for Strategic Studies, Tel Aviv University, 2003.

Feaver, Peter D., and Richard H. Kohn. *Soldiers and Civilians: The Civil-Military Gap and American National Security.* Cambridge, Mass.: MIT Press, 2001.

Finer, S. E. *The Man on Horseback: Military Intervention into Politics.* Harmondsworth, UK: Penguin, 1975.

Foster, Gregory D. "The Culture of Military Bureaucracy: Civil-Military Relations in Democracies Today." *Public Manager* 29, no. 20 (2000).

Gazit, Shlomo. *Between Warning and Surprise: On Shaping National Intelligence Assessment in Israel* [in Hebrew], Memorandum 66. Tel Aviv: Jaffee Center for Strategic Studies, Tel Aviv University, 2003.

———. *Fools in a Trap.* Tel Aviv: Zmora Bitan, 1999.

Gilon, Carmi. *Shin-Beth between Schisms* [in Hebrew]. Tel Aviv: Yedioth Ahronoth Books, 2000.

Golan, Haggai, and Shaul Shay, eds., *Low Intensity Conflict* [in Hebrew]. Tel Aviv: Maarachot, 2004.

Golani, Motti. "The 1956 Sinai War: Political and Military Aspects" [in Hebrew]. PhD diss., Haifa University, 1992.

———. *Wars Don't Just Happen* [in Hebrew]. Ben-Shemen: Modan, 2003.

Gur, Mordechai. *Chief of Staff* [in Hebrew]. Tel Aviv: Maarachot, 1998.

Halberstam, David. *War in a Time of Peace.* New York: Scribner, 2001.

Halevy, Ephraim. "The Role of the Intelligence Community in Planning Israel's Strategic Alternatives" [in Hebrew]. *Maarachot,* July 2003.

Harel, Amos, and Avi Isacharoff. *The Seventh War* [in Hebrew]. Tel Aviv: Miskal-Yedioth Ahronoth Books, 2004.

Harkabi, Yehoshafat. *War and Strategy* [in Hebrew]. Tel Aviv: Maarachot, 1990.

Hedges, Chris. *War Is a Force That Gives Us Meaning.* New York: Basic Books, 2002.

Hirschfeld, Yair P. *Oslo: A Formula for Peace* [in Hebrew]. Tel Aviv: Am-Oved, 2000.

Hirsh, Gal. "From 'Cast Lead' to 'Another Way': The Development of the Military Campaign in the Central Command" [in Hebrew]. *Maarachot,* February 2004, 26–31.

Horowitz, Dan. "Is Israel a Garrison State?" *Jerusalem Quarterly* 4 (1977): 58–75.

Horowitz, Dan, and Moshe Lissak. *Troubles in Utopia: The Overburdened Polity of Israel.* Albany: State University of New York Press, 1989.

Huntington, Samuel P. *The Soldier and the State: The Theory and Politics of Civil-Military Relations.* New York: Vintage Books, 1964.

Inbar, Efraim. *Yitzhak Rabin and Israel's National Security.* Washington, D.C.: Woodrow Wilson Center Press and Johns Hopkins University Press, 1999.

Kagan, Robert. *Of Paradise and Power.* New York: Knopf, 2003.

Kasha, Asa, and Amos Yadlin. "Military Ethics of Fighting Terror: An Isaeli Perspective." *Journal of Military Ethics* 4, no. 1 (2005): 3–32.

Katzenstein, Peter J., ed. *The Culture of National Security: Norms and Identity in World Politics.* New York: Columbia University Press, 1996.

Kemp, Kenneth W., and Charles Hudin. "Civil Supremacy over the Military: Its Nature and Limits." *Armed Forces and Society* 19, no. 1 (1992): 7–26.

Keren, Michael. "Justifications of Conscientious Objection: An Israeli Case Study." *International Journal of the Sociology of Law* 26 (1998): 121–147.

Kier, Elizabeth. "Culture and French Military Doctrine before World War II." In *The Culture of National Security: Norms and Identity in World Politics,* edited by Peter J. Katzenstein, 186–216. New York: Columbia University Press, 1996.

Kimmerling, Baruch. "Militarism in Israeli Society" [in Hebrew]. *Theory and Criticism* 4 (1993): 123–140.

———. "Political Subcultures and Civilian Militarism in a Settler-Immigrant Society." In *Security Concerns: Insights from the Israeli Experience,* edited by Daniel Bar-Tal, Dan Jacobson, and Aharon Klieman, 395–416. Greenwich, Conn.: JAI Press, 1998.

Kissinger, Henry. *Does America Need a Foreign Policy?* New York: Simon & Schuster, 2001.

Klein, Menachem. *Shattering a Taboo: The Contacts towards a Permanent Status Agreement in Jerusalem, 1994–2001* [in Hebrew]. Jerusalem: Jerusalem Institute for Israel Studies, 2001.

Klieman, Aharon. "Israeli Negotiating Culture." In *How Israelis and Palestinians Negotiate: A Cross-Cultural Analysis of the Oslo Peace Process,* edited by Tamara Cofman Wittes, 81–132. Washington, D.C.: United States Institute of Peace Press, 2005.

Kohn, Richard H. "How Democracies Control the Military." *Journal of Democracy* 8, no. 4 (1997): 140–153.

———. "Out of Control: The Crisis in Civil-Military Relations." *National Interest,* Spring 1994, 5–17.

Kover, Avi. "Low Intensity Conflicts: Why There Is a Gap between Theory and Practice." In *Low Intensity Conflict,* edited by Haggai Golan and Shaul Shay, 69–101. Tel Aviv: Maarachot, 2004.

Kriesberg, Louis. "Negotiating the Partition of Palestine and Evolving Israeli-Palestinian Relations." *Brown Journal of World Affairs* 7 (2000): 63–80.

———. "Paths to Varieties of Inter-Communal Reconciliation." In *From Conflict Resolution to Peacebuilding*, edited by Ho-Wong Jeong. Fitchburg, Mass.: Dartmouth, 1999.

———. "The Relevance of Reconciliation Actions in the Breakdown of Israeli Palestinian Negotiations, 2000." *Peace and Change* 27, no. 4 (2002): 546–571.

Levy, Yagil. "After Rabin and Peres: The Personal Dimension of Israel's Turn to Peace." *Security Dialogue* 28, no. 4 (1997): 465–478.

———. "How Militarization Drives Political Control of the Military: The Case of Israel." *Political Power and Social Theory* 11 (1997): 103–133.

———. *The Other Army of Israel: Materialist Militarism in Israel.* Tel Aviv: Miskal-Yedioth Ahronoth, 2003.

Lind, William S., Maj. John F. Schmitt, and Col. Gary I. Wilson. "Fourth Generation Warfare: Another Look." *Marine Corp Gazette* (December 1994): 34–37.

Lissak, Moshe. "The Ethos of Security and the Myth of the Militarized Society" [in Hebrew]. *Democratic Culture* 4-5 (2001): 187–212.

Lomsky-Feder, Edna, and Eyal Ben-Ari, eds. *The Military and Militarism in Israeli Society.* Albany: State University of New York Press, 1999.

Luttwak, Edward N. "A Post-Heroic Military." *Foreign Affairs* 75, no. 4 (1996): 33–44.

Makovsky, David. *Making Peace with the PLO.* Boulder, Colo.: Westview Press, 1996.

Malka, Amos. "The Regional System in the Stability Test." In *Views of the Generals: On the Collapse of the Oslo Process and the Violent Israeli-Palestinian Conflict* [in Hebrew], edited by Yaacov Bar-Siman-Tov. Jerusalem: Leonard Davis Institute for International Relations, Hebrew University of Jerusalem, 2003.

Michael, Kobi. "The End to the Deterministic Distinction: The Age of Low Intensity Conflict as a Paradigmatic Challenge to the Relations between the Political and the Military Echelons." In *Low Intensity Conflict,* edited by Haggai Golan and Shaul Shay. Tel Aviv: Maarachot, 2004, 201–238.

———. "The Army's Influence on the Transition Process from War to Peace: The Israeli Case" [in Hebrew]. PhD diss., Hebrew University of Jerusalem, 2004.

Moskos, Charles C. "Towards a Postmodern Military: The United States as a Paradigm." In *The Postmodern Military,* edited by Charles C. Moskos, John Allen Williams, and David R. Segal. New York: Oxford University Press, 2000.

Naveh, Dan. *Executive Secrets* [in Hebrew]. Tel Aviv: Yedioth Ahronoth Books, 1999.

Nir, Shmuel. "Attrition and the Test of Adaptation." *Studies in National Security* 4 [in Hebrew] (March 2003): 164–174.

———. *The Limited Confrontation.* IDF, 2001.

———. "The Nature of the Limited Conflict." In *Low Intensity Conflict,* edited by Haggai Golan and Shaul Shay, 19–45. Tel Aviv: Maarachot, 2004.

———. "There Is No Catch Here." *Maarachot,* January 2003, 68–70.

Nir, Yaron. "An Elaborated Approach to the Palestinian Viewpoint Concerning the Solution to the Conflict." *Maarachot,* April 2003, 18–23.

Nye, Joseph S. *Soft Power.* New York: Foreign Affairs, 2004.

Operations Short of War/Counter Insurgency Handbook. Camberly, UK: Staff College, 1993.

"The Peace Index," Tami Steinmetz Center for Peace Research, Tel Aviv University, April 2001.

Pedhatzur, Reuven. "Israeli Security Culture: Its Origins and Its Influence on Israeli Democracy" [in Hebrew]. *Politika* 10 (2003): 87–117.

Peres, Shimon. *The New Middle East.* New York: Henry Holt, 1993.

Peri, Yoram. *Between Battles and Ballots: Israeli Military in Politics.* Cambridge: Cambridge University Press, 1983.

———. "Civil-Military Relations in Israel in Crisis." In *Military, State, and Society in Israel,* edited by Daniel Maman, Eyal Ben-Ari, and Zeev Rosenhek. New Brunswick, N.J.: Transaction, 2001.

———. "Israel: Conscientious Objection in a Democracy under Siege." In *The New Conscientious Objection,* edited by Charles C. Moskos and John Whiteclay Chambers II. New York: Oxford University Press, 1993.

———. *The Israeli Military and Israel's Palestinian Policy: From Oslo to the Al Aqsa Intifada,* United States Institute of Peace Peaceworks 47. Washington, D.C.: United States Institute of Peace, November 2002.

———. "Media, War and Citizenship." *Communication Review* 3, no. 4 (2000): 1–29.

———. "Rabin: From 'Mr. Security' to Nobel Prize Winner." Afterword in *The Rabin Memoirs,* by Yitzhak Rabin. Berkeley and Los Angeles: University of California Press, 1996.

———. *Telepopulism: Media and Politics in Israel.* Stanford, Calif.: Stanford University Press, 2004.

Peri, Yoram, ed. *The Assassination of Yitzhak Rabin.* Stanford, Calif.: Stanford University Press, 2000.

Perlmutter, Amos. *Military and Politics in Israel: Nation-Building and Role Expansion.* London: Frank Cass, 1969.

———. *The Military and Politics in Modern Times.* New Haven, Conn.: Yale University Press, 1977.

———. *Politics and the Military in Israel, 1967–77.* London: Frank Cass, 1978.

Priest, Dana. *The Mission.* New York: W. W. Norton, 2003.

Rabinovich, Itamar. *The Brink of Peace: Israel and Syria, 1992–1996* [in Hebrew]. Tel Aviv: Miskal-Yedioth Ahronoth Books, 1998.

———. *Waging Peace* [in Hebrew]. Tel Aviv: Dvir, 2004.

Raveh, Saar, and Maaya Pecker-Rinat. "To Win and Stay Humane." *Maarachot,* September 2002, 21–25.

Rawls, John. *A Theory of Justice.* Oxford: Oxford University Press, 1973.

"Report of the Public Commission on Parliamentary Supervision of the Defense System and Ways to Improve It." Knesset, December 2004.

Reshef, Dani. "A New Approach to Low Intensity Conflict." *Maarachot,* April 2003, 9–11.

Roman, Peter J., and David W. Tarr. "Military Professionalism and Policymaking: Is There a Civil-Military Gap at the Top? If So, Does It Matter?" In *Soldiers and Civilians: The Civil-Military Gap and American National Security,* edited by Peter D. Feaver and Richard H. Kohn. Cambridge, Mass.: MIT Press, 2001.

Rosenhak, Zeev, Daniel Maman, and Eyal Ben-Ari. "The Study of War and the Military in Israel: The Social Construction of Knowledge." In *In The Name of Security,* edited by Majod Al-Haj and Uri Ben-Eliezer, 185–214. Haifa: Haifa University Press, 2003.

Ross, Dennis. *The Missing Peace.* New York: Farrar, Straus and Giroux, 2004.

Rubinstein, Danny, Robert Malley, Hussein Agha, Ehud Barak, and Benny Morris. *Rashomon Camp David.* Tel Aviv: Yedioth Ahronoth Books, 2003.

Sagi, Uri. *Lights within the Fog* [in Hebrew]. Tel Aviv: Miskal-Yedioth Ahronoth Books, 1998.

Sasson-Levy, Orna. "Masculinity as a Protest: Identity Construction among Blue-Collar Soldiers" [in Hebrew]. *Israeli Sociology* 5, no. 1 (2003): 15–48.

Savir, Uri. *The Process* [in Hebrew]. Tel Aviv: Miskal-Yedioth Ahronoth Books, 1998.

Schiff, Rebecca L. "Civil-Military Relations Reconsidered: A Theory of Concordance." *Armed Forces and Society* 22, no. 7 (1995): 18.

Shelah, Ofer. *The Israeli Military: A Radical Proposal* [in Hebrew]. Tel Aviv: Kinneret Zmora-Bitan Dvir, 2003.

Sher, Gilead. *Just Beyond Reach: The Israeli-Palestinian Negotiation, 1999-2001* [in Hebrew]. Tel Aviv: Yedioth Ahronoth Books, 2001.

Sipri Year Book. New York: Oxford University Press, 2002.

Sivan, Emanuel. "The Assassination in Paris, The Assassination in Tel Aviv." In *Political Assassination* [in Hebrew], edited by Charles S. Liebman, 22–32. Tel Aviv: Am-Oved, 2000.

Sneh, Ephraim. *Responsibility: Israel after Year 2000* [in Hebrew]. Tel Aviv: Yedioth Ahronoth Books, 1996.

Stanley, Jay. "Harold Lasswell and the Idea of the Garrison State." *Society* 33, no. 6 (September-October 1996): 467.

Tal, Israel. *National Security* [in Hebrew]. Tel Aviv: Dvir, 1996.

Tamir, Avraham. *A Soldier in Search of Peace.* London: Weindenfeld and Nicolson, 1988.

Tatzpit. IDF Training Division, December 2000.

Wagman, Yehuda. "The Limited Conflict Catch." *Maarachot,* September 2002, 68–77.

Wald, Emanuel. *The Curse of the Broken Tools* [in Hebrew]. Jerusalem: Schocken, 1987.

Ya'alon, Moshe. "Preparing the Forces for the Limited Confrontation." *Maarachot,* December 2001, 380–381.

Yaari, Aviezer. *Civil Control of the IDF,* Memorandum 72. Tel Aviv: Jaffee Center for Strategic Studies, Tel Aviv University, 2004.

———. "Intelligence Assessment in Israel's Conditions of Uncertainty." In *Intelligence and National Security* [in Hebrew], edited by Zvi Offer and Avi Kover, 213–221. Tel Aviv: Maarachot, 1987.

Index

About the Author

Yoram Peri is the head of the Chaim Herzog Institute for Media, Politics and Society and a professor of political sociology and communication in the Department of Communication at Tel Aviv University. Early in his career he served as political adviser to Israeli prime minister Yitzhak Rabin (1974) and as a spokesman of Israel's Labor Party (1970–73). He had a long career with the daily newspaper *Davar*, serving as its managing editor (1988–90) and editor-in-chief (1990–95). He regularly writes for newspapers and journals in Israel and abroad and formerly hosted current affairs programs on television and radio. He has served as president of the Association of Editors of Israel's Daily Newspapers and is a member of the presidium on the Israel Press Council.

Peri has been a senior research fellow at the Jaffee Center for Strategic Studies of Tel Aviv University and a visiting professor at Harvard University, Dartmouth College, and American University. He is a recipient of a Fulbright award and has been a visiting scholar at several institutions in the United States, including the Middle East Institute and the United States Institute of Peace, where he was a senior fellow in 2001–2. In addition to his academic activities, he is deeply involved in Israel's civil society and served as president of the New Israel Fund from 1999 to 2001.

His most recent books in English are *Telepopulism: Media and Power in Israel* (2004) and *The Assassination of Yitzhak Rabin* (2004). An earlier publication, *Between Battles and Ballots: Israeli Military in Politics* (1983), is still considered the seminal work in its field. Peri holds a PhD in sociology and political science from the London School of Economics.

United States Institute of Peace

The United States Institute of Peace is an independent, nonpartisan federal institution created by Congress to promote the prevention, management, and peaceful resolution of international conflicts. Established in 1984, the Institute meets its congressional mandate through an array of programs, including research grants, fellowships, professional training, education programs from high school through graduate school, conferences and workshops, library services, and publications. The Institute's Board of Directors is appointed by the President of the United States and confirmed by the Senate.

Generals in the Cabinet Room

This book is set in Adobe Caslon; the display type is Futura and Symbol ITC. The Creative Shop designed the book's cover; Helene Y. Redmond designed the interior and made up the pages. The index was prepared by Sonsie Conroy. The book's editor was Nigel Quinney.